PHANTOM BOYS
VOLUME 2

PHANTOM BOYS
VOLUME 2

MORE THRILLING TALES FROM UK AND US OPERATORS OF THE McDONNELL DOUGLAS F-4

RICHARD PIKE

GRUB STREET | LONDON

Published by

Grub Street

4 Rainham Close

London

SW11 6SS

Copyright © Grub Street 2017

Copyright text © Richard Pike 2017

Copyright text Chapter 17 © RG Head 2017

A CIP record for this title is available from the British Library

ISBN-13: 9-781-910690-39-0

Cover and book design by Daniele Roa

Printed and bound by Finidr, Czech Republic

DEDICATION

In memory of Roger Colebrook who died shortly after Christmas Day, 2015. He was a fine pilot, a staunch supporter, a good friend.

AUTHOR'S ACKNOWLEDGEMENT

With sincere thanks to the renowned aviation artist Chris Stone whose excellence has featured on a number of jacket covers in Grub Street's Boys series. For *Phantom Boys 2,* Chris was inspired by an aerial combat scene experienced by the late Brigadier General Robin Olds, USAF, during Operation Bolo in the Vietnam War:

> 'The MiG 21 zoomed away and I engaged afterburner... reared up my Phantom inside his turn... he was turning to the left so I pulled the stick and barrel-rolled to the right... I found myself above him, half upside-down... he never even saw me... I could clearly see his silhouette against the sun when I launched two Sidewinder missiles... one of them impacted and tore apart his right wing.'

CONTENTS

PROLOGUE

Author's note: *This was written by the late Brigadier General Robin Olds USAF, commander of the Eighth Tactical Fighter Wing 1966-1967 during which period he was based at Ubon Royal Thai Air Force Base from where he flew over 100 F-4 combat missions against North Vietnam. By kind permission of his daughter Christina Olds whose book,* Fighter Pilot – The Memoirs of Legendary Ace Robin Olds, *was published by St Martin's Griffin, Flatiron Building, New York.*

Like a brooding hen, she squats half asleep over her clutch of eggs. Her tail feathers droop and her beak juts forward belligerently. Her back looks humped and her wing tips splay upward. Sitting there, she is not a thing of beauty. Far from it. But she is my F-4, and her nest is a steel revetment – her eggs are six, M-117, 750-lb bombs. This avian has fangs – very unbirdlike. They nestle under her belly and cling to her wings. She is ready to go, and so am I.

She receives me and my backseater, and we become a part of her as we attach ourselves to her with straps and hoses and plugs and connectors. A surge of juice and a blast of compressed air and she comes alive. We are as one – tied together – the machine an extension of the man – her hydraulics my muscles – her sensors my eyes – her mighty engines my power.

She screams and complains as we move through shimmering heat waves along an endless expanse of concrete. Final checks, then her nose pointed nearly two miles of runway, and we are ready. Throttles forward, then outboard thump, thump – the afterburners kick in. Now my bird roars and accelerates rapidly toward her release from mother earth, leaving a thunder behind that rattles windows and shakes the insides of those who watch.

I look over at my wingmen as we climb effortlessly toward a rendezvous with our tanker. All is well with them, and I marvel again at the transformation of our ugly duckling into a thing of graceful beauty – yet she's businesslike and menacing, thrusting forward and upward with deadly purpose.

Refuelling done, we drop off and lunge forward, gathering speed for this day's task. We hurtle across the Black, then the Red rivers, pushing our Phantoms to the limit of power without using afterburners, weaving and undulating so as not to present a steady target for the gunners below.

Then a plume of dust down to our left, and the evil white speck of a surface-to-air missile rises to meet us. We wait and watch. That missile is steady on an intercept course, and we know we are the target. Then, on signal, we start down. The missile follows – and now hard down – stick full forward – the negative G forces hanging us in our straps. The missile dives to follow, and at a precise moment we pull, pull – as hard as we can – the positive Gs now slamming us into our seats with crushing force.

Our heavy bird with its load of bombs responds with a prolonged shudder, and we are free for the moment, the missile passing harmlessly below, unable to follow our manoeuvre. On to the target – weaving, moving up and down, leaving the bursts of heavy flak off to the side or down below. The F-4 is solid, responsive, heeding my every demand quickly and smoothly.

We reach the roll-in point and go inverted, pulling her nose down, centring the target in the combining glass as we roll into our 70-degree dive toward the release point. My Phantom plunges toward the earth through an almost solid wall of bursting flak. Then "PICKLE!" And the bird leaps as her heavy load separates and we pull with all our force around to our egress heading. There are MiGs about, and my F-4 becomes a brutal beast, slamming this way, then that, snarling with rage, turning, rolling, diving, hurtling skyward like an arrow, plunging down with savage force.

The melee over, the rivers crossed, and headed for our post-strike refuelling, and my bird is once again a docile, responsive lady, taking me home, letting my heart beat slow, giving me comfort in having survived once again. I gather the flock close by, and we slowly circle each other – top, bottom, and each side, looking for flak damage, rips, leaks, jagged holes. None found, we press on to meet our ticket home and gratefully take on fuel from our tanker friends. A bit of follow-the-leader up and over the beautiful mountains of dazzling white nimbus, just to relax – to enjoy the special privilege given us in flying this magnificent bird and the home runway lies ahead there near the little town of Ubon Ratchathani. Landing done, post-flight checks finished, engines shut down, and my F-4 vents its tanks with a prolonged sigh, speaking for both of us, glad it's over, anticipating a brief respite before the next day's work.

It's an unusual pilot who doesn't give his bird a private touch of loving gratitude before he leaves her nest.

CHAPTER 1

INTO ACTION

RICHARD PIKE RECALLS AIR COMBAT IN THE F-4

The best and the worst of times was, for me, an apt description as an operational pilot on McDonnell Douglas's famous F-4 Phantom. Moreover, it was a description that captured the turmoil within my head one evening while I strolled through the streets of Skopje, Macedonia (as one does). There was a potent, almost tangible tang in the Macedonian air that evening...intense and unsettling. Daylight had started to fade and glancing up I noticed that a few stars had begun to appear in the sky. In the distance, about ten miles away, the outline of the Sharr Mountains indicated the border with Kosovo. A hundred miles or so beyond that lay Kosovo's contentious and perilous border with Serbia. I took a deep breath and sighed. The general mood within Skopje was heady and exotic, yet on that July evening in 1999 I held disturbing images in my head – mental pictures of the recent chilling campaign of ethnic cleansing by Serbian troops against the Albanian population of Kosovo. The Serbian actions had led to hundreds of thousands, mainly ethnic Albanians, seeking safety in huge refugee camps set up in Macedonia. The scenes inside these camps were pitiful, furthermore the situation had created unrest within Macedonia itself.

It was about five months earlier, in March 1999, that NATO aircraft had initiated air attacks against Yugoslavia, and just ten or so weeks after that when the president of Yugoslavia, Slobodan Milosevic, had conceded defeat. Now, as a consequence, displaced Kosovans had started to drift back to their own country. Their country, though, bore grim scars from scandalous and brutal acts by the Serbians – acts that amounted to a systematic campaign of terror which included murder, rape, arson and severe maltreatment.

An international effort to assist Kosovo had began, an effort that involved, under a United Nations World Food Programme contract, a team of pilots and engineers from Bristow Helicopters Ltd. As a helicopter pilot with that company, I was part of the team and it was our task to distribute, by Sikorsky S-61N helicopters, food in the form of bread-making flour to remote communities in war-torn Kosovo. Normally we were employed to fly to North Sea oil installations, so to operate in far-flung, often mountainous, corners of Kosovo was, one could say, an interesting contrast. Interesting, too, especially from my perspective as a former Phantom pilot, was the recent news that Luftwaffe Phantoms, as part of the NATO operation, had been in action against the Serb forces in Yugoslavia. The messages about this, though, were mixed.

Various aircraft types had been involved in the NATO campaign. We'd heard how F-16 Fighting Falcons, for example, had been used from the Belgian, Danish, Dutch and Turkish air forces as well as from the lead operator, the United States Air Force. But for me it was the unverified accounts of Phantoms operated by the Luftwaffe that were intriguing. Serb forces claimed to have shot down some of these F-4s and Russian sources said that a crew of one of the aircraft had been killed. Other sources, however, stated that the Luftwaffe operated Panavia Tornado aircraft, not Phantoms. In either case *The Sun* newspaper ran the headlines: 'Luftwaffe and the RAF into battle side by side'.

*   *   *

Suddenly, with my mind still preoccupied, I came across a small scene of desolation on the streets of Skopje. Ensconced on one side of the crowded pavement near the Vardar river, a young mother shifted uncomfortably on the piece of cardboard that acted as her seat. Melancholy was writ across her pale, proud face. "Please..." she said, guessing, no doubt, that I was American or British, "...for the baby." Her tone was clear, if strongly accented – and clear, too, was her need. For a moment I'd gazed at her worried, solemn expression as she clutched her small child. Then I nodded and stooped down to place some local Macedonian coins in her begging bowl. She lowered her head in response but said nothing more.

Impressed by her air of dignity despite the circumstances, I said: "That's okay...sorry if..." but my voice trailed away when I saw her screw up her eyes tightly. She shrugged her shoulders in a small gesture of anguish and her breathing seemed to become laboured. A brief, edgy silence ensued; this was not the reaction that I'd anticipated. If, in my naivety, I'd expected her to say something like: "It's a consequence of temporary privation, but thank you for your concern," clearly I had a thing or two to learn about the straightjacket of grinding poverty, about the meaning of real hardship where beauty and grace were gnawed away by indigence and where health was ruined by hunger. With a strange urge to try to offer a few useful words, or even some useless ones like, "lovely to meet you. I've heard so much. Good. Good. Now let's all have some tea," instead, feeling ineffectual, I merely half-raised one hand in a hasty farewell and turned away, somehow humbled, to resume a walk through the centre of Skopje.

Within this capital city of some half-a-million people, the uneasy atmosphere that evening was inclined to encourage one to think many thoughts and, certainly, my own mood remained philosophical. For one thing, I'd been struck recently with the notion that, shortly to retire as a pilot after some forty years of flying, while not exactly at the Methuselah stage yet, I was nonetheless beginning to feel my age. Of course, I reasoned, one didn't mind the process of growing old (as the ancient joke went, consider the alternative) though it could be hard, even so, not to feel bewildered by those contrary companions, the future and the past.

As I continued to walk away from the young beggar-woman, I began to discern the Sharr Mountains' highest point, Rudoka e Madhe, which could just be made out in the distance. This peak, at some 9,000 feet, provided an impressive visual navigational aid when we took off from our base situated to the north of Skopje. With an involuntary shudder I recalled how, when flying northwards into Kosovo, we helicopter crews witnessed some bad sights. At the border crossing point, marked by massive traffic queues (a helicopter, naturally, provided a most convenient queue-jumper), a cement factory had been the casualty of bombing. A large area was powdered in white layers of cement as if tiny white mites had decided to infest trees, factory buildings, fields, crops, houses, vehicles. As we flew on towards the United Nations helicopter landing site at Pristina, Kosovo's capital city, country villages in superb surroundings would reveal less-than-superb sights: individual houses selected as targets for revenge burning. The war may have ended, but retaliation had not. In merciless scenes where former neighbours had become enemies, occasional black clouds of filthy smoke rising upwards marked where another property had just been torched. Sometimes we'd see villagers clustered helplessly together, dazed, seized by dread, no doubt, as they observed the war's aftermath produce prolonged horror.

Maybe, I reckoned, a reflective mood was an inevitable result of witnessing such events. Perhaps, though, it was just another sign of ageing, especially as it seemed everything was so much worse these days. Of course people had been saying that for a thousand years, but in this case it really seemed to have a ring of truth. For sure, I mused, I'd been more than fortunate to have experienced unusual variety as an aviator, first as a fighter pilot, then as a military helicopter pilot before a move to civilian helicopters – an unconventional progression and one that had avoided becoming an airline pilot, which I'd never really fancied. And that evening, while reflecting on NATO's rumoured use of Luftwaffe Phantoms, maybe this helped to stir up memories of my own flying in the McDonnell Douglas F-4.

*   *   *

My conversion training onto the Phantom had taken place at RAF Coningsby in Lincolnshire. For some years before that I'd been flying the single-seat English Electric Lightning, an aircraft with the need for self-sufficiency and independent thinking, qualities which became deeply engrained. Pilots who graduated from the Lightning to the Phantom sometimes commented that life seemed, somehow, to become a bit more serious. The F-4's two-man crew meant that a different mindset was required; good crew co-operation between pilot and navigator was key. For a number of us this could cause problems, and my own case was no exception, especially when my allocated navigator for the course at Coningsby, a gangly young fellow, seemed unpromising at first. However, in fairness, hidden talents emerged as the course progressed. This was notable during the phase when students were taught the basics of air-to-air combat (popularly, if erroneously, called dog-fighting) in a Phantom.

Copious briefings, as ever, prepared us for the demanding air combat exercises. A number of the navigators regarded these as pilot-orientated activities with violent manoeuvring which they'd not enjoy. I had to admit that if I was a navigator, I probably wouldn't have enjoyed it much either. At first, even my usually ebullient young navigator seemed to be quite gloomy about the prospect. "Don't worry, Nick," I tried to reassure him, "you'll be fine." He said nothing but smiled weakly by way of reply.

With the briefings over, the action began. After an early start one morning, four of us, two pilots and two navigators, carefully checked our anti-G suits and other equipment before we began to make our way to the allocated Phantoms. The aircraft had been specially prepared: fuel tanks had been removed – clean aircraft allowed greater manoeuvrability so we could pull to the maximum G limits as stipulated in special graphs. These graphs, typical of the complexity found in most things to do with F-4s, had been studied diligently.

Now, while the two navigators climbed into the rear cockpits of their respective machines, the pilots signed technical logs before walking out to the Phantoms. The early morning air was chilly as I carried out the ritual of aircraft external checks after which I climbed up the F-4's small steps for access to the front cockpit. The cockpit itself looked quite roomy and well laid-out, especially compared to the likes of the Lightning cockpit with its eccentric arrangements of pipes and wires casually threaded together before the days of ergonomics. A ground crewman helped me to strap in, then he checked that the ejection seat safety pins were removed and stowed. After this he moved to a pre-positioned fire extinguisher which he manned while monitoring the engine start process.

Before long, with the Phantom's engines 'turning and burning', air traffic control gave clearance for us to taxi out to Coningsby's active runway. At the holding point by the runway, where we were instructed to wait while other traffic cleared, I glanced at the surrounding scene. Nearby, a brightly coloured windsock pointed away from distant hangars, camouflaged buildings and the air traffic control tower. Beyond lay acres of flat Lincolnshire farmland that surrounded the airfield perimeter. Above, I noted a sky dappled with occasional towers of cumulus cloud at medium level but overall the weather conditions looked okay.

"Clear for take-off," announced the controller at which I released the Phantom's rudder pedal brakes to follow the leader onto the runway. Approaching the take-off point, I moved to an echelon starboard position on the leader and waited for his signal to increase engine power – a circling motion of one hand. With this signal given, I started to ease the twin throttles forward and glanced at the cockpit instruments. The engine revolutions increased smoothly to around eighty per cent power at which point I stopped further throttle movement. Now, with the Phantom leaning forward onto its nose-wheel as if eager to get going, I awaited a further signal from the leader. This came in the form of a firm nod of his head as, simultaneously, he released his aircraft brakes and pushed the throttles towards the full cold power position. I heard an increase in background noise as the Rolls-Royce Spey engines crescendoed from a low whine to a roar, then a slight hesitation when reheats were engaged following a further firm nod of the leader's head. A positive punch in the back verified that the reheats had lit. I continued to hold a formation position as the Phantom's wheels left the runway surface after which we turned towards the sea and climbed up towards the briefed operating area.

The first exercises, which demonstrated basic combat manoeuvres (BCMs) to illustrate the capabilities and weaknesses of the Phantom in combat situations, confirmed that basic principles had changed little from the earliest days of air combat. In endless struggles as aircraft banked and turned and climbed and dived in attempts to gain advantage, it was as if, for the pilot, the body of the Phantom was part of his body; his arms and legs were at one with the machine. The navigator, meanwhile, had to operate the Phantom's radar and when in close combat he had to focus, too, on the visual picture outside the cockpit. In close combat, a key requirement for both pilot and navigator was to maintain visual contact with the opponent.

When satisfied that we were ready, the lead Phantom now set us up for a full blown one-versus-one practice combat. The two aircraft split up, then turned back to face each other. Like boxers in a ring, one in the red corner, one in the blue corner, a so-called circle of joy was soon underway. I was aware of the leaping shadows of adjacent clouds, the clenching of my teeth, the persistent pressure from my anti-G suit as the device inflated around my legs and stomach during the strenuous manoeuvres. Adrenalin surged through my system. If we lost visual contact with the other aircraft, there was a horrified moment of silence in our cockpit. "Keep looking! Keep looking, Nick," I'd cry. With his top seat straps loosened my navigator could turn his upper body sufficiently to see almost directly behind us. However, he had to struggle to remain conscious: our tight turns meant the need to withstand up to 8 G – eight times the normal level of gravity. In the violent manoeuvres he would be thrown back and forth, and shaken savagely from side to side. "Can you hear me, Nick?" I asked at one point, worried that he may have blacked out.

"Yeah...I hear you," he said, his voice groggy with fatigue.

"The other aircraft's still there," I went on, relieved that he was still awake.

"Mmmm," said Nick, "I know...'cos I think I see the bastard now. He's in our five o'clock low, one mile."

"Okay!" I said. "Well spotted, Nick!"

"Pull up," said Nick, "we'll be better placed then." At this, I levelled the Phantom's wings and pulled up sharply. Soon, with bank reapplied, I could see the other aircraft below us. Nick's excitement and enthusiasm now appeared to grow exponentially. "They've lost sight of us!" he cried breathlessly, "they're still turning...but I reckon they're searching desperately." As our 'enemy' was a staff-constituted crew, for the two of them to lose sight of a couple of rookie students was...well, it was not supposed to happen. My heart thumped in my chest and a dilemma worked through my subconscious, a momentary realm of uncertainty – but not for long. I watched our opponents continue their turn then, judging what I reckoned to be the ideal moment, I lowered our Phantom's nose to drop down into the 'enemy's' six o'clock position.

"We should be in range shortly," said my navigator. Then, with almost unbearable excitement in his voice, he yelled: "Check switches!" With a rapid glance around the cockpit, I double-checked...*guns/missiles selector – Sidewinder – Master Arm switch – check...* "Standby..." I cried as, with one finger touching the trigger lightly, I made a final check of parameters. Everything was as it should be – and there was no time to lose. Firmly, therefore, I squeezed the trigger as, simultaneously, I said to my navigator: "Firing Fox 2!" – by which I meant, of course, a theoretical firing of one missile – a Sidewinder AIM-9 heat-seeker. If it had been for real, we would have been aware of a faint *'whoooosh...'* as the Sidewinder shot forward from the launch rail. When the AIM-9 began to accelerate away from us we would have seen a gentle barrelling as the 'rollerons' on the missile's wings controlled the rate of roll thus replicating the motion of a deadly Sidewinder snake. Within seconds, the target would be despatched, as if in the final thrust of an infantryman's bayonet, rapidly, surely and without hesitation.

"Eureka!" cried my navigator, his tone a blend of elation and shock. While we could not exactly hear cymbals clash and Hollywood choirs resonate in the background, for us this was still a small but significant triumph. Did I feel triumphant? Maybe I did... surely I did. On reflection, though, perhaps the more relevant question was how I would have felt if, in a real situation, the AIM-9 missile had brought down an opponent. Most aircrew would probably try to take the view that their battle was against a machine not individuals. However, there were reports from World War Two that some Luftwaffe pilots had opened fire on Allied aircrew who dangled in parachutes having escaped from doomed machines. The mentality was hard to fathom but maybe an irresistible reflex that welled up from deep inside the psyche of those Luftwaffe pilots (and others too, no doubt) meant that, for some at least, the fight had not been altogether impersonal. Years later I reflected that a similarly intractable mentality had probably led to the outrages in Kosovo.

"Fox 2," I called on the aircraft radio.

"Confirm Fox 2?" said the surprised and worried-sounding voice of the other pilot.

"Roger," I said. "Fox 2!"

A slight hesitation ensued after which he said: "Okay...understood..." Another pause, then: "...and well done, you two!" In an implausible flash of speculation I imagined his face as ash-grey, the earlier robust and assertive look gone.

"You did well," I said to my navigator, "...really well back there, Nick. Our opponents were old hands and hard to outdo!" After his earlier reservations, I could picture a broad grin of success.

"Rejoin in echelon starboard," instructed the formation leader, "we'll return to base now." Tired and curiously light-headed from the exertions, I followed the lead Phantom back to Coningsby where we 'broke' into the circuit to turn downwind in preparation for landing

Later, it struck me that a person who has never experienced the demands placed on a fighter crew during air combat will be unlikely to understand what whirlwinds revolve inside the head. If fear is felt, it is less likely to be caused by the prospect of physical danger as comprehension of the heavy responsibilities involved. Doubtless glad and proud to have been chosen for a serious military mission, trained aircrew will be more than anxious to succeed. Their chief fear may well be that of making a mess of things.

As I wandered through the streets of Skopje more than a couple of decades later on that July evening towards the twilight of the twentieth century, my mind seemed to retreat into a kaleidoscope of vaguely connected images. The wild and exuberant mood stimulated when flying the F-4 in air combat remained deep within the memory cells, as would the febrile atmosphere in Skopje that night when some mysterious feeling in the air suggested that, as if witnesses to a memorable and intoxicating adventure, it was obvious that something important was taking place in the process. Perhaps part of that process should involve relating tales about these adventures, tales that needed to be told, tales for posterity, in which case the reader should be advised to sit back, fasten the seatbelt and enjoy the intriguing, unpredictable, thrilling world about to be entered...

CHAPTER 2

SURPRISE

ARCHIE LIGGAT'S FALKLANDS CONNECTION

With the potential, as they say, to shoot oneself in the foot, there was both irony and surprise in the situation. But there it was, an important day, a day of new beginnings, a day in 1993 that was written down in many diaries. As the colonel himself walked into the crewroom – a colonel who turned out to be large, moustachioed, ebullient – a sudden hush fell across the room. When Squadron Leader Archie Liggat, as officer commanding 234 Squadron, a tactical weapons and advanced training unit at RAF Valley in Anglesey, stepped forward he shook the colonel's hand and said: "May I introduce some of my staff and students, sir..."

And as Archie went through the niceties he was conscious that his every move was under the scrutiny of a group of senior Royal Air Force officers. Perhaps, beneath the "wonderful to meet you..." "How are you today?" "Nice weather isn't it?" routines, he felt, deep down, the press of secondary agendas. Maybe he harboured thoughts that, despite the show of joviality, the colonel could be hard and mean and out for himself – not that Archie had anything against the fellow personally, it was just that, under the circumstances, it was difficult not to feel more than a little bemused by the proceedings. And few would argue that the proceedings were, to put it mildly, rather unusual.

*   *   *

It was three years earlier, one day in October 1990, when Archie was a Phantom pilot based in the Falkland Islands that the scene was set for the remarkable reunion that would take place, entirely by chance, during the colonel's visit to Valley. For one thing, it was quite by accident that Archie, together with colleagues, was on quick reaction alert (QRA) duty on that particular day in the Falklands. The men were primed to react if needed while they waited in a special crewroom next to a hangar with two fully armed Phantom FGR2s. On the day in question, Archie and his colleagues had been made aware of a special request from the Argentine government concerning a large section of Antarctic ice, part of the renowned Wilkins Ice Shelf, which had broken off and was drifting around the South Atlantic seas. The Wilkins Ice Shelf, evidently stable for most of the twentieth century, had now started to break up. Worried about the effects of global warming, scientific researchers from Argentina were anxious to make detailed observations from the air.

As the aircraft to be used for these observations, a Lockheed C-130 Hercules operated by the Argentine air force (Fuerza Aérea Argentina or FAA), had limited range, permission had been sought by the Argentines to fly across the Falkland Inner Conservation and Management Zone (FICZ). Since this would be the first such flight by an aircraft of the FAA after the war of 1982, the issue was a contentious one. Nonetheless, the United Kingdom government had agreed to the flight on condition that the C-130, as it crossed the FICZ, was accompanied by two RAF Phantoms. In order to cope with language difficulties, Spanish-speaking air traffic controllers would be available at the Phantom's base at RAF Mount Pleasant in East Falkland.

So it was that the two QRA Phantoms took off on that spring Falklands day to intercept, identify and escort the Argentine aircraft. The plan worked just as arranged and it was not long before Archie, as pilot of the number one QRA aircraft, held formation on the left side of the C-130. When in position, he noted that the Argentine aircraft, apart from insignia and camouflage paintwork, was similar to the RAF C-130s of 1312 Flight based at Mount Pleasant. The latter had been modified to offer an in-flight refuelling facility which the Phantoms used occasionally. While Archie and his navigator held sentinel on the Argentine's left side, the other Phantom pilot manoeuvred judiciously as his navigator took photographs. The Phantom crews made no radio contact with the Argentine opposite numbers, although a few polite nods of the head took place from time to time. With the C-130's cruise speed of less than 300 knots, progress through the FICZ seemed, after a while, slow – indeed, unaccustomedly slow, in fact tedious to the point that Archie started to become quite bored.

Possibly at that point Archie's thoughts may have meandered in different directions which included, perhaps, mental pictures of home, of his birthplace in Grantown-on-Spey in the highlands of Scotland... Suddenly, Archie was struck with an idea; an idea which he discussed with his navigator who seemed quite amused by the preposterous proposition. For while in formation they'd spotted that their charge was one of the FAA's two KC-130s, a type of Hercules based on the US Marine Corps variant used for in-flight refuelling. Archie decided to ease his twin throttles forward to reposition the Phantom; he wanted to be fully visible to the Argentine flight deck crew. He then dropped his left hand from the twin throttles to the fuel panel below. With his eyes still watching the Hercules, Archie's fingers felt carefully for the in-flight refuelling probe switch. The distinctive shape of this switch was readily identified. Now, when

The view from Archie Liggat's Phantom as number two Phantom breaks away from the C-130, following escort duties. (Reproduced with permission of the MoD)

he operated the switch, Archie and his navigator heard the typical thumps and clunks that signified movement of their flight-refuelling probe. As the device, normally flush with the fuselage by the pilot's cockpit, broke out of its housing the movement signalled a standard silent procedural message interpreted by aviators as: "I'd like some fuel please!"

The response from the Hercules' flight deck crew was immediate: both of the pilots' heads whipped round to stare at their escort. Meanwhile, several other crew members, their facial expressions quizzical, began to crowd against side windows. The repartee could be imagined:

"They're off their tiny little rockers!"

"How can we deal with these people?"

"They must be under stress!"

"It's a ruse."

"No, it's just a lark. Let's play along." At this, one of the Hercules' men grinned at the Phantom crew and gave a thumbs up sign. Thus encouraged, Archie manoeuvred backwards to adopt the standard refuel 'wait' position. After a moment or two, to his astonishment the Hercules' refuel drogue gave a slight lurch before it began to emerge from the hose drum unit. As the fuel line slowly extended, Archie followed it back and started to move to a refuelling position. At this juncture, however, the Hercules' captain must have decided that the prank had gone far enough: the hose jerked to a stop, paused, then was reeled swiftly back into its housing. Archie now eased his twin throttles forward to resume his former position abeam the Hercules' cockpit. When there, he dropped his oxygen mask briefly to make an exaggerated glum expression. The reaction from the Hercules' crew was intriguing: even more faces appeared at the side windows, all smiling broadly. Some shook their heads from side to side and wagged fingers as if at a naughty schoolboy.

Meantime, the Hercules' captain raised his coffee cup in salute, a sign which Archie construed to mean 'no hard feelings'. He therefore retracted his refuelling probe and held a slightly wider formation as if to indicate: 'Okay. That's agreed!' For the next hour or so Archie maintained this position while the formation flew on the planned course which took the aircraft directly overhead Mount Pleasant airfield then on towards the eastern boundary of the FICZ. When there, Archie complied with the internationally agreed signal 'you are clear to proceed' before he gave a cheery wave and broke away sharply to the left as he headed back to Mount Pleasant.

After landing, Archie and the other crew members were duly debriefed by intelligence officers who asked suitably intelligent questions. As usual, there were forms to complete, documents to sign, this and that to do to ensure satisfactory bureaucratic progression, but before long, in the bustle of a busy life, the incident began to recede to the back of Archie's mind. Indeed, three years went by before the memory was stirred, three years during which he moved from Leuchars to 74 Squadron at RAF Wattisham in Suffolk where, among other duties, he was the Phantom aerobatic display pilot – the last on type in the Royal Air Force. In the autumn of 1992, coincident with RAF Wattisham's transition to the Army Air Corps, he was posted to RAF Valley as officer commanding 234 Squadron, a training unit whose motto 'ignem mortemque despuimus' might have instilled a sense of awe within the student body (especially when they learnt the meaning – 'we spit fire and death').

*   *   *

Perhaps such a motto may have been appropriate, too, when issues concerning Argentina arose although, as some ten years had elapsed since the Falklands War, efforts were underway to normalise relations. As part of that process, a new Argentine air attaché had been appointed, a colonel who was in the throes of introduction to personnel at various Royal Air Force stations around the country, including RAF Valley. With the selection of 234 Squadron as one of the units to be visited, on the day in question staff and students were lined up ready to meet their important guest. To greet the colonel, the officers' mess had provided tea with proper teacups, silverware, posh biscuits, sandwiches, stewards and all.

When the colonel eventually arrived, he turned out to be a big man with an exuberant nature that seemed to go well with a moustache that might have made the legendary 'Biggles' proud. To accompany the colonel, smartly-uniformed members of the air attaché's staff were joined by a group of senior Royal Air Force officers. In contrast, Archie and his men wore their normal day-to-day flying suits. When Archie made suitable introductions, he was relieved to see that the colonel was an affable fellow who chatted freely with everyone present. Maybe it was all the more of a surprise, therefore, when the colonel suddenly stopped speaking to stare, mouth agape, at a badge he'd just spotted on Archie's flying suit. The badge, innocuous enough so Archie thought, revealed the achievement of 1,000 flying hours in a Phantom.

"Have you ever been to the Malvinas?" asked the colonel. An embarrassed hush descended on the room.

"Yes, sir. On several occasions," said Archie, "though we called the islands something else." He glanced nervously around the room. Some of the senior Royal Air Force officers scowled their disapproval.

"On several occasions?"

"Yes. I was detached there to fly Phantoms."

"Interesting," said the colonel. After a pause he went on: "I've flown there myself, actually."

"You have?"

"Indeed. That is...in a manner of speaking."

"Sir?"

"It must have been about three years ago. I was on board a C-130 which had permission to overfly the Malvinas – the first FAA aircraft to do so since the war. We had to be escorted by a couple of Phantoms, one of which pretended to need an in-flight refuel from our C-130." The colonel laughed and went on: "It was all a bit of fun, of course. But it broke the ice, so to speak, and the C-130 captain was willing to play along up to a point."

At once, Archie beckoned one of his students, whispered a message which sent the student scurrying off to return after a moment or two with Archie's flying logbook. Thumbing hastily through it, Archie found a particular page with a photograph loosely inserted. He extracted the photograph and showed it to the colonel whose face, as he studied the picture, at first looked shocked, then bemused, amused and amazed. "This is you...?" said the colonel. "Yes, sir. I was on duty that day – I was the Phantom pilot who pretended to need an in-flight refuel."

"My God..." The colonel stared at Archie then, in a spontaneous act, clapped him on the shoulder, shook his hand vigorously and grabbed him in a bear hug. Now, in an escalating spirit of munificence, the colonel fumbled in his pocket to pull out a small leather pouch which contained a medal from the Argentine air academy. Without further ado, the colonel solemnly pinned the medal to Archie's flying suit before, his moustache bristling with pride, he stepped back and saluted our gallant protagonist.

At this, the buzz of conversation in the room started up again while poor Archie, as he struggled to recover from momentary vertigo induced by such extravagance, was relieved to see that the group of senior Royal Air Force officers now looked rather less mournful. Maybe Archie felt a little light-headed, caught off-balance by the bizarre, unplanned experience. Was it, though, altogether unplanned? On reflection, Archie reckoned that the colonel seemed, somehow, pre-prepared. If not, why carry such a medal anyway? Surely not on the off-chance of meeting some random individual who instantly needed one?

At length, when the colonel and his party made moves to leave, he came up to Archie to shake his hand warmly. "Goodbye, my friend. Please pay a visit to the Argentine air academy one day, huh?"

"Thanks, sir. That would be…" Archie suddenly noticed the way the colonel was looking at him. When the colonel nodded and turned around to leave, Archie was left with the distinct impression that he knew all along who Archie was. He could never be sure, of course, and as he watched the Argentine officer and his party leave, Archie realised that the entire, strange episode would have to remain as one of life's little surprises.

CHAPTER 3

NAVAL HAZARDS

ALAN WINKLES' BRUSH WITH FATE

The day started as a good one, an ordinary Wednesday in February 1976. The term ordinary, of course, was a relative one and Squadron Leader Alan Winkles' position on board an aircraft carrier in the middle of the Atlantic Ocean might be seen by some as really rather – well – not very ordinary at all, even rather extraordinary. Nevertheless, he had been at sea with the ship, HMS *Ark Royal,* for nearly three weeks by that stage and his sea legs had become quite seaworthy as he settled into new routines. As an air force man recently appointed to take command of the Royal Navy's Phantom Training Flight based at RAF Leuchars, he was scheduled to be on board the *Ark Royal,* nicknamed the 'Mighty Ark', for several weeks in order to gain experience in naval ways – one of which, he soon discovered, was an unashamed capacity to stretch 'several weeks' into six months. The ship, while it steamed westwards, was heading for the east coast of the United States of America. In the wind were pungent oceanic odours which mingled with those from the flight deck as crews prepared 892 Squadron Phantoms for flying operations.

Such preparations were not always possible, however, for on occasions, when mighty and mysterious meteorological millibars began to herald a deep Atlantic low, flying operations had to be suspended. On such days, Alan Winkles would sometimes make for the so-called 'goofers' gallery' to observe an approaching storm. With the elements in charge and with the ship having to cope with giant waves, he'd watch with a mix of fascination and alarm as crests of waves exploded against the nearby superstructure. He'd peer into the storm but see nothing apart from rain, marauding waves of dark ocean and savage seaborne flotsam. From the crest of a wave one moment, a mountain would seemingly collapse to leave a great emptiness as the ship plunged down into the next trough. He'd watch as spray pelted down the bridge windows to end up on a wave-washed flight deck. One time he took film of 60-foot blue water waves crashing into the bridge as the ship battled a hurricane off Halifax, Nova Scotia. On that occasion, aircraft on deck had been moved to the ship's stern spots and lashed down with sixteen chains each, but a liberty boat, violently wrenched from its davits, was lost in the storm.

For the unfortunate crewmen whose duties forced them outside in such conditions, navy-issued oilskins provided a measure of protection. Seamen, though, would wince when raw seas bit against fingers and hands, against ears and cheeks, and these men, hampered as torrents compelled them to half-close their eyes, would have to grip handrails tightly to steady themselves. With the wind's howl rising to a shriek, spray as solid as streamers would lash against oilskins before heading for scuppers in a rush of grumbles and gurgles. When men slithered along the drenched flight deck they'd feel the ship shudder beneath their feet as the aircraft carrier struggled to tackle the conditions. Behind the ship would appear great plumes powered high by the screws. The air would be filled with many kinds of odd noises as the ship's structure creaked and groaned in protest. However, the steady background beat of the carrier's four sets of Parsons-geared turbines provided a measure of reassurance. With eight Admiralty three-drum boilers in four boiler rooms, and with these huge mechanical contraptions pitted against the forces of nature, the aircraft carrier would ride the storm.

Individuals might lose track of time as the onslaught persisted but eventually the sky would begin to clear and the waves would seem to flee with the clouds. With an eeriness emphasised by the swift silence that followed, the rain would cease. While the storm abated, so the frayed nerves of crew members eased. The change of scene could appear to be as rapid and radical as moving to a different ocean.

When flying operations had been cancelled one time, Alan Winkles decided to make for the officers' wardroom. The

Pilot performs pre-flight checks on naval Phantom. Note wings folded.

wardroom atmosphere tended to be tense in stormy weather and, as a newcomer on board and also, perhaps, as the ship's senior member of the Royal Air Force ('crab' in naval parlance) his entrance caused a semi-circle of naval officers in the room to turn and stare before, as a door banged shut, they about-faced again to resume an eye-to-eye nautical huddle. With thoughts about naval ways, the fetishism for correct navy terminology, the stifling of outsiders and even the repression of revolutionary energies, he crossed the room.

When he sat down and picked up a newspaper, it was several days out of date. While some of the old sea dogs on board moaned about this as well as complaining about the manner in which modern broadsheets printed far too much in the way of sanctimonious, humourless drivel, he was interested, nonetheless, to read reports of Concorde's first commercial flight a month earlier. The newspaper commented on the design parallels between Concorde and the English Electric P1/Lightning – the aircraft he had flown operationally before his move to Phantoms. The article pointed out the problems of achieving commercial and economic viability and that for the four Rolls-Royce turbojet engines to attain the required levels of fuel efficiency, they had been specially designed and manufactured. The engines, though, were highly inefficient at low speeds and evidently used some two tonnes of fuel (almost two per cent of the maximum fuel load) just taxiing to the runway for take-off. However, thanks to advanced aerodynamic characteristics, fuel-guzzling reheat (afterburner) was not used apart from take-off and between the airspeeds of Mach 0.95 and Mach 1.7. The report highlighted how Concorde's air intake design was particularly critical so a number of features had been constructed including, as with the Phantom, variable intake ramps.

It was following a recent exercise in the Mediterranean Sea that the *Ark Royal* had set sail for America. Now, with the carrier positioned over 600 miles from the nearest diversion airfield, Lajes Field on the Azores, the ship's aircraft would have to operate on a so-called non-diversion basis. If needed, a specially equipped Blackburn Buccaneer could be launched as an in-flight refuelling backup to allow a Phantom or Buccaneer a little more time to resolve an airborne emergency, but if that failed the pilot and observer would probably be committed to ejection from their aircraft.

As this was the ship's first day of non-diversion flying and in view of his inexperience in naval routines, Alan Winkles was a little surprised to see himself programmed to fly. For one thing, he had yet to practise in-flight refuelling from a Buccaneer. However, having completed eight successful launches and 'traps', he felt reasonably confident. The sea state was moderate and the weather had settled. After a detailed briefing, he and his observer walked out to their Phantom where he carried out a walk-round inspection while the observer strapped in to the rear cockpit. When satisfied, he climbed the small access steps to enter the front cockpit where, having strapped in and completed the cockpit checks, he waited for orders to start engines. The sequence of aircraft launch – Fairey Gannets (for airborne early warning) followed by Buccaneers then Phantoms and lastly Wessex helicopters – reflected fuel constraints when airborne. The sequence was reversed for recovery to the carrier.

While proceedings got underway, aircraft initiated engine start. Meanwhile, the ship began to turn into the natural wind. As the first Fairey Gannet taxied onto the catapult, the pilot spread his Fairey wings and the deck crew prepared for catapult hook-up. In due course, when the Fairey Gannets and Blackburn Buccaneers had been launched, it was the turn of the 892 Squadron Phantoms. As number three in a four-ship Phantom launch that day, Alan duly waited his turn before he began to taxi as instructed by the deck crew. After the previous Phantom's launch, jet blast deflectors were lowered to allow him to manoeuvre his aircraft to the take-off spot. He dutifully followed every twitch of the hands and fingers of the launch controller who marshalled him onto the 180-foot long 'waist' catapult which was thirty feet longer than the bow catapult. The launch controller's movements were just as skilful and subtle as those of a concert pianist tackling a Rachmaninoff piano concerto (with the possible exception of number three in D minor). The most intricate movements were required to ensure that the Phantom's twin nose-wheels were positioned in precisely the right spot just in front of the catapult shuttle. A wire strop attached to the shuttle was then secured to two huge hooks, one under each of the Phantom's engine intakes. Simultaneously, a rear 'holdback' cable was fastened behind the nose gear to maintain tension in the catapult system against the thrust of the aircraft engines.

Dramatic shot of a naval Phantom positioned on the steam catapult ready for take-off.

It was at this point that trouble loomed although Alan had no inkling at the time. The ground chief, who stood just below the Phantom's cockpits, activated a nose gear extension switch which was situated in the nose-wheel bay. At once, the nose-wheel oleo leg extended to twice its normal length thereby adjusting the aircraft attitude to the fourteen degrees angle of attack needed for take-off. Alan, as he felt the aircraft rise, set the tail-plane to the required angle so that the Phantom did not lose height after launch. He reached for a restraining cable fixed to the instrument panel and attached the cable to the control column; this would help to prevent the control column from moving rearwards during launch. He glanced outside the cockpit. The launch man began to twirl a flag to indicate that the pilot should advance his throttles to full power. Alan eased the Phantom's twin throttles forward as he monitored the engine instruments...*temperatures and pressures in limits, nozzles steady, no cockpit warnings.* The low whine of the Rolls-Royce Spey engines began to increase to a roar. These engines, manufactured by the same company that made Rolls-Royce motor cars, had a reputation for reliability and sheer down-to-earth excellence which gave the aircrew a sense of security. Soon, with full reheat selected, the Phantom's airframe shook as if in nervous anticipation of what was about to follow. "All set?" he asked his observer. "Yup...I'm all set," came the reply.

Alan Winkles now saluted the launch man. To make sure that the twin throttles did not slip back during launch, he locked his left arm against them. He pressed his right elbow into his stomach and placed his right hand behind the top of the control column. He held his 'bone dome' (flying helmet) hard against the headrest of his Martin-Baker ejection seat...and he waited. He did not have to wait long. Suddenly, he spotted the launch man's flag being lowered to the deck. One-and-a-half seconds later he felt a tremendous punch in the back as the catapult operator discharged the steam catapult. A combination of 250,000 pounds of thrust from the steam catapult added to 46,000 pounds from twin Rolls-Royce Spey engines in full reheat propelled the Phantom from zero airspeed to 145 knots in less than three seconds. The resultant acceleration of five-and-a-half G caused the aircrews' peripheral vision to 'grey out'. Even so, Alan managed to retain his eyes' main focus on the cockpit indicator which displayed the correct function of the engines' twin reheat nozzles; any engine malfunction at that stage would almost inevitably mean an immediate ejection before the Phantom plummeted into the sea.

Very soon, as the Phantom was hurled clear of the carrier's deck, the aircraft adopted normal acceleration and the aircrews' full vision returned. Alan unclipped the control column's support cable and he went through the after take-off checks. These included operation of a lever on the left side of his cockpit to raise the undercarriage. Usually, a slight thump would be felt as the nose gear retracted into its housing; concurrently the cockpit gauge would show that the undercarriage was 'up'. On that day, however, he felt no thump and within moments his eyes were drawn to a red light which glowed on the cockpit warning panel. The warning panel read 'NLG CAT POSITION' – the extended nose oleo, designed to shrink to normal size after take-off, had failed to operate correctly. This meant that the extended leg, ten feet in length, was too long to fit into its housing, furthermore it would break off unless a smooth and gentle landing could be guaranteed; there was no 'give' in its suspension. Landings on aircraft carriers could be described in various ways but smooth and gentle was not one of them. Pilots' Notes were unambiguous: this was a rare emergency but if the nose oleo remained extended, landing on an aircraft carrier's deck was prohibited; if a suitable diversion airfield was not available, the aircrew members were to eject.

The moment was a blur; Alan took time to absorb the implications. Out of instinct, however, he carried on with necessary procedures. He cancelled the Rolls-Royce Spey reheats and he climbed cautiously ahead in the hope that the fault would clear itself. His eyes became almost glued to the undercarriage cockpit indicator which, instead of indicating up, persisted to show a 'barber's pole' warning. On the aircraft radio he declared an emergency. He selected the undercarriage down again – a successful selection as the cockpit gauge confirmed that the nose wheel and the main wheels were down. However, because the carrier was operating on a non-diversion basis, the problem remained. His observer, therefore, read out the emergency procedures which included various manoeuvres while the pilot pulled positive G and pushed negative G. None of these procedures, though, cured the problem; the 'NLG CAT POSITION' warning light still glowed obstinately on the cockpit warning panel. The aircrew, committed to flying at or below 250 knots (the maximum permissible airspeed with the undercarriage down), had no option but to fly in circles close to the *Ark Royal* in the hope that the defect would clear itself before the Phantom ran out of fuel. Meantime, the crew of the carrier's in-flight refuelling Buccaneer was brought to cockpit readiness while Alan continued to fly endless manoeuvres in attempts to rectify the fault. Alas, his efforts were in vain. As the Phantom's fuel reduced bit by bit, he and his observer became increasingly anxious. They had trained for an emergency ejection when prodigious amounts of adrenalin would help, no doubt, with the proceedings. They had not trained for the pre-meditated situation and the dire feelings which haunted the mind as the *moment critique* slowly but surely crept up on them.

Gazing out at the clouds on the horizon, Alan realised that he seemed to become more vulnerable and isolated as the minutes ticked by. The sweep of the ocean appeared somehow ever vaster and more worrying. Within his head he began to dwell on the details of what felt like an inescapable abyss. His brain seemed to split into two halves with mixed messages whirling through his thoughts: one side of the brain presented intelligent, shrewd insight; the other side suggested doubt, indecision and – yes – downright fear. There was fear of the known; even worse, there was fear of the unknown.

Some people, apparently, were not prone to the sensation of fear; including the legendary naval test pilot Captain Eric 'Winkle' Brown who once said that in dangerous situations he did not feel fear but instead his mind developed an icy focus (he also described himself, incidentally, as a curious mix between an academic and a cowboy). For many, however, fear was an inherent part of their make-up – nature's way, perhaps, of facilitating survival, and for these people fear would root out their weakest spot and find it with the least amount of effort. One moment Alan would consider his position in the light of reason, then fear, initially in the guise of slight uncertainty, would force its way into the thought processes like an enemy agent. But he knew that he should make every effort to fight the contradictions, contentions, and concerns within his head. The successful outcome of this ordeal could depend on remaining level-headed.

Apart from discussing actions detailed in the emergency cards, there was little conversation between the two aircrew. One time, when Alan made a general comment, in the cockpit's rear-view mirror he saw his observer nod abstractedly but say nothing. The two of them, therefore, sat in silence in their individual cockpits. Alan decided to recap, within his mind, the survival drills which had been covered in the many briefings he'd attended over the years. Before he initiated the ejection process, he planned to position the Phantom at an altitude of 5,000 feet in the vicinity of the aircraft carrier and its accompanying Type 42 destroyer. The latter, he'd noticed, had closed up to be nearer the *Ark Royal.*

Before the ejection itself, he would make sure that he tugged at his seat straps to tighten his harness as much as possible. He'd force himself to adopt a good posture with his back pressed hard against the seat. He would order his observer to eject first, then he'd count a few seconds before pulling his own ejection seat handle. He could anticipate a loud bang and a violent upwards thrust as he was propelled away from his warm, high-tech cockpit. After the ejection, the Martin-Baker mechanisms should automatically separate the seat frame from the parachute itself, and from his altitude of 5,000 feet he could expect to spend quite a few minutes in the parachute before he approached the sea. In the parachute descent he should check carefully that his dinghy pack, designed to dangle some distance below him, was properly secured. When, eventually, he was close to the sea's surface and just before his feet touched the water he would prepare to operate the Koch fasteners to release his parachute. When released, the parachute canopy should, hopefully, be caught by the wind and blown clear so as not to impede his survival actions once in the water. He'd have to remember to inflate his lifejacket and to hold his breath when he was about to be plunged into the cold sea; the lifejacket should help him to bob back up to the surface quite rapidly. Then he'd have to haul in a shroud line to pull the dinghy pack towards him. With the pack in his hands, he'd tug at the dinghy's quick-inflation device. At once, a CO_2 gas bottle should crash into life to cause the compact dinghy pack to undergo metamorphosis into a one-man rubber dinghy – a frail but crucial refuge and his key to survival. He'd have to locate and grasp two handles on the side of the dinghy, then haul himself on board before twisting round into a sitting position.

By this stage he'd probably have a taste of sea water in his mouth, his eyes would smart from the salt-laden air and his face would feel stung by the wind. Despite these hazards, he'd have to concentrate on the next priorities. As speedily as possible he should confirm that the dinghy's small canvas sea anchor had deployed to keep his back into the wind. He should set up the dinghy's built-in protective canopy to cover his back and his head. He should blow some air into the special mouthpiece designed to inflate the dinghy's floor. He'd have to commence the laborious, relentless task of baling. If he was sufficiently close to his observer's dinghy, the two aircrew would attempt, no doubt, to paddle towards each other. If events went according to plan, the time spent in their individual one-man dinghies should be minimal as a Wessex helicopter would be on standby to swoop down to pick them up. However, if a helicopter unserviceability arose, or if rescue was delayed because of a problem with the ship, the aircrew might expect a long period spent in their lightweight life rafts. Tossed by wind and wave the two men could anticipate an uncomfortable time. They knew, though, that from the naval perspective the ship's security and ongoing efficiency were of prime concern, and they understood that the navy's attitude in this respect could be brutal.

It was while these and other notions played through his head that the situation was resolved as promptly as it had begun. He was about to ask for the air-to-air refuelling Buccaneer to be launched when he and his observer both felt a familiar thump as the nose oleo adjusted itself. At the same time, the warning light in the cockpit went out. For some moments, with a poignant sensation of deliverance, the two aircrew continued to remain in silence in their cockpits. The men could barely believe what was happening. Had fate intervened? Their new situation, though, was true enough and perhaps, for some reason, fate had wanted to deliver its message, make its point, have its moment, but now, at last, had decided that enough was enough. For those with eyes to see, the episode had been a visionary process, a glimpse of yin and yang, of inner and outer, of flesh and spirit but now, as if fate's obscure objects had been sufficiently tempted, it was time to go home.

At length, with a degree of relief that he's never before or since experienced, Alan informed the *Ark Royal.* He was cleared for an immediate visual join and deck landing. The landing was normal; the nose wheel functioned as it should. The in-flight refuelling Buccaneer's two crew members were stood down; the facility had not been required. That was just as well. Two days later, when needed for another task, this Buccaneer was ordered airborne but was found to be unserviceable when one of its engines failed to start. For some days, the Mighty Ark's programme of non-diversion flying had been based on a false premise.

CHAPTER 4
FIGHTER CONTROLLER
FLIGHT LIEUTENANT PENELOPE 'PENNY' SMITH (NÉE WILD), WRAF

A newspaper headline stated: 'Penelope in a Phantom', another said: 'Penny joins the jet set', comments that, for Flight Lieutenant Penny Wild, encapsulated the thrill she'd felt during her one-hour flight in the back seat of a Phantom based at Royal Air Force Coningsby. As a fighter controller, she was used to the orange glow from the radar screens in a darkened room, the muted light from the operational tote board and the hushed tones of the operations room personnel. The chance to fly as a passenger in one of the fighters she normally knew only as a blip on a radar screen, a flight in which the pilot allowed her to handle the controls for much of the time, was a rare opportunity and one which she'd relish for years to come.

Born in Portsmouth three years after the end of World War Two, her father was a boat builder who had spent the latter years of the war in the Royal Navy. Both of her grandfathers were seamen, one in the Royal Navy, the other in the Merchant Navy, and no-one in her family had shown interest in aviation apart from an uncle, a crack shot who had served with the Royal Air Force Regiment. It came as a complete surprise to her naval-orientated family, therefore, when Penny announced that she wanted to join the Royal Air Force. Evidently her decision was prompted when, as a fifteen-year-old, she'd watched a formation of naval Supermarine Scimitars conduct a fly-past over Portsmouth harbour. The exhilaration of watching those aircraft swoop their way through the skies was, for her, an extraordinary sensation and a defining moment. Suddenly she knew that this was what she wanted to do. However, it was the early 1960s, there were no female military or airline pilots and the Air Transport Auxiliary, which had famously employed women pilots to ferry aircraft in World War Two, had been disbanded in November 1945.

Undaunted, she sought another way to become involved with aircraft and decided to apply to become an air traffic controller. After interviews at the Officer Aircrew Selection Centre at RAF Biggin Hill she was selected for training at the officer cadet training unit at RAF Henlow. Her excitement at passing the course, however, was tempered by the news that, unlike other colleagues on her course, she had been posted to RAF Bawdsey. "Where on earth is Bawdsey?" she asked, "and what goes on there?"

"I don't know," said one of her friends, "but I don't think it's got anything much to do with air traffic control."

It seemed that no-one knew until eventually a member of staff explained to Penny that RAF Bawdsey was not part of air traffic control but was a unit within Fighter Command. "Fighter Command?" she asked in astonishment.

"Yes, Fighter Command. It's all a bit hush-hush, but there's a radar unit there. Their job involves controlling fighter aircraft tasked with the interception of intruders."

"Are there any aircraft based at Bawdsey?"

"No. It's a radar unit – there aren't any aircraft." At this, Penny's heart sank for her aim had been a posting to an active flying unit.

Despite her misgivings, when Penny arrived at Bawdsey she was, in some ways, placated by what she found there. Situated on the east coast of Suffolk, the set-up was dominated by an imposing Victorian property, Bawdsey Manor, which had been taken over by the air ministry three years before the outbreak of World War Two. Penny learnt that, positioned some 200 yards from the manor house, there was a research station where the legendary Robert Watson-Watt had developed, as superintendent, the new and ingenious radio direction finding (RDF) system, later known as radar. As the site for the first of the 'Chain Home' stations to be built, Bawdsey's eight tall masts, four for transmitting, four for receiving, would help to prove pivotal to the outcome of the Battle of Britain. With the outbreak of war in September 1939, and with fears of a possible German commando raid on the coastal unit, the top secret research group had moved to Dundee in Scotland while the RDF system was left active at RAF Bawdsey.

Many years later Penny learnt about a remarkable, and probably less well-known, episode which had occurred in 1940 when the British Army had staged a practice landing against Bawdsey. Warning was given to the commanding officer but the message failed to reach the sentries on duty. When rubber dinghies were spotted creeping up to the beach area, the sentries released gas-filled barrels which then were set alight with tracer rounds from machine guns. In the morning, the sentries found dozens of charred bodies which initially they took to be Germans dressed in British uniforms for disguise. However, further investigation revealed the awful truth. When the authorities realised the full extent of this 'own goal' disaster it was decided that details should be kept secret until, remarkably, as far in the future as the year 2014. Despite this, information was gathered before then by a newspaper which released the story in 1992.

As her ground control intercept (GCI) training got underway at the School of Control and Reporting located at Bawdsey, Penny soon learned that intercepting a target aircraft with a fighter was in effect the antithesis of air traffic control: far from using radar to arrange safe separation between aircraft, the fighter controller's job was to facilitate the merging of blips on a radar screen. She learnt that at the heart of a master radar station, of which there were several around the country, was a control centre built deep underground and termed 'the hole' or 'R3'. These bunkers were part of the ROTOR programme set up in the 1950s to provide an operational environment capable of withstanding a near miss by a nuclear weapon. Entrance was made through a guard room intended to look like an ordinary farmhouse so that, hopefully, enemy observers were fooled (although the massive radar heads nearby might have offered a clue). Within the R3, a central control room known as a master allocation room or MAR, was dominated by a large Perspex plotting map with the overall radar picture projected onto the map. Along a nearby corridor were several fighter control cabins to which controllers, when allocated a practice sortie or a live interception, were sent by the chief controller in the MAR. A typical cabin team comprised a controller, an assistant and an airman or airwoman who kept a small tote board updated with information such as weather conditions and diversion airfields. Interception controllers spoke directly with fighter pilots to guide them during the interception process. The fighter control students were taught various techniques although in practice a successful outcome was as much an art as a science. The complex technology – state of the art for the period – required a considerable depth of understanding; the students were taught the need for a flexible mentality and that they may have to apply their skills in a 'seat-of-the-pants' way, especially when confronted with an evading target.

As she settled into life at Bawdsey, a film crew arrived one day to record scenes for a documentary on Britain's air defences, including coverage of the unclassified part of the ROTOR programme. When filming started, Penny was allocated the position of 'scrambler' in the master allocation room. She was not, however, allowed to recite the standard patter

used when scrambling a fighter aircraft as it was considered classified information. Instead, she was instructed to read the weather forecast. Watching from an observation platform were some high-ranking visitors from NATO countries, including a USAF general who, amused by the weather forecast ruse, had a good conversation with Penny in the officers' mess later. A couple of weeks after that, during her liaison visit to a fighter squadron at RAF Wattisham, the

Bawdsey Manor.

day was warm so Penny wore no coat or service cap. Suddenly, she spotted a highly polished staff car sweep into sight. The car drove up to park near an English Electric Lightning aircraft on the flight line where she and her escorting officer stood, and she was amazed when 'her' USAF general stepped out to walk across to greet her – "Good to see you again."

"Thank you, sir."

"How are you?"

"I'm very well, sir." She came to attention as one should but, lacking the all-important service cap, she was unable to salute. It seemed that the US military were unabashed by saluting without a cap

The Cold War operational room at RAF Neatishead. (Crown Copyright)

so she was embarrassed when the American general, despite her lowly military rank, offered young Penny the smartest of salutes. Faced with this dilemma, not to mention the bewildered expressions of the officers who accompanied the general, she was more than a little relieved when the senior officer, after further pleasantries, continued with his planned tour.

*   *   *

On completion of her training at Bawdsey, Penny became a qualified member of staff there before, in September 1968, she was excited to receive news of her posting to 280 Signals Unit, Cyprus. This radar unit, situated at Cape Gata in the south of the island, was adjacent to RAF Akrotiri, an airfield first constructed in the mid 1950s and which formed a British Overseas Territory administered as a sovereign base area. Penny was one of four female fighter controllers at Cape Gata who inevitably earned the sobriquet 'Gata Girls'. Naturally, the Gata Girls were appreciated by the fighter crews for various reasons, one of which, and perhaps a less obvious one, was the clarity of their voices on the aircraft radios. This could prove operationally significant especially in hectic circumstances when a clear and easily identifiable voice could be crucial during GCI procedures. Sometimes crews of specially-equipped English Electric Canberras designed to 'jam' radars and radio transmissions would simulate Soviet-built swept-wing Tupolev Tu-16 strategic bombers, NATO code-name 'Badger', whose Egyptian crews were known to approach the coast of Cyprus occasionally. To be as realistic as possible, the Canberra crews would also transmit spoof messages in attempts to confuse our fighter pilots. Such efforts, though, invariably failed when the Gata Girls were in control. It was believed that, to counter this effect, unfriendly crews might resort to verbal intimidation, even bad language but the Gata Girls learned to ignore the abuse and to keep on talking. Indeed, they became proficient in coping when, at times, it was hard to get even one word across to a fighter pilot. The results could be chaotic, on occasions hilarious, nevertheless the Gata Girls became expert at pilot-controller teamwork and at making every word count.

An unusual interception took place one weekend when the Cypriot authorities reported to the fighter controllers that an aircraft had filed a flight plan to head south after take-off from Nicosia Airport. This aircraft, however, had headed north instead of south. Furthermore, the authorities had received intelligence that the aircraft, a Martin 2-0-2, was carrying contraband of some kind, possibly guns, and could the Royal Air Force therefore carry out an interception? The watch commander brought the pilot of the QRA Lightning to cockpit readiness, then ordered an immediate scramble and sent Penny hurrying to a control cabin. The Lightning rapidly caught up with the Martin 2-0-2 approaching the island's north shore. At this point, however, the Lightning pilot experienced problems in view of the disparity in airspeeds – the Martin 2-0-2, a twin-engined piston airliner built as an intended replacement for the Douglas DC-3, flew at a cruising airspeed close to the Lightning's stall speed. To keep the Martin 2-0-2 in sight, therefore, the Lightning pilot had to fly a series of 360-degree turns until ordered to break away when a Phantom from the United States Sixth Fleet took over and forced the Martin to land. The incident, reported on the BBC World Service, resulted in arrests when quantities of cannabis were found on board.

Rear view shot of an F-4 on the pan at RAF Akrotiri.

From time to time, following the 1967 Arab-Israeli Six Day War and the subsequent three-year War of Attrition, Soviet-built bombers manned by Egyptian crews would fly towards Cyprus thus prompting the scramble of a fighter aircraft to intercept. To monitor activity in the area, Lockheed U-2 reconnaissance aircraft of the United States Air Force, rumoured to be flown by operatives of the United States Central Intelligence Agency (CIA), were based at RAF Akrotiri for a period. Occasionally, Penny would glimpse one of these clandestine aircraft being towed outside from a closed-off hangar before an expeditious departure. The take-off itself looked relatively slow but once airborne the single Pratt and Whitney turbojet engine (later versions used General Electric turbofan engines) powered the U-2 at a remarkably steep angle of climb to very high altitudes. After take-off, a couple of American officers would appear at Cape Gata in order to monitor the U-2s on radar. These men, however, never wore uniforms and never spoke a word about why they were there.

One time, Penny was the recovery controller when she picked up a radio message from an unknown call sign on the emergency frequency; from the pilot's American accent she deduced that the pilot of one of the U-2s was in difficulty. She duly offered navigational assistance to steer the pilot towards Akrotiri after which he was able to land there safely. Later that day, just as she was leaving the officers' mess, an American in civilian clothing came up to her. "I just wanted to thank you, ma'am," he said.

"Any time," she said, a little perplexed.

"You won't know me," he went on, "but you helped me back to base earlier."

"How do you know it was me?" she asked. The agent just gave a wry smile before he went on his way to leave Penny with little doubt about the way CIA operatives worked.

On occasions, Penny was detached to RAF Troodos, a remote signals station on the summit of Mount Olympus in the Troodos Mountains and, incidentally, the oldest British military base in Cyprus dating from 1878. When the aircraft carrier HMS *Ark Royal* was in the area one time, a pair of Blackburn Buccaneers simulated a low-level attack against RAF Akrotiri. Tension was high, reflecting the fierce inter-service rivalry between the navy and the air force. At Cape Gata, the display controller and his team huddled around their radar screens while Penny did the same at Troodos. Poised at the end of Akrotiri's runway a pair of Lightnings waited, their pilots at cockpit readiness and desperate for the word to proceed. The embarrassment was immense, therefore, when Penny and the other fighter controllers were informed by the Lightning pilots (air traffic controllers had been sworn to secrecy) that the two Buccaneers had just performed victory rolls over the airfield.

It was some months later when HMS *Ark Royal* returned for a further exercise which included another attack by Buccaneers against Akrotiri. This time, the fighter pilots and the fighter controllers were determined to avoid humiliation. Worried discussions and head-scratching took place as all and sundry tried to work out the best way to cope with the problem of these Buccaneers and their ability to fly at ultra-low level from take-off to target. The key factor, an early radar pick-up, seemed virtually impossible to achieve with the equipment then available. For days, various types of interceptions were practised in attempts to fine-tune the best procedures against such a difficult target. With the looming of the exercise itself, Penny had mixed feelings when allocated the task of fighter controller for, although honoured to be selected, the sense of responsibility was, she felt, somewhat unenviable. As it turned out, in her team was an experienced sergeant who was probably, she believed, the best display controller in the entire Royal Air Force. Perhaps that was as well for it was this sergeant who, assisted by the skilled engineers' ability to 'tweak' the radar equipment, managed to pick out a small radar blip at the remarkable range of around 200 miles. "I think that might be them," he muttered. The raw radar equipment used in those days was liable to attract spurious radar returns, nonetheless the sergeant had a strong feeling that he'd glimpsed the Buccaneers.

"Okay," said the chief controller, "let's mark it", and trusting the sergeant's judgement he sent Penny to the nearest fighter control cabin to mark on the radar screen the possible initial sighting. Now, with a Chinagraph pencil and using dead reckoning (DR) techniques, she began to track a predicted flight path based on the Buccaneers' likely approach speed and on the assumption that the aircraft would head directly for Akrotiri. Even though another radar blip was never seen, the chief controller decided to scramble his fighters anyway. Penny directed the fighters to the south of Akrotiri, then turned them onto a heading towards the threat but with lateral separation. Fine judgement was needed while her Chinagraph dead reckoning marks and the fighters closed on each other. At what she trusted was the right moment, she nervously ordered the fighters to make a ninety-degree turn. When she saw that the pilots had rolled out onto the new heading she cleared them to descend to very low level for the interception. At such low altitudes, both radar and radio contact were lost and it was with a sense of elation, therefore, when, a few minutes later, the fighter pilots climbed up to report a successful interception and that both Buccaneers had been 'splashed' (theoretically shot down).

* * *

In November 1970, by which time her spirit of determination had gained her a private pilot's licence, Penny was posted away from the island idyll at Cape Gata to take up a new post at RAF Buchan, a bleak, windswept radar station in northern Scotland. It was mid-winter, distant Scottish hills were grey with low cloud and the Cypriot landscape felt like another world. At Buchan, rain seemed permanently poised to swirl out of the sky, and the wind, sounding loud and high, came from the north to sweep through the officers' mess until dying away again, defeated, only to return feigning a light blow until an abrupt violent gust made everyone flinch. "I keep listening to the wind," said Penny to a friend. "You'll get used to it."

In time Penny did, nevertheless for a while she could not avoid thoughts of the lifestyle she had left behind in Cyprus. She would reminisce on the diverse experiences during her time there, including a particular event shortly before she left the island. A member of staff in the officers' mess at Troodos, a Greek Cypriot steward called Michael, had invited her and four other officers to dinner at his home. It was an unusual invitation and a rare opportunity for them to sample real Cypriot life away from air force routines. When the officers entered Michael's home they were directed to a dining area with a large refectory-style table in the centre of the room. Numbers of family members were summoned to sit down for dinner at which point she suddenly realised that all of her fellow diners were men. This would not normally have bothered her except that the meal itself was served by the household's womenfolk who, by tradition, were not allowed to eat in the same room or at the same time as the men. Michael proved a model host as he tried to put her at ease, nonetheless she could not avoid an ongoing sense of culture shock, especially at the end of the meal when the women were expected to hurry into the room to clear the table as the men had finished.

As Penny settled in to her new life at Buchan, she was allocated accommodation within a small building set aside for WRAF officers. In addition to the seemingly endless howl of the wind, she could hear waves crashing onto the rocks below for her room was close to the edge of cliffs. Her peace was regularly shattered, too, by the sound of an unbelievably loud foghorn nicknamed the 'Boddam Coo' (the Scottish word for 'cow') which blasted away during the frequent local fogs. Despite these drawbacks she grew to appreciate the area and its attractive countryside with scattered sheep and cattle farms. She was delighted when, on her journey to work, she drove past a field of long-haired highland cattle with their fierce expressions and equally fierce horns ready to protect the young. She found that she adapted quickly to the work pattern at Buchan, the radar unit that handled most of the country's Cold War activity.

For a while Penny had been aware that, at times, there was poor rapport between fighter control stations and the fighter squadrons. Crews were often unhappy with the quality of control, or with the lack of full co-operation that they felt was offered by the chief controllers. In turn, chief controllers were annoyed by what they perceived as excessive demands from the squadron crews. In an attempt to rectify the problem, it was decided that two fighter controllers at a time should join IWI (intercept weapons instructor) courses for selected and qualified Lightning pilots and run by 226 Operational Conversion Unit (OCU) at RAF Coltishall. The aim was to improve mutual co-operation and a better understanding of each others' point of view.

A few months after she arrived at her next duty station, RAF Neatishead in Norfolk, Penny was excited when asked if she would like to join one of these courses – the first woman to do so. Furthermore, there would be opportunities for her to fly in the two-seat versions of the fighter aircraft she controlled. Before she could fly, however, she had to complete three requirements: undergo fittings for a full set of flying gear; attend a lecture on ejection seats; and go through a simulated parachute landing in the station swimming pool. These requirements presented, in general, no problems – except, that was, for the anti-G suit fitting. With no women aircrew at that time, the flying clothing section was run entirely by men, so the aircrew changing room, in preparation for Penny's anti-G suit fitting, had to be cleared of all personnel apart from one man, a quiet, grey-haired chief technician whose acute sense of embarrassment was all too obvious. In those days the anti-G suit was placed under the flying suit, so aircrew wore long underwear to prevent skin chaffing. To be ready for the fitting process, Penny needed, therefore, to remove her uniform skirt and to replace it with a pair of male long-johns while still wearing her uniform shirt and tie as well as her service court shoes. When the chief technician set about his work, the awkwardness of the moment was emphasised by a drawn-out, uncomfortable silence. Conscious that the situation was at once absurd and hilarious, Penny could not fail to appreciate the humorous side. "Oh, Chiefie," she wanted to say, "how lovely to see you running round in circles just for me."

"Anything to oblige, ma'am."

"But please be cautious. I gather that this is a French invention notable for its elegance and ingenuity."

"Quite possibly, ma'am."

"Even though it's a work of genius, be careful to avoid injury. The psyche of French-men cannot be trusted."

"Definitely not, ma'am."

"Can you speak French, Chiefie?"

"No, ma'am. It is not possible."

"Hmmm. Perhaps you're right. I have to admit, however, that I quite like Frenchmen although they do tend to be a bit...well...you know..."

"Indeed I do know, ma'am. Shall we tweak your adjusters now?"

When it came to the swimming pool procedure, Penny was winched up to the top of the pool's high diving board. Dressed in full flying kit, which included a heavy immersion suit, flying helmet and oxygen mask, she was left dangling in simulated parachute straps with a dinghy pack slung underneath. At the whim of the instructor, the parachute straps were released and she was dumped unceremoniously into the water. To add realism, an airman used more straps to pull her through the water to replicate a parachute as it was dragged along by the wind. With the possibility, in a real-life situation, of drowning unless the parachute quick release box (QRB) was operated in time, Penny dealt with the QRB 'twist and press' system energetically after which she had to retrieve and inflate her dinghy, then clamber aboard. Now she had to attend to a mass of detail – check that the sea anchor was deployed, bale out water, erect and activate the SARBE personal locator beacon, prepare the signal rockets, bale out more water...suddenly, when she glanced up, Penny realised that quite a few interested observers had begun to congregate around the sides of the station swimming pool: the OCU's first ever female student had clearly aroused a fair degree of inquisitiveness.

As an IWI student, Penny had to deliver a number of lectures to staff members and fellow students. For her first lecture she was assigned the HF200 height finder, dubbed the 'nodding horror' in view of its tendency to spew hydraulic fluid every-where. She carefully researched her subject, wrote lecture notes and produced good visual aids. On the day itself, however, as she stood up to deliver the lecture, she began to shake with nerves, her voice started to tremble and she had to struggle to continue. By the end, convinced that her performance had been abysmal, she worried about her future on the course and that she'd let down the whole of womanhood. About three weeks later, however, her mood of under-confidence began to change following what she subsequently saw as an unexpected watershed moment. With the introduction of a new computerised system to control fighter aircraft, Penny felt strongly that the human judgement aspect was being ignored, a facet that was par-ticularly significant with an evading target, or where electronic jamming was used. A computer, she argued, lacked the skills of an experienced controller with the ability to make considered decisions based on an understanding of the overall situation.

She thought about it, and thought about it some more, then at her next morning briefing Penny launched politely but passionately into an explanation of her views. This time she was gratified to see her audience with expressions of rapt attention; some listeners even had mouths agape. At the end of the briefing, when she asked if there were any questions, a stony silence dominated the room. As she returned to her seat, one of the fighter pilots put his arm to his face in a gesture of feigned terror. A debriefing officer would normally have commented on the lecture at this point, but he was motioned by the chief instructor to remain seated. The chief instructor himself then stood up and said simply: "Penny, you were magnificent...but wrong!" However, she felt vindicated when, at the end of the course, the chief instructor told her that that part of the syllabus had been removed.

Her confidence started to grow as she settled into the IWI course which included an armament practice camp (APC) at RAF St Mawgan. During her time there she was given the opportunity to fire an Aden 30-mm cannon against a target towed by a Canberra – although she hit neither the target nor (perhaps more to the point) the towing aircraft. Towards the end of the course, when she was interviewed for a radio programme, the interviewer's first question: "What's a pretty girl like you doing on a course like this?" seemed so ridiculous that Penny began to giggle and the interviewer had to start again. Shortly after this, a final dinner was held for course members who presented the staff with toy aeroplanes – replicas of the real thing to thank the instructors for their stalwart efforts despite numerous problems caused by aircraft unserviceabilities during the course.

One afternoon, when she was back in the chief controller's chair at Neatishead, she had to explain the goings-on to a visiting Phantom crew. Perhaps a little overwhelmed by the unfamiliar surroundings, the crew said little at first although the stiffness of the atmosphere eased eventually. With a finger held high as if about to draw an exclamation mark, one of the Phantom men said: "There's a lot to handle."

"Yes," said Penny, "but you learn how to manage it with practice."

"There are so many different things to co-ordinate," said the Phantom man who made Penny smile when he went on: "It's like a circus juggler trying to keep a dozen plates spinning on sticks."

*   *   *

In October 1973 Penny was detached to RAF Coningsby as a student on No. 2 Phantom Qualified Weapons Instructors' Course (Air Defence). The following year she returned for a further detachment to assist instructors with the training of fighter control students. It was at this time that the opportunity arose for her to fly in the back seat of a Phantom at Coningsby. However, she was faced with an unforeseen dilemma. She'd anticipated flying in a twin-stick aircraft designed for pilot training, but in view of her experience on the airborne intercept radar (AI) trainer the senior navigator instructor suggested that she might like to fly without the rear-cockpit's stick thus enabling her to operate 'for real' the AWG-11 intercept radar. Penny found this to be a head versus heart conflict. In her head she knew that it would be good to apply the skills learnt in the AI trainer, on the other hand her heart told her that for this once in a lifetime opportunity it would be wonderful to have a chance to handle the flight controls of a Phantom. She chose the latter and to this day she can recall the senior navigator's look of disappointment.

The aircraft for her flight, Phantom XT893, was lined up on the Coningsby dispersal pan as she walked towards the machine with her pilot, the squadron commander of the operational conversion unit. He guided her while she climbed the access ladder into the rear cockpit, then helped her to strap in before he stepped down again to carry out external checks. Standing nearby, a ground crewman placed a fire extinguisher to one side of the aircraft ready for the engine-start procedure. Before long, she saw the pilot climb into the Phantom's front cockpit and strap in after which he spoke to warn her about the racket heard during engine start – a shrill sound followed by an abrupt crashing noise which indicated the first engine's start cycle. This process was swiftly repeated for the second engine. Meanwhile, the leader of their two-ship formation obtained clearance from air traffic control to taxi out to the runway take-off point.

As the two Phantoms progressed along the taxiway, she tried to absorb all that was happening around her. In the Coningsby air traffic control tower she thought that she could spot the local controller, a distant figure behind long panes of darkened glass. She had fleeting memories of her own aspirations all those years ago to become an air traffic controller. This was no time for reverie, however, for the take-off point was looming and the controller had given clearance for the formation to enter the runway-in-use. The lead

No.2 Phantom QWI(AD) Course. (Crown Copyright)

Phantom pilot moved smartly to one side of the runway centreline while Penny's pilot positioned his Phantom judiciously, ready for a formation take-off. As both aircraft came to a halt, Penny looked across at the pilot of the lead Phantom. He made a circling signal with one hand – a visual order to increase engine power. Both aircraft began to lean forward against the brakes, like greyhounds ready for the 'off'. Penny knew that this was it. There was no turning back now. Her heartbeat racing, she saw the lead pilot give a positive nod of his head. At once, both Phantoms leapt forward as their pilots released the aircraft brakes.

Penny was aware of small, rapid movements of the flight controls as her pilot maintained his formation position. She saw the lead pilot give another emphatic nod of his head and she was conscious of a firm forward movement of the twin throttles next to her left hand. She noticed a slight hesitation, then an abrupt roar and a powerful punch in her back...the Rolls-Royce engines' reheats had lit. While the rate of acceleration increased, her peripheral vision picked up a blur as the runway edges rushed by. Her main focus, though, was on the lead Phantom whose every move her pilot followed with precision. As the lead Phantom's nose wheel lifted from the runway surface, shortly followed by the main wheels, and as her own aircraft followed, she felt a surge of adrenalin and a strange sensation of freedom as if at the release of earthly bonds.

Her pilot held close formation for a while longer before he moved away to take up a looser 'battle formation' position. It was at this stage that he invited Penny to take over the Phantom's flight controls. She found the lightness of the hydraulically-operated controls to be a little unnerving at first but soon, when the two aircraft split for practice interceptions, she was exhilarated to think that this was no dream but that, yes, here she was in real life actually handling the potent, famous Phantom. The sortie that day involved three practice interceptions for which her aircraft was permanent target. These were flown at low altitude with her pilot at the controls although between interceptions he climbed to a safe altitude so that Penny could resume control for a while. By the end of the sortie, when the two Phantoms re-joined in close formation for the recovery to Coningsby, she was mindful of her privileged opportunity, one that she would never forget.

Not long after this flight, the time approached for Penny to retire from the service. In February 1975 she was offered a job with Hawker Siddeley Dynamics (later absorbed into British Aerospace) to assist with trials conducted in California, USA on a new air-to-air missile to be known as Skyflash, a medium-range semi-active radar homing missile derived from the US AIM-7 Sparrow.

By the end of the three years of trials she was engaged to be married to an American. Following marriage and motherhood, Penny was widowed in 1990. Her son was just seven years of age. Six years later she remarried and in the year 2003 she was anxious to share a little of her past life with her new husband and her by-then twenty-year-old son. The three of them visited Neatishead and the adjacent RAF Air Defence Radar Museum, an experience that brought mixed emotions. The fighter control branch of the Royal Air Force no longer existed in its Cold War form. With more compact, mobile equipment and with radar data transmission, the branch had become part of an integrated system of battle management. There were no more 'nodding horrors', no more spewing of hydraulic fluid, no more massive radar antennae. The world had moved on.

Penny felt humbled when she thought about the significance of radar for the country's defence and for the part that she herself had played. Before she and her family left Neatishead, no doubt she had a sense of nostalgia when she walked outside where, for a brief moment, while gazing at the faint horizon, she saw the sun diffused through trees and a halation of the light reaching across. The effect expanded, captured everything in a sudden flash, and quickly caught her thoughts too. As the sun sank below the horizon, the Norfolk countryside became engulfed in shadow.

Penny descends after completing her Phantom flight.

CHAPTER 5

STARS AND STRIPES

COLONEL SCOTT SONNENBERG, USAF

It was July 1970 when First Lieutenant Scott Sonnenberg's pilot training with the United States Air Force finished and he was assigned to fly the McDonnell Douglas F-4. War in Vietnam was raging at the time and his training had included techniques in escape and evasion as well as instruction on how to cope with interrogation and other aspects as a prisoner of war. On completion of this, he was posted to George USAF base, so named after Brigadier General Harold H. George, a World War One fighter ace. When the lieutenant arrived at the base, which was situated some 75 miles north-east of Los Angeles in southern California, he was briefed on various local aspects. The base was adjacent to the south-western edge of the Mojave Desert, and not far from the Mojave river. He learnt that the river would wind and twist sporadically until it reached its terminus, a large inland delta that flowed mainly underground although occasionally the surface channels, usually dry, could fill up to cause extreme flooding. Another significant local feature, earthquakes, meant that each year many thousands of movements were recorded although most of them were too small to be felt.

Lieutenant Sonnenberg's first day on duty at George AFB prompted vivid memories. He was a brand new, recently married, first lieutenant and perhaps it was with a degree of trepidation that he entered the squadron building to walk right up to the duty desk. He signed in as required then he asked what was planned for him. At this, the captain who manned the duty desk jumped up, grabbed a microphone connected to the squadron's loudspeaker system and announced excitedly to the whole squadron: "Hey...our very first first lieutenant 'front-seater' has arrived for training!" At once, heads popped out of every door to observe this new and unusual creature that had imposed itself upon a well-established and revered, if somewhat ancient, men's club. Impressed and perhaps a little daunted by such a reception, the lieutenant learnt that the policy within the USAF up to that point had been to allow only senior pilots to be aircraft commanders (front-seaters) of the F-4, the USAF's most advanced fighter at the time. The back seats were manned by junior pilots

Lieutenant Scott Sonneberg standing beside a fully-armed F-4.

called PSOs (pilot systems operators) who, after a couple of years in this lowly status, would aim to upgrade to the front cockpit. In 1970, however, the USAF decided to change its policy. In future, as an experiment to see how they got on, new first lieutenants would begin their training in the front seat. Under the revised system, Lieutenant Sonnenberg was the first of the class to report for duty.

Once the initial shock of such a novel regime had subsided, the lieutenant's training began. He learnt that the primary tactic used in air-to-air combat was the so-called 'fighting wing'. For this, the lead F-4 of a pair would engage an adversary while the second F-4 would follow the leader through the twists and turns of violent manoeuvring. In theory, the wingman's crew members were supposed to check behind to ensure that enemy aircraft did not sneak up from the rear. In reality, the wingman was so absorbed with the all-consuming task of hanging on for dear life that it was highly unlikely that the crew had any opportunity to do much checking of the six o'clock area. Sometime later, the powers-that-be within the USAF fortunately saw sense and a more flexible tactic was adopted whereby the wingman kept the leader in sight but was able to manoeuvre and engage as a second attacker.

During his course, Lieutenant Sonnenberg was programmed one day for a sortie led by his squadron commander. After take-off, the pair headed for a designated area where the squadron commander, having initiated a series of vigorous air combat manoeuvres, tried hard to 'shake off' his rookie wingman. The rookie wingman, however, was determined not to be shaken off – so determined, in fact, that the squadron commander ended up devoting the entire mission to his shake-off attempts. The squadron commander was evidently so impressed that he regarded this student pilot as his 'golden child' for the remainder of the course. Golden child status, however, could have its drawbacks especially when the other course members enjoyed reminding Scott Sonnenberg of his distinction.

One time, excitement was in the air when a squadron open day was arranged and spouses were invited along to be given a series of briefings and tours which would aim to explain just what their husbands did all day. As part of the event the wives were driven to a practice bombing range to witness at first hand their husbands' bombing skills. The wives were driven to an observation spot, a safe area to one side of the range but a place where they couldn't see very well. As a result, they had to rely on information from one of the squadron officers who provided an ongoing commentary. From Scott Sonnenberg's point of view, this was just as well. His intention of demonstrating to his new wife just what a stud she had married seemed to go seriously awry when his bombing results, normally his strong suit when flying F-4s, proved to be so inaccurate that he felt lucky even to have hit the earth. Fortunately, from the observers' perspective every bomb looked like a bull's eye, duly confirmed by the reassuring narrative of the escorting officer. In truth, while a hero at home, he had to pay out, as previously agreed, quite a few quarters of financial redress to his wingman.

The night flying aspect of his training at George AFB would cause serious problems in the long term. It had been decreed that for training purposes night flying should begin at sunset, for example if sunset was at 6 p.m., the students would take off at 6.01 p.m. for a so-called 'night' flight. Scott Sonnenberg could recall a night training mission of flight refuelling which, after take-off, involved a climbing turn to the west directly into the setting sun. The sun was so bright that, even though it was officially night-time, he had to carry out the refuels with his sun visor down. Following this, he turned towards the bombing range which, from the sky, resembled a miniature version of Las Vegas lit up like a Christmas tree. The result, ultimately, was in his opinion a dereliction of duty by the leaders that sent dangerously ill-prepared students to war missions in South East Asia.

Lieutenant Scott Sonnenberg's F-4 training lasted six months at the end of which, in March 1971, out of twenty-six students he was one of thirteen to be selected for a combat assignment in South East Asia. He was excited – elated, even – to be told that he was heading for the Royal Thai air base at Ubon in Thailand. Little did he understand what awaited him at this United States Air Force front-line facility.

War in Vietnam
Scott Sonnenberg's arrival at Ubon was at a critical time during the infamous, merciless conflict between communist North Vietnam and the anti-communist government of South Vietnam – a war that had such a profound impact on the American psyche, especially on the men and women who fought it as well as on the millions of US citizens who supported it or protested against it. The clash of regimes included guerrilla action by the Viet Cong, a South Vietnamese communist common front aided by North Vietnam and whose activities involved the use of terror as a standard tactic, monthly assassination quotas and other barbarous conduct which left a deep and enduring legacy. The United States presence in the war had swelled from a trickle of military advisors in the 1950s to the dramatic operations involving thousands of soldiers in the 1960s. At the time of Scott Sonnenberg's arrival in 1971, the war still raged without let-up (Saigon finally fell in 1975) and the use of air power was a key aspect of operations. As the war progressed and as the casualty figures became ever more alarming, the US and South Vietnamese

forces grew increasingly reliant on air power. For many, the Phantom was seen as an iconic symbol of that air power.

The F-4's rugged design and flexibility meant that it could be employed in a number of different roles. One of these, known as Spectre escort, was flown at night and Scott was soon involved with such missions. He would be briefed as part of a formation, typically three F-4s, whose task was to escort an AC-130 'gunship', a heavily-armed variant of the Lockheed C-130 Hercules transport aircraft, which had been assigned to a working area. Once the gunship was airborne, the F-4s would take off from their Ubon base at twenty-minute intervals in a rotational sequence: one F-4 would escort the gunship within the target area, a second would head for an in-flight refuelling tanker while the third F-4, when relieved, would fly from the target area to the tanker. In theory, this plan achieved constant escort coverage over a period of two or so hours.

To make this work, the gunship had to fly a relatively predictable pattern at an altitude and airspeed that was in the heart of the North Vietnamese air defence systems. The gunship, therefore, was vulnerable to an abundance of different small-arms fire as well as to larger air defence guns and cannon. The gunship's objective was to detect the movement of trucks along the Ho Chi Minh trail, a sobriquet coined by US troops after President Ho Chi Minh of North Vietnam. The trail provided a logistical support system that ran from North Vietnam through Laos and Cambodia to South Vietnam and, according to the US National Security agency's official history of the war, was 'one of the great achievements of military engineering of the twentieth century'.

A gunship equipped with on-board sensors, including infrared and TV, would set up an orbital pattern while the crew made use of a chain of audio sensors that the US had placed along the Ho Chi Minh trail. If the gunship's sensor operators detected enemy trucks, the AC-130 would focus its guns in attempts to destroy the vehicles. Meanwhile, the F-4 escort would try to fly a circular pattern similar to that of the gunship, only higher and larger. For this, the F-4 pilot faced some daunting challenges. The first of these, a gratuitous one, was the design of the Phantom's interior lighting system. This was controlled by a single switch which, if adjusted to the right level of brightness for one cockpit light, would make the others far too bright or too dim. The solution was basic but effective. Scott Sonnenberg learnt quickly from the other pilots to take along a roll of insulating tape – yes, insulating tape – to spend a good five or ten minutes before flight carefully taping up the cockpit lights to achieve a workable level of brightness. The engine fire warning lights were a special problem – if one came on in flight the glow was particularly bright and the lights couldn't be turned off. The remedy was an artfully placed piece of tape which left a small corner of the warning light exposed. Eventually, the problem was eased when the USAF installed individual rheostats for each light.

In order to keep track of the gunship, the F-4 pilot had to fly at, or slightly above, stall speed. To conceal the AC-130 from the enemy below, the gunship was blacked out apart from a series of lights along the top of the fuselage and from wing-tip to wing-tip. On clear nights these lights were visible but dim; on less than perfectly clear nights they were very hard to see. Thus the Phantom pilot, as he manoeuvred his aircraft close to stall speed and heavily laden with fuel and ordnance, had to fly in a virtually blacked-out cockpit while struggling to keep track of a slow and vulnerable gunship which was at times barely discernible. In time, the F-4 inevitably overtook the lumbering gunship which meant an awkward adjustment to the escort pattern.

The primary role of the F-4s was that of deterrence. The crew, therefore, to discourage hostile fire and in the hope that enemy agents were eavesdropping, would make radio calls to let everyone know that an F-4 was on duty. On some nights, however, when the enemy either didn't hear or didn't care, the hostile fire started anyway. This would appear in the form of dazzling strings of red 'balls' which would shoot up from the ground and last for just a few seconds before ceasing. In theory, the F-4 pilot had to mark the spot on the ground then roll in to attack the hostile gun. In reality, however, Scott Sonnenberg and his colleagues found this less than straightforward – once the firing stopped they were back to a scene of pitch blackness, furthermore the use of a bomb, in daylight the most effective weapon against an air defence gun, turned out to be far too inaccurate when delivered at night. The F-4 crews became aware that the most effective ordnance was a combination of M-36 thermite munitions and CBU 24/52 cluster bombs. The first time an enemy gun opened up, a Phantom would drop a single M-36 which produced a pattern about the size of a football pitch. The thermite would burn for some two to three hours thus providing a ground marker. If an enemy gun opened up again, the F-4 pilot could plot the gun's position relative to the ground marker and, with a high degree of confidence about accuracy, drop cluster bombs. While cluster bombs may not destroy the gun itself, the gunners would be taken out so that the AC-130 could complete its mission unchallenged. In this way and using these weapons, the F-4s would rule the night.

During the year or so that Scott was operating in South East Asia, gunship escort duty was

Lieutenant Sonnenberg on the wing of an F-4 ready for action.

his squadron's most frequent mission although other missions, including night strikes, came up from time to time. Often these night strikes were affected by the area's volatile weather conditions and quite commonly, therefore, once the F-4s were airborne, plans were changed from visual procedures to attacks using the aircraft's on-board systems. In 1971-1972 ground positioning system (GPS) did not exist and laser systems were still relatively new. However, for better or worse, Scott's squadron was one of the few to be equipped with long-range aid to navigation (LORAN). On one notable occasion when the weather was not suitable for visual bombing, he was directed to an in-flight refuelling tanker where he was joined by other strike aircraft not equipped with LORAN. After refuelling, he was tasked by the night-time airborne command post, call sign Moonbeam, to lead an attack against a new target. Nobody else airborne realised that Scott was a green lieutenant on his first tour; for all they knew he was a crusty lieutenant-colonel on his third combat tour. Intriguingly, therefore, it was this green lieutenant that ended up guiding some two dozen fighters who, while holding formation positions on his aircraft, followed his every move. He led a combination of air force, navy and marine fighters to a target where, on his command, they dropped their ordnance – and all because his aircraft was equipped with LORAN and theirs were not.

Sometimes, after take-off, aircraft from Scott's squadron would be diverted from a pre-planned mission to support a contingency operation, for example when a fellow aviator had been shot down and rescue was in progress. The F-4 would be given altitude separation from other aircraft and sent to a holding point where the pilot would declare his weapons load and fuel state to the controller. One time, Scott and his weapons operator were on a single aircraft pre-planned mission when they heard that a US aircraft had gone down in the Mu Ghia pass, the principal entry point to the Ho Chi Minh trail and a heavily defended mountain pass in dense tropical forests between North Vietnam and Laos. Moonbeam asked Scott if he had any air-to-air missiles. "Affirmative," Scott replied, though in truth he had little confidence in his one AIM-7 Sparrow.

"Copied," said Moonbeam, "proceed to the Mu Ghia pass and set up combat air patrol."

"Okay. Proceeding there now." Boldly, he set a heading directly for the pass. It was later that he realised the full significance of how, at the start of one of the dramatic rescues of the Vietnam War, the United States airborne defence had relied on a 'green' lieutenant with a suspect missile and no gun. As he said: "No wonder we lost the war."

He continued to fly on a direct course to the pass when his weapons systems officer in the back seat advised: "I suggest we don't fly directly over the pass, Scott. We'll be better off holding a few miles to the west." The prudence of this suggestion became clear a couple of minutes later when a bright flash appeared abruptly below, then began to rush up towards them – a surface-to-air missile. Immediately, Scott took the pro- scribed defensive action: he rolled the Phantom to initiate a steep dive while manoeuvring to place the missile on his left side. "They've fired a SA-2!" cried his back-seater breathlessly. Within moments the SA-2 Guideline missile, a Soviet-designed system that had gained international fame when used in May 1960 to shoot down the U-2 high-altitude reconnaissance aircraft flown by Gary Powers, started to turn back down to follow the F-4. "Standby!" Scott warned his back-seater as, in a violent manoeuvre, he initiated a climb. Now, as the Phantom rapidly gained height again, the crew watched the SA-2 disappear behind them.

Later, at the mission debrief, Scott and his back-seater excitedly reported what had happened only to learn that several other US aircraft had been in the same area, all of them convinced that the SA-2 had been fired at them. As he said: "Well, at least we'd felt like heroes for a few minutes."

Of course, heroic activities by US aircrew during the Vietnam War have been well documented and perhaps none more so than an incident in the late-1960s involving Captain Bob Pardo, a colleague of Scott Sonnenberg – they'd flown together and he was 'a good guy' according to Scott.

Pardo's Push

Some thirty miles north of Hanoi at a place called Thai Nguyen, an area in Vietnam renowned for the quality of its tea, a North Vietnamese steel mill was used for the production of essential war materiel. In March 1967 units of United States F-4s and Republic F-105 Thunderchiefs were briefed to attack this heavily defended mill, and as part of the plan Captain Bob Pardo with his back-seater, First Lieutenant Steve Wayne, were to fly their F-4 leading another Phantom flown by Captain Earl Aman with First Lieutenant Robert Houghton as his back-seater. Their task was to defend other US aircraft against enemy MiG action but if no MiGs appeared, these two F-4s were to join their colleagues in attacking the steel mill.

Powerful monsoons and extensive low cloud had delayed this mission for nine days until, on Friday 10 March 1967, skies cleared. An air of nervous anticipation was apparent when crews walked out to their aircraft lined up at Ubon Royal Thai Air Force base; the men all knew that a hazardous mission was in

Bob Pardo and Stephen A. Wayne, after Wayne's 100th combat mission.
(Taken from thisdayinaviation.com)

prospect with the high possibility of casualties. Before long, with engines started and weapons and other checks completed, the aircraft took off to head north towards the target area. The initial part of the flight may have felt surreal as crews flew above the rich and diverse vegetation and the tropical forests that spread like an intricate tapestry across Vietnam. Reality struck, however, when the aircraft were still some distance from the target and ground defences began to open fire. Suddenly, Aman and Houghton's aircraft was hit by flak and their F-4 started to shake violently. They discussed whether to turn back but, despite the problems, decided to proceed.

No MiG fighters appeared but anti-aircraft fire persisted as the F-4s and F-105s continued towards the target. Aman and Houghton managed to drop their bombs, as did others, although several of the US aircraft were shot down near the steel mill. Then Aman and Houghton felt their aircraft take two more hits. Aman radioed Pardo: "We're losing fuel fast!"

"Okay," said Pardo, "we'll head for the tanker." He wanted to lead his wingman to a pre-briefed rendezvous point with an in-flight refuelling tanker, however it soon became clear that Aman and Houghton's aircraft was losing fuel too rapidly to reach the tanker in time.

"We'll have to eject!" cried Aman on the aircraft radio.

"Standby," said Pardo, conscious that an ejection at that point would mean a descent by parachute into enemy territory. In his mind were bleak thoughts of communist treatment of US forces, especially aircrew, which was known to be barbaric.

By this stage, as Pardo and Wayne's Phantom had also been hit by flak, warning lights flashed in Pardo's cockpit when his F-4 lost electrical power and started to lose fuel – fortunately, though, the aircraft's handling remained normal.

"We'll climb," radioed Pardo to his wingman while he eased the Phantom's throttles forward, "follow me up!" He wanted to gain height so that the aircraft could glide as far as possible if the fuel ran out. As the two Phantoms climbed towards 30,000 feet Pardo radioed his wingman again: "Earl, you've been hit bad. I can see you losing fuel."

"Yuh...okay...we're preparing to bail out, Bob."

"Don't jump yet! We'll do our damnedest to help you out of here!" cried Bob Pardo. After a pause he went on: "Jettison your drag 'chute, Earl." Following this action Pardo planned to position the nose of his F-4 into the empty drag 'chute receptacle; this, he hoped, would allow him to 'push' his wingman along. The attempt, though, was foiled by jet wash from Earl Aman's aircraft. "Standby, Earl," Pardo warned, "I'm gonna try something else." At that, he manoeuvred very carefully to attempt to position the top of his Phantom's fuselage directly beneath the other's 'belly' but this, too, failed. Pardo, though, had not run out of ideas yet. "Drop your tail-hook!" he cried.

The steel tail-hook, designed to halt the aircraft after landing on an aircraft carrier, was nothing if not strong – seriously strong. Slickly, if warily, Pardo manoeuvred his F-4 towards the tail-hook, now locked down. Closer and closer he moved, his task hardly helped when the hook began to sway from side to side. Still he persevered, easing forward bit by bit until the one-inch-thick armoured section at the base of his windshield touched the hook. He eased forward a little more. Intense concentration no doubt crowded out dark thoughts that might have occupied his mind – feelings, perhaps, of anger, of fearfulness, of determination that his superb flying skills should not let them down at this crucial point.

'Pardo's Push' by S. W. Ferguson.
(Taken from thisdayinaviation.com)

With the rate of descent of the linked-up F-4s at around 3,000 feet per minute, Pardo began to push his aircraft a little harder against the tail-hook. It was a courageous thing to do; if his windshield gave way, the steel hook would smash into his face. But his plan was starting to work: as he persisted, the rate of descent was gradually reducing. Suddenly, though, he had to pull back when zigzag cracks began to form at the base of his windshield. He needed to think of something else. Pardo, therefore, repositioned slightly to place the tail-hook against a square of metal at the junction of his windshield and the radome. That led to a moment of 'eureka' for by pushing hard for a few seconds at a time he discovered that the rate of descent was halved to some 1,500 feet per minute.

But now Aman radioed: "We're out of fuel! Both our engines have just flamed out!" Undaunted, Pardo continued to push and push – to such effect that the rate of descent was still kept under control. His situation, though, took a dramatic turn for the worse when, suddenly, a red fire warning light began to shine in his cockpit: the left engine was on fire. "Standby!" cried Pardo to his back-seater, "I'll have to close down the port engine." This action, however, meant that with just one engine to propel two aircraft the rate of descent increased drastically. Pardo therefore re-lit the engine only to close it down again a minute later when the light reappeared.

Despite the perils, Pardo carried on pushing for another ten or so minutes, the catalogue of complex thoughts within his head facilitated, no doubt, by that most mysterious yet beneficial compound – adrenalin. Eventually, he managed to push his wingman a total distance of nearly ninety miles. The two F-4s were down to an altitude of some 10,000 feet when Laos loomed. In sight was the border between Vietnam and northern Laos, marked by the Black River known locally as the Song Da. Pardo radioed his position to US search and rescue crews which resulted in the scrambling from Thailand of several Douglas A-1 Skyraiders (single-seat propeller-driven ground-attack aircraft with the call sign 'Sandy') and two HH-43 Jolly Green Giant helicopters. With this 'posse' underway what followed became a race against time.

By this juncture, with the Phantoms' rate of descent starting to accelerate, even the resourceful Pardo was devoid of further ideas. They had made it, though. Pardo had pushed his colleagues beyond the Black River and into Laos and now, finally, Aman and Houghton were forced to abandon their aircraft. At an altitude of approximately 6,000 feet the two men pulled their ejection seat handles to escape immediate dangers even though further hazards faced them very shortly – dangling in his parachute, Houghton could spot a band of armed guerrillas with dogs running towards him. The guerrillas shouted and fired weapons at the parachute. Houghton landed in a small tree but despite back pain after his high-speed ejection he managed to extricate himself and to stagger, revolver in hand, through elephant grass towards a small stream. There, he radioed the rescue posse to report his situation as well as the armed guerrillas' position and that of Aman who had ended up below a slippery cliff. Aman, luckily, had not been spotted by the guerrillas.

Meantime, Pardo and Wayne flew south for another minute or two before Pardo turned towards a United States Special Forces camp in Laos. With their Phantom nearly out of fuel, he ordered Wayne to eject first. Following a successful ejection, Wayne landed by parachute to the north-west of Houghton and Aman. Wayne hid in nearby bushes until the A-1 'Sandys' came in very low and drove off the guerrillas without having to fire a shot. A 'Jolly Green Giant' helicopter then flew in to winch up Houghton and Aman before rescuing Wayne.

Pardo, meanwhile, had ejected but was knocked unconscious in the process. He sustained two fractured vertebrae in his neck and when he came to after his parachute landing he heard shouting and gunfire in the vicinity. At once, he radioed the 'Sandys' to strafe the hillside near his position before, in considerable pain, he stumbled, revolver in hand, a distance of about half-a-mile up a hill where he waited for some forty-five minutes until a 'Jolly Green Giant' helicopter finally located him and winched him to safety.

Despite his remarkable courage and tenacity, the United States Air Force leadership, sensitive to high combat losses at the time, far from commending Pardo reprimanded him for the loss of his F-4. It was over two decades later, following a re-examination of the case, that the injustice was at last acknowledged. At a ceremony in 1989, Major Bob Pardo and his colleagues were awarded Silver Star medals given in recognition of gallantry in action against an enemy of the United States of America.

Scott Sonnenberg
The ironic conclusion to the now-renowned 'Pardo's Push' may have surprised many, nonetheless the mastery and sheer boldness demonstrated during that epic episode soon became the stuff of legend. The event highlighted the demands placed upon aircrew

during the war in Vietnam, a war that provoked, and continues to provoke, such deep divisions of opinion. The fierce debates in the United States and elsewhere were summarised by a popular, if not universally concurred, expression at the time, 'better red than dead', an outlook for which Scott Sonnenberg said, when asked, that he could neither agree nor disagree. He expressed the view that if the people of the United States elected a communist system of government, he'd be discouraged but he would not fight against it. If, however, a communist society was forced upon the people against their will then he would fight against it to the bitter end. Such a view was held, no doubt, by many and Scott's experience on one of his first missions in South East Asia turned out to be a tough test of this philosophy.

His flight leader on that day had dropped bombs in a wooded area next to a clearing and the forward air controller was pleased with the result. The controller called on the radio: "Okay, number two. Your leader's got the whole unit on the run and they're trying to make it across that clearing. You're cleared in!"

At this, Scott manoeuvred his F-4 for attack. As he rolled in to strike the enemy he re-checked the cockpit switches which, when operated, would release the cluster bomb units (CBUs) attached to his aircraft. Unlike bombs, CBUs were designed to kill people, not to destroy equipment. The skills he had acquired during his training were about to be applied in reality. When he spotted people running across the clearing – a total of some 200 individuals – the abysmal thought occurred to him that they were less than a minute away from dying and he was their executioner; a young man in an apocalyptic situation for which he had been trained and now it was his duty to proceed. As he lined up the target in his sights, clouds passed from beneath the sun and the tropical forests by the clearing and the grasses ahead appeared to gleam where the sunlight caught small droplets, survivors from an earlier rain shower.

When it was all over, there was no sense of triumph, no sound of bells, just the forward air controller's voice: "Nice drop number two. There's not a soul moving. It'll take quite a while to count the bodies – I'll call the count back to you later. Thanks again!"

On reflection, some might say: "I don't understand it. How could you do such a thing?"

"I was just doing my job!"

"But all those people…"

"They were our enemies!"

"They were still human beings. Would you have done the same thing if they'd been innocent women and children?"

"No…no I wouldn't. For one thing, I've not been trained to do that. Anyway, there'd be no point – it would be counter-productive. I've been trained to attack legitimate military targets." Scott would seek to persuade detractors that he was not some robot reacting without thought or reason, that he was a sentient man who abhorred killing. By the end of his tour in South East Asia, with 177 combat missions logged, if asked whether he'd be willing to fight and kill again his affirmative response, he'd say, was justified by a conscious decision that was based on an absolute conviction that life without freedom was not life at all. In the same way that humble ripples on the sea's surface could swell to mighty waves, so it was that mild-mannered individuals could be stirred to apply maximum force when cardinal human freedoms were threatened. While others throughout history may have lacked the power to achieve or maintain their freedoms, as a member of the armed forces of the United States of America he possessed considerable powers and, while deterrence remained his primary intent, he would not hesitate to use these powers if necessary, a principle emphasised in President Kennedy's inaugural speech on 20 January 1961:

> *Let every nation know, whether it wishes us well or ill,*
> *that we shall pay any price, bear any burden, meet any*
> *hardship, support any friend, oppose any foe to assure*
> *the survival and the success of liberty.*

These weighty responsibilities had to be carried day-to-day throughout Scott's time in South East Asia, a working day that would start, typically, at around 5 p.m. After a meal in the officers' club, he would be driven to the squadron set-up where he'd check the scheduling board for information on that evening's line-up with call signs, take-off times, mission numbers and other details. Together with his back-seater he'd receive intelligence and weather briefings then carry out any planning that was needed. While, in peacetime, special emphasis was placed upon pre-flight briefings, those at Ubon tended to be cursory at best; the real mission information was given after take-off by the airborne command centre (Moonbeam).

At this juncture he and his back-seater would proceed to the locker room to change into flight suits that had been stripped of all identification: no patches, no places for patches, no rank or other insignia, just plain, dark green Nomex flight suits. Flight crews were issued with portable radios for communication with search and rescue teams, if needed. Small arms were issued too, usually a .38 calibre revolver; he knew of one individual who insisted on taking hand grenades; this was unusual but as he had been shot down once and wished that he'd been equipped with hand grenades, his insistence was accepted by the powers-that-be.

When 'booted and suited' Scott and his back-seater would walk out to their allotted F-4. Following pre-flight checks and take-off procedures, during the climb-out from Ubon he'd contact Moonbeam by radio to confirm his mission number and the aircraft's ordnance fit. Moonbeam would give details about that evening's mission with instructions on where to fly and what to do when there. If in-flight refuelling was needed, he would make for the specified area where refuelling tankers flew a racetrack pattern to refuel whoever showed up; unlike peacetime, there were no assigned times or off-loads and the refuelling was conducted on a first-come, first-served basis. On bad weather days, the refuelling tankers could be used as rendezvous points while Moonbeam drew up alternative plans; on such days impressive sights would form spontaneously as dozens of fighters lined up by the wings of the tanker.

On completion of a mission, as the F-4 crews flew back to base they might practise night-formation flying and other skills. Some would enjoy flying high-speed approaches to the airfield; normally flown at an airspeed of 250 knots, an approach at over twice that amount could present air traffic controllers with some interesting (and from the aircrew perspective, hilarious) challenges. After landing, and after maintenance and intelligence debriefs, crews were driven back to the officers' club for a night-flying meal. Following this, Scott and his room-mate liked to head for the base tennis courts. Their tennis session would invariably draw a crowd of Thai children, not necessarily to observe the tennis skills but mainly to enable the children to collect swarms of rice bugs attracted by the powerful floodlights. The large flying insects were quite edible and full of protein so, between tennis points, the players would use their tennis racquets to carry the bugs to the youngsters who used large bags to store their next meal.

The days seemed to merge as this routine continued and Scott found that he lost a sense of time. The only break in his one-year tour in South East Asia was a fourteen-day mid-tour period of rest and recreation for which his wife flew to Bangkok before they spent two weeks travelling around Thailand. When it was time for her to leave, however, the Pan Am flight was cancelled. With the next flight ten days away, Scott's commanding officer suggested that she should stay at the Ubon base. This turned out to be a strange period as she had the painful experience of sending him off to work each day knowing that he may not come back. Fortunately, the ten days passed relatively uneventfully.

*   *   *

For the following six months Scott flew combat missions up to and including his final mission on Thursday, 20 April 1972. This flight, as if encapsulating the whole period that he'd spent in South East Asia, managed to yield a lifetime of memories. The mission, which lasted for 2.6 hours, was in aircraft F-4D tail letter #8743 armed with nine Mk.82 unguided bombs. Aware that as a last flight he and his back-seater, Lieutenant Steptoe, would be greeted with champagne on return to Ubon (assuming they made it back), Scott and his back-seater unbuckled their seat straps just before take-off. The two men hastily changed from their regular flight suits into party suits – lightweight, short-sleeved versions of the regular ones but much brighter in colour and covered in patches and various forms of identification. If shot down, the men knew that hiding was not an option. Following this quick change, they swiftly strapped back in to be given clearance from air traffic control to proceed.

After take-off, Scott headed directly for the in-flight refuelling tanker. When fully topped-up, and having received a target briefing from the forward air controller, he flew a high orbit over the battlefield. As the weather conditions were good, he was able to pick out the target although the downside of good weather meant that enemy gunners could readily identify an aircraft, especially one as prominent as a Phantom trailing smoke. In view of this, Scott flew a descending spiral approach; he ensured that he never rolled his aircraft's wings level or tracked in just a single direction, techniques which determined that the enemy gunners were faced with a difficult target. However, Scott's own problems were compounded although, with his experience of over 170 combat missions, he was, as he put it, at the peak of his game. Flying towards the target he was aware of tracer rounds from a 57-mm Soviet anti-aircraft gun streaming over the cockpit and wings of his Phantom. He released ordnance at the appropriate point and when pulling off the target he was gratified to see a Soviet-built 122-mm field gun explode.

When working with forward air controllers, the Phantom pilots developed an informal system for rating enemy gunners: a level three was not very good – the gunner's shots were going behind the aircraft; if the tracking was pretty good this merited a level between five to seven; a level-nine gunner meant that the pilots were in for a pretty rough time. So it was that, on that day, as the anti-aircraft gunners were earning themselves a level nine, the forward air controller decided that the situation was too dangerous and that the Soviet 57-mm anti-aircraft gun needed to be eliminated. Scott and his number two, therefore, were allocated this task and with the sun behind them as a helpful distraction, initiated a roll-in for a curvilinear approach. They were met with a hail of tracer as the level-nine gunner emptied the ammunition from his 57-mm gun onto the attacking aircraft. Approaching the required altitude, Scott rolled his aircraft's wings level and released all of his remaining ordnance. Employing violent defensive manoeuvres as he pulled away from the target area, he looked back over his shoulder for signs of anti-aircraft fire. Instead of this, however, he saw a massive explosion where the 57-mm had stood. Suddenly he knew with a sense of high satisfaction that his colleagues about to follow would be saved from the perils posed by that level-nine gunner. Later, he and his number two were credited with one 57-mm anti-aircraft gun destroyed, one 122-mm field gun damaged, and the forward air controller reported that he believed the two Phantoms had taken over 200 rounds of 57-mm fire.

With his aircraft now out of ordnance following this attack, Scott met up with his number two, call sign Fenway 2, so that they could conduct mutual visual inspections of their Phantoms for signs of battle damage. When satisfied, the two set off to rendez-vous with the in-flight refuelling tanker for a top-up before heading home. The weather on that Thursday remained good and for their return to Ubon air base Scott decided that, for his last combat mission, something different was required. Normally, he and his number two would have flown over the runway before performing a left turn through 180 degrees to the downwind position. That day, however, on a pre-briefed signal Scott turned left and his number two turned right in a co-ordinated sequence that created a degree of confusion, not to say consternation, to the duty air traffic controller. After landing, they taxied the two Phantoms to the squadron dispersal area where, eager to celebrate the occasion, squadron colleagues and the director of operations were lined up to greet them. The director of operations, evidently unamused by the landing stunt, was even less amused when the Phantoms' canopies were opened to reveal aircrew in their party suits. The upshot of all this was that Scott's award of the Distinguished Flying Cross was received at the same time as a letter of reprimand.

*   *   *

As a postscript to the episode, some weeks later, when First Lieutenant Scott Sonnenberg reported for duty as a fighter pilot instructor on the F-4 at Luke Air Force Base, Arizona, a note on the message board instructed him to report to the director of operations for the 58th Tactical Training Wing. Normally, a full 'bird' colonel in the United States Air Force would not be too interested in the arrival of a new first lieutenant, so it was with a fair degree of curiosity that Scott made his way to see the senior officer. When politely ushered into the colonel's office, Scott saluted smartly then waited while the senior officer, who was sitting behind a desk, continued to study paperwork. Eventually, the colonel looked up slowly and said: "Welcome to Luke Air Force Base."

"Thank you, sir."

"Now tell me about your last flight in South East Asia."

Scott straightened his back, took a deep breath and gave his account. When he'd finished, a period of silence followed at the end of which the colonel said: "Mmmm... well, I have to admire your spirit and initiative. However, you're about start as an instructor training a new generation of fighter pilots. I expect you to show a bit more maturity and professionalism." The colonel paused then went on: "This is what I'll do. I'll sit on this letter of reprimand and see which way you go. Dismissed."

Scott Sonnenberg never saw the letter again. Years later, though, he would comment dryly that the threat had him walking the straight and narrow for quite a while.

Author's note: *With sincere thanks to Colonel Scott Sonnenberg for his co-operation with this chapter and for his advice on the 'Pardo's Push' section. Unfortunately we were unable to trace Major Pardo but I have pieced together his remarkable story with information from a number of different sources.*

CHAPTER 6

OPEN SESAME

JACK HAMILL AND PETER DESMOND IN AIR COMBAT

As he taxied the Phantom towards the take-off point at RAF Leuchars, Flight Lieutenant Jack Hamill (far left) noted seasonal changes across the airfield. It was March 1975 and in places, buried within the airfield grasses, thick fringes of wild snowdrops appeared on either side of the taxiway. Behind him a variety of camouflaged buil-dings and great air-craft hangars were arranged in a somewhat haphazard manner. To one side of the taxiway the air traffic control tower was adjacent to a series of aircraft shelters designed for use by his unit, 43 (F) Squadron, in the event of war or during exercises. To the south of the taxiway lay the main runway, a black scar that carved through the airfield grasses. Before long, as the Phantom approached the runway entrance point, Jack made a terse radio call to air traffic control: "Chequers 43...take-off."

"Chequers 43, standby one," said the controller, "hold clear of the runway for now." After a few moments the controller continued: "Previously conflicting traffic is currently due north of the airfield. You can line up and take off, Chequers 43."

With the completion of the pre-take-off checks, Jack moved swiftly onto the runway. "All set?" he asked his navigator, Squadron Leader Peter Desmond. "Yup. All set."

Jack now advanced the Phantom's throttles and he monitored the instruments of the twin Rolls-Royce Spey engines which, as if impatient to proceed, began to crescendo from a low growl to a roar. His peripheral vision picked up a blur to each side as he released the brakes and the aircraft accelerated. Soon, as the Phantom became airborne, he turned onto a southerly heading and climbed to an altitude of 5,000 feet. The good visibility that day presented ideal conditions for the planned task – a low-level affiliation training exercise against a formation of Hawker Siddeley Harrier 'jump-jet' aircraft. Earlier, during a telephone briefing, Jack and Peter's stipulated aim was to try to spot the 'enemy' without being seen themselves, then to simulate a 'splash' (shoot-down) of as many in the formation of four Harriers as possible.

This, both men knew, would be no easy task; the Harrier's unconventional performance meant that the crew of an intercepting Phantom had to be wary. Developed in the 1960s, and the most successful vertical/short take-off and landing jet aircraft among many attempted designs, the Harrier could operate effectively from temporary bases such as fields, forests, jungle clearings and car parks; large and vulnerable air bases used by the likes of Phantoms were not needed by the versatile Harrier. It was this selfsame flexibility, however, that presented intercepting fighters with special problems. For instance, in an air combat 'circle of joy' situation, by operation of a single lever to rotate the four nozzles under the wings, a Harrier pilot could reduce his airspeed below the fighter's stall speed thus forcing the latter to overshoot. When the fighter had overtaken and was in the sights of the Harrier pilot, he could rotate the nozzles again to accelerate and 'splash' the fighter. The fighter crew, therefore, had to employ particular techniques to avoid this danger.

"Standby..." Peter interjected to his pilot. "We'll fly over the Firth of Forth shortly and pass to the east of Edinburgh, then we'll overfly the Lammermuir Hills and set up the briefed CAP." The CAP (combat air patrol), normally an elliptical pattern, was planned that day to be flown by the Phantom crew at an altitude of 5,000 feet, a height which would allow target identification at a useful range on the aircraft's radar operated by Peter. "Just to remind you, Jack," went on Peter, "as part of the safety brief, the Harriers will remain below 1,000 feet initially."

"Okay," said Jack, "but we can depart from briefed safety heights when we've visually identified the targets?"

"That's correct."

While Jack established the first leg of the combat air patrol, Peter worked at the Phantom's Ferranti AN/AWG-12 multi-role radar to fine-tune the equipment. As a fighter navigator since 1953, firstly on the Gloster Meteor, followed by the de Havilland DH-112 Venom, then the Gloster Javelin, Peter Desmond was well acquainted with the art of airborne controlled interceptions. Nonetheless, despite his previous experience, he could recall tensions at the Phantom Operational Conversion Unit at RAF Coningsby when, two years ago, he was a student on the course there. He'd discovered that, following a successful airborne sortie, he would struggle to explain the hypothesis of what he'd just done in practice. In debriefs he would be confused by instructors intent on academic explanations. Perhaps unhelpful, too, was the age-old division between instructor and student where one talked about how it was done while the other did it, although the theory about how it was done did not necessarily coincide with what was actually done.

Admittedly, thought Peter, the Phantom's renowned complexity could create baffling issues. He reflected that, for one thing, the Phantom was one of the first fighter aircraft to be fitted with the ingenious invention that could detect a target hidden within 'ground clutter' – clutter that would swamp traditional pulse radar screens. This invention, called pulse/Doppler, offered potential that was at once remarkable, complicated, confounding. With an ability to recognise Doppler shifts in the radar return, then eliminate all non-moving objects such as the ground and buildings, the Phantom's advanced electronics were revolutionary. With Doppler selected, only objects moving at the speed of an aircaft would appear on the navigator's radar screen, so the Phantom, unlike previous generations of interceptors, was equipped with technology that could discern the bearing and velocity of a low-level target. For the imminent task that day, this facility was about to prove key.

Another aspect about to prove key, that of visual air-to-air combat, had caused difficulties for a number of navigators on the course at Coningsby, including Peter. With fuel tanks and some missiles downloaded, the Phantom's performance envelope allowed the pilot to pull up to eight times the force of gravity at an airspeed up to Mach 1.4 – again, revolutionary for the period, as well as remarkable, complicated, confounding...and a few other things too. Peter remembered how instructional lectures at Coningsby had not been helped by deep didactic discussions accompanied by difficult-to-follow diagrams scribbled on blackboards. In short, he became downhearted and he worried about his ability to pass the course. This was especially the case after the first two practice combat sessions which had left him feeling disorientated and exhausted by the sheer physical effort needed. For the second time at Coningsby, Peter had spoken with the commanding officer, an astute man with high expectations. "Okay," said the CO, a former Cranwell cadet and future air chief marshal, "I'll crew you with my best air combat pilot. He should sort you out."

When Peter flew with this pilot, a USAF major with combat experience from the Vietnam War, a fog of understanding began to clear. Peter felt that the major was always in complete command of the situation which allowed him time, therefore, to explain what he was doing and why. In a practice combat flight against the two staff pilots who'd managed to confuse Peter comprehensively, the major fought solo with sufficient expertise to dispose of the opposition one by one. From that point, Peter's self-assurance developed, an abyss was bridged, and he was able to cope confidently with air combat sorties. This was all thanks to the USAF major's instructional and other skills which made the news even more shocking when, later, Peter heard that the major had been killed in a road accident in France.

"I'll turn onto the reciprocal heading now," Jack said as he continued to fly the combat air patrol. "Copied," said Peter.

As he applied bank, Jack concentrated his visual search in the known threat direction. Jack was an experienced pilot, although not on Phantoms; as an ex-Avro Vulcan bomber pilot his route to the fighter world had been circuitous. Five years earlier he had been posted as a student to the Central Flying School, the establishment that trained pilots destined to become flying instructors. After this, out of forty students he was one of just four to be posted as instructors on the Folland Gnat, the RAF's advanced training aircraft at the time. Three years later, in July 1973, he'd been posted onto the Phantom fleet and, following the operational conversion course at Coningsby, he and his family moved north to join 43 Squadron.

"Rolling out on reciprocal now," Jack informed Peter as the Phantom remained in the combat air patrol pattern.

"Roger," said Peter. "Nothing seen on radar yet."

*   *   *

Jack understood that Peter had been taught at Coningsby by a veteran of the Vietnamese War, and he held respect for his navigator's new-found proficiency in air-to-air combat in the Phantom. The United States pilots, Jack knew, had developed particular prowess in air combat, although when he thought about the broader aspects of war in Vietnam and the latest news reports from that tortured country, he wondered about the enormous scale of effort. Just now, as the North Vietnamese swept south towards Saigon, there were predictions that hostilities could end by next month. While North Vietnamese troops progressed towards the coastal city of Da Nang, accounts of a general state of panic were illustrated by astonishing scenes at the airport. Jack had read reports of how, on arrival at the airport, the president of World Airways discovered that one of his Boeing 727s was about to make its fourth and final flight to safety in South Vietnam. However, pushing aside the women and children were some 400 South Vietnamese soldiers forcing their way onto the aircraft – an aircraft designed for just 150 passengers. A number of individuals who failed to make it on board attempted to climb into the Boeing's wheel-bays and when, eventually, the airline captain managed to take off it was with the rear stairway still open.

"Standby, Jack," Peter's voice had a sudden urgency. "Hold this heading for now, but I have a faint radar contact..."

"What's the range?"

"Around twenty miles." Peter hesitated for a moment or two, then said sharply: "Turn onto a heading of two zero zero!"

As Jack turned the Phantom, he felt his stomach in knots as he searched anxiously for the Harriers. He sat upright in the cockpit, his right hand resting lightly against the stick while his left hand eased the twin throttles forward slightly. From years of habit and training his head moved ceaselessly while his eyes scanned above and below, from one side to the other, ahead and behind. Today, though, as he had to focus more specifically on the area ahead and below, he knew that a low-level target was going to be helpful – a high target positioned directly into the bright sun would be hard to spot with the naked eye. This was not a problem for Peter, however, as he stared at the movement of the blip on his radar screen. "Turn right ten degrees," he said, "we'll offset the target to the left."

While the Phantom flew on, the minds of the two crew worked on many things. Out of instinct and with a quick glance that did not interfere with his lookout, Jack checked his cockpit instruments. The glance, no more than a second or so, allowed his mind to record like a computer key information...*airspeed, altitude, heading, fuel contents, oxygen, engine temperatures and pressures...*

"Target's range fifteen miles," said Peter. "Maintain current heading and height for now."

Jack knew that he and Peter had the advantage at this stage: the Harrier pilots had yet to see the Phantom and they were unlikely to do so for a while as Peter worked out a suitable interception profile. With the Harriers well to the Phantom's left and several thousand feet below, Peter aimed to maintain this until abeam. At that point he'd order a turn while Jack, flying a wide berth, tried to remain out of sight as he moved stealthily into missile-firing range behind the Harriers.

"Range ten miles," said Peter. "I won't use the radar's lock-on mode – it'll alert them."

Jack continued to fly precise parameters while Peter concentrated on the Phantom's radar picture.

"Range approaching six miles," said Peter.

Suddenly Jack muttered, almost to himself: "Got 'em."

"Say again?"

"I've got visual contact with one aircraft," said Jack, "....left, left...ten o'clock low."

"That checks with radar."

"Okay. Commencing a lazy left turn..." Jack hesitated before he went on: "I can see five of the buggers altogether."

"Five? We were briefed there'd be four."

"The fifth is acting as escort for the main formation of four."

For a moment Jack looked up at the sky which remained clear and blue and cloud free, meanwhile his mind continued to calculate the optimum line of approach to the Harriers below. Still keeping a discreet distance, he began to reduce height from 5,000 feet as he turned. He noted that the four Harriers were in a classic low-level battle formation. Above them, at an altitude of approximately 1,000 feet above ground level, was the escort aircraft. "Target's range three miles," said Peter.

Jack's fingers moved briefly, surely around the cockpit as he checked that switches were set for a simulated missile firing. "Levelling at 500 feet," he said to Peter.

"Range two-and-a-half miles from the target," interjected Peter.

"I'll aim for the Harrier on the far right."

Jack manoeuvred slickly to place the selected target in his sights. The Harrier pilots, though, had still failed to notice the Phantom behind them; the four-ship remained in neat battle formation as if set up for a right royal fly-past. Swiftly, Jack verified the parameters for a theoretical launch of an AIM-9 Sidewinder missile. He double-checked the switches; he squinted through the sights; he rechecked the target's range...then he pulled the trigger. "Fox 2 on the starboard Harrier," he cried excitedly to Peter, "moving left onto the next one."

It was at this point that the Phantom was spotted. "Harrier formation...break left," yelled the escort. At once, as Jack followed in a tight turn, he and Peter were subjected to increasing G with mounting pressure around their legs and stomachs as anti-G suits began to inflate. Now with four Harriers and one Phantom following each other in line astern, the five aircraft manoeuvred aggressively this way and that in efforts to gain advantage. In a helter-skelter of movement, the lead Harrier pulled up sharply, applied bank, slammed back down again, rolled abruptly. In the Phantom's rear cockpit, as he tried to brace for the next violent lurch, Peter had to rely on Jack's intermittent commentary. "I'm worried about the escort," cried Jack, "I've lost sight of him."

"I think he broke out to the right."

"Watch our six o'clock position!"

At this, a sudden explosion was accompanied by dust and debris swirling around the Phantom's cockpits. Jack instinctively pulled back on the stick and the Scottish landscape disappeared as the aircraft nose came up. In the climb, Jack checked the flight controls for full and free movement. Still uncertain what had happened, his immediate thought was one of collision – that he'd collided with the Harrier escort. He glanced inside his cockpit to verify that the briefed safety frequency was selected before he shouted on the radio: *"STOP...STOP...STOP..."*

A stunned pause followed this transmission. Then a small voice from the Phantom's rear cockpit said: "I'm..okay..." Jack, however, still confused by noise and debris, remained convinced that a collision had occurred. His cockpit shook with the rush of slipstream and he heard a high-pitched shriek from the airflow. At an altitude of 5,000 feet he levelled the aircraft and turned due north. Still sure that he'd collided with the Harrier escort, he wondered whether to test the undercarriage and flap systems but decided to wait until nearer the airfield. But which airfield? Should he fly back to Leuchars or should he divert to another airfield?

It was while these thoughts worked through Jack's mind that he heard the still, small voice from the Phantom's rear cockpit again: "Can you slow down, please? It's uncomfortable back here without a canopy."

"Canopy?"

"Yes!"

"What about it?" said Jack, struggling to hear in the noisy environment.

"My canopy's gone!" said Peter.

"Where's the Harrier escort?" asked Jack.

"No idea. Who cares, anyway?"

"Well…didn't we collide with it?"

"No."

"No?"

"Yes…no!"

"What happened then?"

Peter sighed. "When you asked me to look out for the Harrier escort, I turned sharply…"

"And?"

"And I knocked the canopy jettison handle."

"*What?*" said Jack.

"I said…" but at this point Peter's explanation was interrupted by the pilot of the Harrier escort who wanted an explanation of his own. With this given, Jack decided that the most appropriate action was to return to Leuchars. He flew at 200 knots, the lowest practical airspeed under the circumstances. Peter, meanwhile, had to bend himself almost double in attempts to avoid the worst of the wind blast. Eventually he was released from this torment when Jack landed the Phantom safely and taxied back to his squadron dispersal area where the senior engineering officer waited. Hands on hips, this officer stared quizzically at the Phantom while Jack closed down the engines then waited for Peter's ejection seat to be checked by specialists.

When, at length, they climbed out of their respective cockpits, Jack and Peter both felt subdued – uncharacteristically so. They glanced at each other, then promptly turned to look due east at signs of an ominous change in the weather. The heavens had darkened and the low howl of March winds presaged rain showers rolling over the sea. After their 'open sesame' experience a soaking now would seem a little unreasonable, thought Jack, as the two of them began to run for shelter.

CHAPTER 7

FALKLANDS PHANTOMS

JOHN WALMSLEY IN THE FALKLANDS

Life, at times, can seem perverse. It certainly felt that way to Squadron Leader John Walmsley when, in June 1986, after a long-distance flight in a Lockheed TriStar from the United Kingdom via the Ascension Islands to the newly-constructed Falkland Islands' airfield at Mount Pleasant, he made for his cabin on board a so-called Coastel positioned on one side of Stanley Harbour. A Swedish-built floating accommodation barge, the Coastel would end up eventually in the United States of America as a prison ship (for which purpose, incidentally, significant upgrading was required). John Walmsley's cabin, a metal box that measured approximately twelve feet by eight feet and which had to be shared with another aircrew member, had no window and consequently felt quite claustrophobic. He was keen, therefore, after depositing his somewhat meagre belongings, to head for the Coastel's top deck where he'd observe some of the legendary wildlife.

He had learnt that the Falklands archipelago was home to five different penguin species, some of the largest albatross colonies in the world, and to marine mammals such as the enormous southern elephant seal and the not-so-enormous but still rather big South American fur seal. He'd heard about untamed acres of peat scrub and ragged hills, dark fringes of rock beneath the hills and beside rivers and streams, and thick spreads of grasses that led to scattered settlements like San Carlos, Goose Green, Bluff Cove – names delivered from obscurity by the Falklands War of 1982 and which were generally inaccessible other than by horseback, helicopter or specialist vehicle. The Falklands wind-resistant vegetation consisted mainly of dwarf shrubs, and virtually the entire land area of the islands was used as pasture for sheep which accounted for the predominance in the local diet of lamb or mutton followed by more lamb and more mutton. It was the cormorants and other bird life, though, that John Walmsley watched with fascination from the Coastel's top deck. The cormorants, as they dived for fish, could be seen clearly through the harbour's waters. These waters were marked by

65

various shipwrecks including, near the Coastel, the *Lady Elizabeth,* a three-masted freighter which sank in 1913 after the ship hit a reef and limped into Stanley Harbour – known also as Port Stanley (although originally it was called Beau Port then later named Port Jackson).

Before long, John and his navigator, Flight Lieutenant Steve Chaskin, were ready to be driven by Land Rover from the Coastel to the airfield, a tented encampment which comprised Royal Air Force Stanley. The two of them chatted with the driver about local aspects including some of the terms used by the military in the Falklands. "There are many helicopters here," said the driver, "small ones like Scouts or Gazelles are nicknamed 'teeny-weenies', larger ones like the Sea Kings are termed 'wokkas' and Chinooks are called 'wokka-wokkas'. A civilian company, Bristow Helicopters, has a contract to operate a couple of Sikorsky S-61N helicopters known as 'Erics' after the darts player Eric Bristow. Apparently this annoys the company boss, Mr Alan Bristow himself….hold tight!…" as the Land Rover left Stanley's tarmac roads it began to bump along a pot-holed track which passed as the main route to the airfield, "…we're coming to an interesting section of road."

"It's a good job these vehicles are versatile," said John hopefully as he clung on for dear life.

"The army use caterpillar-tracked vehicles for driving around the 'camp'," said the driver.

"What camp?"

"Anywhere in the Falklands outside Stanley is referred to as the 'camp'."

"So what about normal cars? Are there any here?"

"A few in Stanley…crap cars, mind – just crap cars."

"How do they scrap the crap cars?"

"Along with the rest of their rubbish – great piles of the stuff in landfill sites. And

there's another problem, too. Mines!" The islands are covered in the wretched things, a grim reminder of the war. They reckon there are over a hundred minefields – in total around 20,000 mines. You'll find taped-off minefields with warning signs spread across the islands, a sad, bad legacy."

Soon, as they drove onto the airfield, John could spot Phantoms parked in the dispersal area allocated to 23 Squadron, the unit to which he'd been posted as a

Mines! (Richard Pike)

Building Mount Pleasant and the famed corridor – early 1986. (Richard Pike)

flight commander. He'd left his previous unit, 43 Squadron based at RAF Leuchars, as summer approached so now, since a Falklands June marked, more or less, the middle of winter, it would mean for him a year of pretty much continuous winter. There was little time to worry about this, however, as he settled into his new role for he soon discovered that life in the Falklands was, to say the least, unusual and that the set-up at RAF Stanley was no exception. During the Falklands Conflict between early April and mid June 1982, three Phantoms from 29 Squadron had been stationed at Ascension Island to provide air cover for aircraft flying to the war zone. A couple of months after the war's conclusion, these and other Phantoms from 29 Squadron (later re-named 23 Squadron) had been detached to RAF Stanley to provide air defence of the Falkland Islands. The short runway at Stanley had been patched up with AM2 aluminium matting, after which arrestor cables were installed for the Phantoms' landing run. A total of five arrestor cables were available: two at the approach end, one in the middle in case the first two were missed, then, as a last chance, two more cables were provided at the runway end. Beyond the runway end, crews faced rough terrain, rocks and almost inevitable ejection.

However, all changed a week or so after John's arrival at RAF Stanley when the entire organisation prepared to move some thirty miles south-west to the new set-up at RAF Mount Pleasant whose motto 'Defend the Right' logically followed the Falkland Islands' motto 'Desire the Right'. The name Mount Pleasant was selected from nearby hills (normally a Royal Air Force station would adopt the name of a local village, but no such village existed). As the nearest hill was called Mount Misery, and as this sounded altogether far too downcast, the name of its neighbour, Mount Pleasant, was picked instead. At the new airfield, changes were conspicuous for, in place of the Rubb tents at Stanley, the Phantoms would operate from hangars partially set into the rocks, and the main runway was suited to fast-jet operations. Furthermore, a second runway, though shorter, could be employed if necessary. One aspect of the accommodation that qualified for the record books was the half-mile-long corridor (dubbed 'Death Star Corridor') which linked barracks, messes and recreational areas and which was said to be the longest corridor in the world.

It was during the move to Mount Pleasant that John was summonsed one morning by his commanding officer. "You're just the chap, John," he declared.

"Yes, sir...what for, sir?"

"You're smart...keen...in good spirits."

"I am?"

"Definitely! And you have a quick grasp of procedures, a commanding presence..."

"So what exactly..." said John, his voice now croaky with unease.

"Well," said the commanding officer, "as you know, we have to mark our departure from Stanley with a parade." John's eyes blurred then refocused and his jaw developed a twitch. "After that," went on the CO, "there will have to be a second parade to celebrate our arrival at Mount Pleasant. And you, my dear chap, are the ideal candidate to act as flight commander for both parades."

"Are you sure, sir?" asked John peevishly.

"Quite sure! As the last man in, you've drawn the short straw!"

So it was that, when the parades took place as planned, Squadron Leader John Walmsley ended up as a flight commander responsible for leading officers and other ranks, including a number of Gurkha soldiers, all dressed in natty disruptive pattern camouflage. Many years later, when listening to an inappropriately named piece of music called *Aviators' March* by André Rieu, an eccentric Dutchman, John was reminded of this parade and the need to explain to Mr Rieu that aviators do not march unless ordered to do so and even then begrudgingly.

As a final flourish, and to mark Queen Elizabeth II's birthday, a five-ship Phantom fly-past was performed over Stanley Harbour before the aircraft landed at their new base at Mount Pleasant. The event was duly mentioned in *The Penguin News,* the only newspaper produced within the islands and which, incidentally, was respected locally for a defiant approach to the policies of the Falkland Islands government.

*   *   *

When training at Mount Pleasant began in earnest, most sorties were flown with a pair of Phantoms alternating as target and fighter for practice interceptions. A number of these were flown at night for, during a Falklands winter, daylight was brief and by mid-afternoon, when the last feeble vestiges of sunset had faded, there was still work to be done. The intensity of darkness on a Falklands night could be unnerving for the faint-hearted, and John and his colleagues found that the absence of brightly-lit villages and towns tended to confound the innate sense of orientation. Even out at sea, the whole great Southern Atlantic Ocean was opaquely black apart from cloud-free nights when the light from stars merged with any moonlight to give the impression of bouncing off the watery abyss with an eerie fluorescence. When the night sky was streaked with high, thin clouds or filled with a density of dark and blustery rain clouds, all life seemed to vanish within immediate inkiness. A clear night, though, could create the illusion of entering a vast planetarium for with the lack of light pollution, especially over the 'camp' area, there were rare opportunities to spot shooting stars, the greenish glow of the aurora australis (Southern Lights), and wandering planets against the backdrop of the Milky Way and southern constellations. The latter's eleven circumpolar constellations, including Carina (the keel), the Crux with its cross-shaped or kite-like asterism commonly known as the Southern Cross, Alpha Centauri (one of the brightest stars in the sky and the closest star system to our solar system), looked alien to the northern hemisphere-based aircrews familiar with the Plough or Polaris or the North Star.

In-flight refuelling of the Phantoms was provided by a Lockheed C-130 Hercules aircraft modified to hold a refuelling rig and an extra fuel tank and which always remained on standby in case bad weather interfered with recovery of the fighters to Mount Pleasant. If needed, the Hercules would be ordered airborne to refuel the Phantoms while waiting for an improvement in the weather conditions or, as a last resort, to accompany them for a diversion to Brazil.

Although four years had elapsed since the conflict, Anglo/Argentine relations remained prickly with the ongoing possibility of further hostilities, including the potential scenario of a 'lone wolf' Argentine pilot bent on revenge. For this reason, all of the Phantom sorties were flown with the aircraft fully armed. As a reminder to pilots, the 'master arm' switch was lightly taped over for the aircraft's weapons' fit – normally four Skyflash radar-guided missiles, four Sidewinder infrared missiles and a single Vulcan 20-mm six-barrelled Gatling gun mounted in an under-fuselage pod – was a potent one. The Phantoms' inboard pylons were fitted with chaff (or 'window', a radar countermeasure) and dispensers for infrared decoys. When at Mount Pleasant, where a QRA force was kept at permanent readiness, John Walmsley flew five QRA scrambles during his Falklands detachment although no targets materialised for most of these flights.

As winter set in and heavy snowfall began to limit flying operations, John had a bemusing conversation one time when he was summonsed to speak to someone on the telephone.

"I'm a farmer on West Falkland," said the caller whose gritty voice seemed to fit this description.

"Oh, yes?"

"Aye. I wish to register a complaint," said the farmer, his Falklands accent a mix between that of a New Zealander and a Scotsman (with subtle differences).

"Okay...well... what have we done to upset you?"

There was a pause, then: "It's not what you've done."

"There's surely been some mistake?" John was worried now – and intrigued.

"No mistake," the farmer appeared adamant.

"What's happened then?"

A long-ish silence ensued before: "It's not what you've done but what you've NOT done!"

"Hmm, I see," said John who did not see at all. "Well...what haven't we done?"

"You've not made enough noise."

"Ah...yes. That's a common complaint, I suppose."

"Aye. We're all worried that you might have packed up and gone home."

"If only..."

"What?"

"If..." went on John evasively, "if only we could overfly you more frequently, that would be nice would it not?"

"It might."

"I'll try to arrange it."

"Okay. Good. Don't make too much noise, mind," said the farmer.

"Why?"

"You'll frighten the sheep."

Apart from this issue, snowfall sometimes overwhelmed the Mount Pleasant snow-clearing efforts although the hardworking teams would manage to keep the main runway open for any QRA activity. Taxiways to the runway, however, remained snowbound until John and his colleagues came up with an unconventional plan. They discovered that a Phantom with engines running, if pushed backwards by a tractor, acted as an efficient snowplough, although the Rolls-Royce engines had to be restricted so the tractor itself was not pushed backwards. The Phantoms' weapons were not removed but made safe with safety pins, though John resisted the temptation to contact the *Guinness Book of Records*' people to claim the world's first fully-armed snowplough.

John's work routine, one day off in seven, meant limited opportunity to experience local Falkland life, although one time, when granted a two-day break, he and his navigator were flown in a 'teeny-weenie' to a settlement in West Falkland. The sense of isolation was considerable as the two aircrew, having been dropped off by the helicopter, stood by the settlement's landing pad and waved farewell to their pilot. The two of them, grasping their overnight bags, then began to walk towards the nearest house. It was not long before they came across a man who cried out: "Welcome! You must be the Phantom crew. We had a telephone call to say that you'd be coming."

"Hope that's okay?" said John.

"Of course it's okay. Delighted to meet you. We'll be putting both of you up in our house tonight."

"Marvellous! Thank you so much."

"Come in and meet my wife and two young daughters. After that, you can help with loading wool if you like."

The aircrew learnt that this wool, renowned for its purity and high quality, was the islanders' main export. After loading onto an amphibious truck, the wool bales were driven to a small coaster for onward shipment. In addition to that task, the coaster was used to restock the settlement shops across the Falklands and to deliver any individual items ordered by islanders...a new refrigerator, a Land Rover tyre, a book, plumbing equipment – everything had to be delivered this way.

John and his navigator Steve stayed in a house close to Port Howard, the largest settlement in West Falkland and situated on an inlet off Falkland Sound. They learnt first-hand accounts of the Falklands War from the islanders' perspective, for this settlement had

Crashed aircraft and scrap metal dump post-war. (Richard Pike)

been occupied by about 1,000 Argentine troops and consequently became a target for Royal Naval ships and Harrier aircraft. On 21 May 1982 one of the Harriers was shot down by a Blowpipe missile fired by an Argentine commando company. The Harrier pilot, Flight Lieutenant Jeffrey Glover, ejected from his aircraft, an event witnessed by the islanders as he parachuted into the sea where he nearly drowned. Eventually, the pilot was picked up by enemy troops and, after medical treatment for serious injuries, he was taken to the Argentine mainland as a prisoner of war, the only British POW of the war. About three weeks after this incident, and four days before the Argentine surrender on 14 June 1982, a British secret observation post on a ridge above Port Howard was discovered by an Argentine patrol. During the ensuing fire-fight, Captain John Hamilton, a member of the Special Air Service, was killed and his signaller captured. Hamilton became the first posthumous recipient of the Military Cross and he was buried with full military honours in the Port Howard cemetery by the Argentines whose patrol commander praised the heroism of this officer.

It was thought-provoking for John and Steve when they discussed these events during dinner with the Falkland family kind enough to host them. Conversation centred, too, on the unique Falkland lifestyle. "We have to become DIY fiends in the Falklands," said the family's dad, "there are no electricians to call up for help, or car mechanics or roofers or anything like that. If something busts then it's a case of fix it yourself or do without! Before I came here I used to be a steel worker in Sheffield, so I'm a fairly practical type."

"You're a long way from Sheffield," said John.

"I got bored with my life there so I decided to try the Falklands. I got married here and became a sheep farmer. And now we have two bonny daughters."

"What about their schooling?"

"There's a system of travelling teachers for rural communities like ours. A teacher will stay in the settlement for a week or two before moving on. When the teacher has left, we have 'telephone teaching' whereby lessons are dispensed by 'phone and the kids listen on audio headsets. The older children attend a secondary school in Stanley."

"Does the system work out okay?"

"It seems to. It's highly individualised, our girls are doing well and we try to open their eyes to the wider world with magazines like *The National Geographic*. I must admit, though, that they miss out in some respects. Little things on the whole…" the dad paused, "…a small example is nuts in shells. Our girls have never seen any. Unfortunately, the basic supplies sent to the settlement shop do not include such luxuries."

"Well, well," said John who made a mental note to advise other Phantom crews to rectify this when visiting settlements in future.

The following day, when John and his navigator were picked up by the teeny-weenie, both men felt glad of their rare opportunity to have sampled the 'camp'. The routines on a Falkland settlement were worlds away from flying Phantoms, nonetheless both men felt that they had gained worthwhile insights into the life that it was their duty to defend.

*   *   *

When back at the squadron, John was briefed on a new and unusual task. Recently arrived were the Royal Naval Type 12M anti-submarine frigate HMS *Rothesay* and the Type 22 frigate HMS *Brilliant,* and the navy had requested that Phantoms conduct mock attacks against these ships. To add realism to the exercise, an O-Class submarine was also in the vicinity.

One evening, when the submarine was moored in Stanley Harbour, John and a few other squadron members were invited on board for a cocktail party. The evening proved to be no exception to the navy's general reputation for unorthodox concoctions served at their cocktail parties. When, at length, debates to put the world to rights led to a discussion about the merits of going to war in a submarine or a Phantom, opinions were strongly divided. "There's no way I'd want to go to war in a submarine," said John glancing around his cramped surrounds.

"And there's nothing on this earth that would persuade me that it was a good idea to be in one of those bloody Phantom things."

"Just think of the advantages," said John.

"And think of the advantages of being in a submarine," said the submariner.

"I can't think of a single one."

"Oh, but you're wrong there," grinned the submariner. "For one thing, where else but on board a submarine could you go to war wearing carpet slippers? Nice woolly ones with a tartan motif."

"Sounds..." said John, hesitating as everyone burst into laughter, "...quite comfortable." The hilarity persisted until eventually it was time for the air force men, or 'crabs' in naval parlance, to wave farewell to their naval hosts and confront the twisty road home.

Back at Mount Pleasant John was faced with an ongoing issue of some complexity. Before leaving for the Falklands, he'd been the president of a Board of Inquiry following an accident in the United Kingdom. A Phantom had been flying at low level at an airspeed of 500 knots when the aircraft went out of control in pitch. Both aircrew ejected but suffered injuries – near-fatal in the navigator's case. The wreckage of the Phantom had been delivered in some 400 large plastic sacks to the Royal Aircraft Establishment at Farnborough where the wizards of the Aircraft Accident Investigation Board had set about their tasks. Now, having just received the accident report, John had to finalise his findings even though he was nearly 8,000 miles away from the original site of his Board of Inquiry.

The accident report had revealed that, on impact, the Phantom pilot's pitch trim gauge was indicating full nose-down trim. John made the judgement that the root cause of the accident was unlikely to have been trim runaway – a fault easily countered by the pilot. He decided, therefore, to conduct high-speed, low-altitude experimental flights in the Falklands. These flights progressed as planned and on completion it was concluded that the most likely reason for the accident was blockage of the pitch feel bellows which caused the pilot to trim fully nose-down without realising. A sudden clearance or rupture of the bellows would make pitch control over-sensitive as well as pitching the Phantom nose-down.

Shortly after this episode, John became involved in a clandestine plan to intercept an Argentine electronic intelligence (ELINT) aircraft, a modified Boeing 707. Coincidentally, he had been in Cyprus some two years previously when this aircraft, following modification in Israel, was intercepted by Phantoms on its return flight to Argentina. Now, though, the ELINT machine was known to patrol near the Falklands to gain information about UK military electronic emissions. The ministry of defence in London was keen for 23 Squadron Phantoms to intercept and photograph the intruder, but a recent QRA scramble with Hercules in-flight refuelling support had failed to achieve an interception; the elusive eavesdropper had managed to escape. Clearly, new tactics were required, so plans were made for a silent scramble: there would be no radio calls; the Phantom's 'identification friend or foe' device would be switched off; the airborne radar system and even the radio altimeter would be kept firmly off. Meanwhile, the ground radar controllers at Mount Byron and Mount Alice, both located in West Falkland, were carefully briefed on their part in the ruse.

The time was 0600 when, on Friday 13 June 1986, John began his take-off run from Mount Pleasant airfield. The airfield name seemed apposite on that day for the sky was clear, there was not a breath of wind, and all was well with the world as the Phantom climbed up in radio silence. Soon, as he levelled the aircraft at the planned altitude of 25,000 feet, John gazed down at the terrain below which reflected a fine winter morning with the Falklands looking at its best. It was not long, however, before the benign scene showed signs that would lead to complications. As John flew above Falkland Sound and West Falkland, layers of cloud started to accumulate and by the time he initiated a combat air patrol at 25,000 feet due west of West Falkland, the Phantom was flying in thick cloud.

Meantime, as the ground-radar controllers watched the Phantom's blip on their screens, they prepared to put into action the pre-briefed plan. In a deliberately relaxed voice one controller now passed to his colleague occasional weather updates for Mount Pleasant airfield. The weather updates, however, were adjusted so that the wind direction and speed elements acted as a code to indicate the Phantom's range and bearing from the ELINT aircraft. John maintained the required heading as the range was counted down towards fifteen miles at which point luck appeared to be on his side for the cloud began to thin until, suddenly, the Phantom broke out of cloud and he saw the ELINT aircraft heading directly towards him. He descended to increase the height separation, then executed a hard turn to end up below the Argentine machine which continued on its course with the crew evidently oblivious of the Phantom's presence.

John now manoeuvred to hold a safe formation position on the Boeing 707. The Boeing, he noticed, had been painted white with a smart blue band along the fuselage as if to suggest an ordinary airliner. This was clearly not the case, however, for John could see copious aerials of various shapes and sizes on the Boeing's belly – aerials, he surmised, which must have been installed when the aircraft was fitted-out in Israel. "Can you count up the aerials, Steve?" John asked his navigator.

"Hang on...still counting!" replied Steve. At length, when both of them agreed on the tally, they began to discuss the true nature of the Boeing 707's role.

"It appears to be more of a communications eavesdropper than a real ELINT machine," said John.

"I agree," said Steve. "This thing's hardly in the same category as, say, a USAF RC-135C with its distinctive 'cheek' pods, a camera position on the aft fuselage plus a few other signs of a genuine ELINT aircraft."

By this stage Steve had started to take photographs using the special QRA camera supplied with black and white film, then he took more photos using his own personal camera with colour film. "This should keep the intelligence boys happy," he said.

"Well done," said John, "but before we leave, perhaps we should make our presence known?"

"I think we should," said Steve. "I reckon the crew are still unaware that they've been rumbled."

At this, John manoeuvred to a position above and behind the Boeing before he began to move forward slowly to place the Phantom abeam and to the left of the pilots' cockpit. He climbed slightly so as to give the pilots a good view of the Phantom's eight air-to-air missiles, then he waited, and waited and continued to wait until an abrupt jerk of the Boeing suggested that the pilots had, finally, looked out of their 'office'. Their state of shock can be imagined as, like small boys caught in the act of petty theft, they realised that they'd been ambushed. Their next move was to turn hard towards the Phantom as if to ram it out of the sky. A Phantom's superior manoeuvrability, however, allowed John to perform a graceful barrel roll around the Boeing's cockpit before he engaged the Phantom's reheats and headed back towards Mount Pleasant airfield.

Meanwhile, the Mount Pleasant weather reports, by now in uncoded form, announced that the weather conditions had deteriorated to state 'red' with a cloud-base below 300 feet.

"The wind direction's across the runway and gusting up to fifty-five knots," said John. "We should think about your rolls of film," he went on. "If the worst comes to the worst we may be forced to eject into the sea."

"I'll stow the film in the most waterproof way available," said Steve. At this, he loosened his ejection seat straps, unzipped his immersion suit and placed the film rolls under the suit.

As they continued to fly towards Mount Pleasant, John pondered a further problem – that of the Phantom's weaponry in the event of a possible diversion to Brazil. Should he land the Phantom in South America with the aircraft still fully armed, or should the weapons be ditched into the sea before landing? He decided to put this to headquarters for a decision if and when the issue arose.

The weather conditions at Mount Pleasant, meantime, showed no signs of improvement. "Request clearance for a let-down over the sea," John asked air traffic control.

"There's no conflicting traffic," said the controller, "you're clear to descend over the sea."

Despite any superstitious omens about 'Friday the thirteenth', the let-down worked out well and the Phantom broke through cloud at a safe altitude of around 500 feet. John now reduced the Phantom's airspeed while he flew back towards Mount Pleasant as he maintained visual contact with the ground. When the airfield came into sight, a glance at the windsock confirmed the prospect of a difficult landing. Buffeted by turbulence, he had to kick off a large amount of cross-wind drift immediately before touchdown. The good judgement of an experienced 'top gun' pilot paid dividends, though, as the Phantom landed firmly but safely on the runway after which he taxied the aircraft back to its QRA hangar.

"Glad to have missed that sea dip," John quipped to his navigator as the two of them climbed out of their cockpits. "And now we must send the films post-haste to London."

It took a few days but when John heard back from London, the intelligence officer's comments were highly satisfactory. "They were pleased with your colour photos," John said to his navigator.

"Did they realise that I used my own camera?" asked Steve.

"Probably not. From their point of view it was just part of a day's work."

"After all that effort?"

"Afraid so," chuckled John. He nodded slowly and glanced up when he heard the distinctive cry of a passing bird, one of the area's profuse number of oystercatchers. For a moment or two he thought about conditions in the Falkland Islands, the abundance of wildlife, the barren surroundings, the 'camp' settlements, the particular lifestyle. "Just part of a day's work," he confirmed.

CHAPTER 8

PERSEVERANCE

By early evening it was all over. Perhaps I should say all over bar the shouting for there was quite a bit of that still to come. Furthermore, I may have thought that it was all over but from another perspective things were only just beginning. The telephone call gave me a clue. "It sounded important," the flight commander said, "I got the feeling that you should hurry."

Several hours earlier I'd been on standby in the 43 (F) Squadron crewroom at Leuchars where, along with my navigator Bill and other crews, we remained on ten-terhooks in anticipation of a scramble call. It was the last day of September 1975, a run-of-the-mill Tuesday except that we were preoccupied with an exercise which was far from run-of-the-mill for it involved co-operation (a lot of co-operation) with the Royal Navy. Sometimes the common apothegm 'naval co-operation exercise' felt like a contradiction in terms but despite this, like it or not, we were required to follow naval procedures many of which appeared arcane, annoying, complex to the point of absurdity and apparently designed to ensure that errors were pretty much inevitable. This, indeed, was the cause of much discussion as we waited.

We discussed, too, recent affairs on the world stage for some remarkable events had occurred this month including not one but two determined attempts to assassinate US President Gerald Ford. We talked about how, at the beginning of the month, a woman called Lynette 'Squeaky' Fromme was thwarted by a US secret service agent with the equally implausible name of Larry M. Buendorf. Our crewroom conversation discussed in amazed, almost hushed, terms how Lynette Fromme was some three feet from the president when she aimed a .45 calibre automatic pistol at him and pulled the trigger. Unfortunately (from her point of view) she'd failed to operate the pistol's loading mechanism. Grabbed by Larry M. Buendorf she evidently screamed: "Oh shit! It didn't go off! It didn't go off!" We learnt later, however, that Lynette Fromme did go off – to prison, that was, for the next thirty-four years. And we talked, too, about the way, a mere seventeen days after the first attempt and just a week ago, another woman, Sara Jane Moore, had fired a single shot from a .38 revolver but narrowly missed the president. She'd raised her arm for a second attempt but a nearby ex-marine called Oliver Sipple dived at Sara Jane Moore, grabbed her arm and wrestled her to the ground. We did not know at the time, of course, that thirty-two years later, on release from prison at the age of seventy-seven, she'd say that she 'was very glad that she did not succeed'.

If the crewroom atmosphere was tense that day, the reasons were many and varied. For one thing, a worrying accident a month earlier involving a US Marines Phantom had caused other Phantom operators to take note. The Marine Phantom from the United States ship *Nimitz*, at the time positioned some distance off the coast of south-west Scotland, had collided mid-air with a Grumman A-6E Intruder during a flight-refuelling manoeuvre. While the two members of the Phantom crew had been recovered, the two Grumman Intruder men had not. "Bad business," muttered one of the navigators in our crewroom.

"Wonder what went wrong," said someone else.

"Impatience…incorrect use of procedures…blinded by the sun…who knows?"

"Perhaps similar reasons applied to that in-flight refuelling accident near Sunderland earlier this year."

"The Victor and the Buccaneer?"

"I think it was a handling problem. The Buccaneer pilot was new and inexperienced. His aircraft struck the Victor's tailplane which caused the tanker to pitch nose-down into an out-of-control dive."

"Were there any survivors?"

"The Victor plummeted into the sea killing four of the crew, though I believe that the captain managed to eject."

At this unfortunate turn in the conversation I glanced at Bill. Our eyes met and he raised one eyebrow in a knowing gesture. We were both aware of how, during another recent exercise which involved in-flight refuelling, we'd battled not so much with a lack of skill but with a lack of sleep. "I keep nodding off," Bill had said at the time.

"I'm struggling not to do the same," I'd said.

"What?" He could barely believe that the man at the controls of a twenty-ton fighter flying in the dead of night and in close proximity to a Victor tanker could be anything other than wide awake.

The exercise, though, had been underway for some days, we'd been scrambled as the hour approached midnight and the plain truth was that Bill and I were both tired – very tired. When, in the small hours of the night, we'd been sent to the Victor tanker to refuel, our fatigue was hardly assuaged.

"On the subject of disasters," the crewroom conversation was resumed by one of the pilots, "what about that Italian air force Starfighter saga last week?"

Someone let out a low whistle of astonishment. "They'd just taken off, hadn't they?"

"Yes – four of them in formation. But the weather was bad and the leader must have become disorientated. The F-104s crashed in line, all four of them."

One navigator stood up to make himself a mug of coffee. I couldn't help noticing how the unsteadiness of his hand caused the rim of the mug to jog against his lower lip.

I realised that, despite any superficial bravado, all of us were, in truth, quite anxious. Regardless of outwardly unruffled appearances, it was the nervous smiles, the little secret glimmers of apprehension in the eyes that could portray real thoughts.

Such anxiety, however, seemed to ease quite quickly at signs of activity; waiting around was the worst part. So it proved on this day when, shortly before midday, Bill and I received the order to scramble. We jumped up from our seats, grabbed lifejackets, headgear and other accoutre-

FG1 F-4 of 43 Squadron at high level over the North Sea.

ments and began to dash towards our allotted Phantom XT874. As we ran outside, I was aware of the smell of bonfire smoke. The smoke, rising from a small farmhouse beyond the airfield, was drifting across to fill the air with the nostalgic scent of autumn and burning leaves. The atmosphere felt damp; the weather man had warned of the prospect of haar fog, particularly later in the day as warm air passed over the cold surface of the North Sea.

Soon, as Bill and I clambered aboard XT874, I went through the scramble-start procedures. With the Rolls-Royce Speys swiftly fired up and all checks completed, within moments I was taxiing the aircraft at a fast pace towards the take-off point. Cleared by air traffic control, I moved directly onto the runway and without stopping moved the throttles forward for a rapid 'rolling' take-off. In practically no time at all we were climbing up on a north-easterly heading ready for 'trade'. As we climbed, the misty layers at lower levels disappeared and we entered a world of brilliant sunshine interrupted only by a few patches of cumulus cloud at about 10,000 feet. Below, we caught occasional glimpses of North Sea oil installations and Sikorsky S-61 helicopters flying to the Forties Field and other platforms. In the Phantom's rear cockpit Bill had started to search for signs of a target. Poor Bill: little did we know just then that when he left the service to gain his civil pilot's licences he would be killed in a flying accident. As his former CO put it: "Bill was a great navigator. But as a pilot he was in the wrong job."

That day, though, Bill was in good form when he exclaimed: "It's distant but I think I'm picking up the first signs of a target."

The fighter controller at the radar station at RAF Buchan in north-east Scotland confirmed Bill's suspicions. "There's a high-speed target in your ten o'clock position," she said, "You're authorised to intercept and identify." In other words, we were not permitted to conduct a head-on attack with a simulated Sparrow missile but we'd been cleared to approach the target from behind.

"Standby to increase airspeed," said Bill. Running through my mind I had thoughts of high fuel consumption and the need for an in-flight refuel following the high-speed interception.

"Confirm that a tanker will be available." I said to the controller.

"Affirmative," she said.

"Accelerate to Mach 1.3," said Bill, "the target's closing fast."

As I selected reheat on both engines, a glance at the machmeter revealed our increasing airspeed...*Mach 1.0...Mach 1.1...Mach 1.2.* At a reading of Mach 1.3 I eased the throttles into the mid-reheat range. "Turn right twenty for displacement," commanded Bill while he worked out the interception geometry. Fine judgement was needed, especially at these high airspeeds: if Bill got it wrong we could end up way behind the target. Worse still, if we ended up in front and therefore in the target's sights we'd become, as they say, 'tomato soup'. Glancing around the cockpit I double-checked the armament and other switches. I kept a wary eye on the fuel gauges as the engines' reheat system gobbled up reserves in a very Rolls-Royce way. "Turn a further right ten," said Bill, "then standby for a hard left turn." He began to count down the ranges: "Twenty miles from the target. I've got him on pulse now." This meant that Bill had switched his radar from pulse-Doppler to the short-range pulse mode. "Fifteen miles." I noted that even though the weather conditions were still good, the target was likely to be hidden by the sun's brightness. "Ten miles." The tension was mounting; my heartbeat seemed to increase as did the sense of restlessness inside me. "Six miles. Standby to turn!"

And when, within moments, Bill gave the order to turn hard left, I monitored the Phantom's attitude indicator while applying an accurate seventy-five degrees of bank. In the turn, I looked visually for the target while Bill, meantime, continued to call out the ranges. "It's hard to make out against the sun," I said when rolling out behind the target, "but I think it's a Lightning."

"You're right," cried Bill who'd glanced up from his radar screen. "It is a Lightning. One of your old mates!" But now, even though we had rolled out at a reasonable range, the target seemed to be accelerating away.

"I'll have to increase to Mach 1.5," I said.

"We'll use a hell of a lot of fuel trying to catch him up," said Bill.

"One thing's for sure," I said, "a Lightning will run out of fuel before we do."

"In that case we should persevere."

At this I pushed the throttles forward again to the maximum reheat position. *Mach 1.4... Mach 1.5...*as before, with the lack of outside reference points the only indication of our airspeed was the machmeter. "We're closing again," said Bill, "range now one-and-a-half miles."

Unusual shot of an FG1 preparing for an interception over the North Sea.

"Okay. I've got good visual contact," I confirmed and before long, as our Phantom drew up alongside the Lightning, the pilot rocked his wings to acknowledge the intercept. At this, I gave the pilot a friendly hand wave, disengaged reheat and spoke to the Buchan controller: "Target splashed. Breaking away to starboard. Any more trade?"

"Negative – no further trade at present," she said, "you're clear to steer two-one zero for the tanker."

As we headed for the specified in-flight refuelling area, I heard a few notes from Bill which suggested that he was singing again. On the aircraft radio we picked up sporadic messages from the Buchan controller, otherwise there appeared to be little exercise activity. We completed a rendezvous with a Victor tanker after which, following a refuel to full tanks, the controller ordered us to fly to a defined area to set up a combat air patrol as required by the navy. This involved maintaining an orbital pattern until called for further action. By that stage we'd been airborne for an hour or so and now, after the initial flurry of excitement, the time seemed to drag. Another hour ticked by, then another and another. Further in-flight refuels followed but the dearth of target activity was marked. Indeed, we spent the next five or more hours circling like an airliner awaiting a landing slot at Heathrow airport. "I'm bored," moaned Bill at one point, "and I'm hungry and k-knackered – and I need a pee, but not necessarily in that order. Wake me up if anything happens."

At length, however, as if in response to Bill, any sense of lethargy was dispelled when the controller piped up: "We've just heard from Leuchars that their visibility is deteriorating rapidly in haar fog. You've been cleared to leave the combat air patrol. Edinburgh airport is the nominated diversion if your approach to Leuchars is unsuccessful." At this, I turned the Phantom towards Leuchars and prepared for a bad weather recovery.

"It'll be touch and go," I said to Bill.

"But you're the squadron instrument rating examiner."

"So?"

"So you'd better not screw it up."

"Just for you, Bill," I quipped, "one will try one's jolly little best," a remark to which he merely grunted in reply.

Before long, as we flew towards the airfield and just as I levelled at the procedural height demanded by air traffic control, the Phantom entered the top layers of a fog bank. Now I had to fly by reference to the flight instruments alone. While Bill called out the approach checks, I eased the throttles back to allow the aircraft to settle at the required airspeed for an instrument landing approach (ILS). I waited for the first of two needles to swing into the centre of the cockpit dial; this would show our position relative to the airfield's extended centreline.

Soon, when this needle (the 'localiser' needle) moved, I turned the Phantom onto the final approach heading. Now with small, fine heading adjustments I worked to ensure that the needle remained centrally placed in its dial. Then, as the second ILS needle (the 'glide-path' needle) began to indicate that the Phantom was approaching the ideal glide-path, I lowered the aircraft nose slightly and reduced engine power. I had to continue to fly with finesse: both needles needed to be positioned accurately within the dial; if a needle scooted off to full-scale deflection it became effectively useless. And needle sensitivity increased as the aircaft came ever closer to the ILS transmitter placed near to the runway touchdown point.

Beneath the Phantom, the sheen of the fog bank meant that the sea's surface remained invisible. As if we were flying through strands of grey cotton wool, the fog whirled around the Phantom while I persisted with the approach. Outside the cockpit, with visibility down to near zero, there was no form, no shape, no size, no substance, just an endless stretch of nothingness. A quick double-check around the cockpit showed that everything was ready for landing: the wheels were down, the flaps were down, the boundary layer control system was puffing away quite happily, there were no cockpit warnings, the ILS needles were neatly crossed in the centre of the dial. There was no more banter from Bill; he knew that his pilot's concentration had to be total and uninterrupted.

As the ILS took us ever closer to the decision height, from time to time I glanced up in attempts to see ahead. The nothingness, though, was ubiquitous and I thought: 'This is not looking hopeful. Looks like we'll end up in Edinburgh.' On the verge of increasing engine power for an overshoot, however, I suddenly spotted the dim glow of airfield approach lights through the fog layers. "Visual," I said to Bill; he did not reply but his sigh of relief was almost audible as we continued down for a landing.

"That's seven hours and fifteen minutes to log," said Bill after we had landed. With fog still swirling around the airfield, I taxied back to the squadron dispersal site and followed the marshaller's directions before parking and closing down the Phantom. As Bill and I climbed stiffly out of our cockpits, we were met, unusually, by one of the squadron's flight commanders. "That was quite a marathon," he said by way of polite conversation. We did not disagree. "I've just had a phone call," he looked at me, "it sounded important." I turned and stared at the flight commander. He knew that my wife was due to give birth and this was probably why, for a normally cheerful individual, his expression seemed uncharacteristically serious. "I got the impression that you should hurry home," he said.

"Okay," I said, "thanks for that." If I sounded a little terse, maybe this was caused by the transition as earthly matters interrupted the airborne mindset, the intense concentration needed when flying the likes of a Phantom. But now I was aware of a different reality. Clearly, the situation was urgent; just a few hours away a whole new life dawned – a bonny boy, it would turn out, full of fun, a mass of mischief. I was tired, yes, but that could not be helped. Other, more pressing, priorities had to be faced. Perseverance was needed and there was no time to lose.

CHAPTER 9

HYDRAULIC HASSLE

ALAN WINKLES IN THE FAR EAST

In place of the obvious reply, which would have rung hollow by its very obviousness, Flight Lieutenant Alan Winkles merely grunted and looked cross. With difficulty he squinted at his surroundings which, with visibility reduced to a matter of yards, had almost vanished into the rain-soaked gloom. Formidable fingers of rainwater reached out at Alan and his colleagues as the men searched anxiously for shelter. The rain made a drumming sound on the roofs of nearby buildings. On the ground, where great puddles of water had accumulated, the deluge caused a hissing noise as if a nest of angry snakes had been disturbed. Shifts in the wind direction, typical of a tropical storm, accentuated the men's troubles as the downpour seemed to grow stronger, the racket louder. "Let's go over there," yelled Alan as he pointed at a building. At this, the group of five men began to dash from their temporary refuge under a palm tree towards a likely-looking building.

As they ran, streaks of lightning flickered down menacingly from the electrically-charged heavens. The crack of thunder, like cannon-shot from towering cumulonimbus directly overhead, reverberated through the air base buildings. "Quick...quick..." cried Alan, "try the door." The door of the chosen building, however, was locked. "It's no good...we'll go to the next one." That building, fortunately, was accessible and the men, looking less than magnificent in their sodden clothes, tumbled inside where, not so fortunately, attempts to dry their clothing were less than successful. In the absence of other ideas, the men stared glumly outside to observe with awe the rain-washed environs of the Royal Australian Air Force base at Butterworth.

Though invisible through the monsoon bedlam, Alan knew that directly opposite the air base at Butterworth lay the island of Penang and its capital city of George Town. "There's some intriguing background to this place," he'd said to colleagues earlier. He'd learnt that Butterworth had originally been opened in 1941 as a Royal Air Force station built as part of the British plan to defend the Malayan Peninsular against an imminent threat of invasion by Imperial Japanese forces. The airfield, however, was captured in December of that year and remained in enemy hands until the end of hostilities in September 1945. Control of the station then returned to the RAF, and Japanese prisoners of war were made to repair and improve the air base which went on to play an active role in helping to curb communist insurgency during the Malayan Emergency. In 1957 the station was transferred to the RAAF although the RAF maintained a presence for, among other factors, the air base was used regularly by transport aircraft and Avro Victor in-flight refuelling tankers tasked to support Lightning and Phantom fighter aircraft en route to Singapore. This involved Phantoms from Alan's squadron, 54 Squadron, including Phantom XV420 which was currently the cause of engineering and operational anguish. It was late December 1969 and this aircraft, sent to Singapore as part of an exercise, had suffered 'PC1' failure (failure of one of the flight controls' hydraulic systems) and consequently had diverted to Butterworth. Although not part of the original crew, Alan had been detailed, along with his navigator and three members of ground crew, to act as rescue party.

The storm took an hour to clear, a valuable hour which the engineering team could ill-afford to waste but eventually, as the rain abated, the five men emerged from their shelter to resume work on XV420. With limited equipment as well as limited time, the three engineers faced extra challenges but these men, thought Alan, displayed admirable commitment and versatility. A particular problem was the lack of a key item, a hydraulic test unit, which was not available at Butterworth. The chief technician in charge therefore asked Alan to start one of the Phantom's engines and to operate the flight controls in the hope that this would reveal the source of the leak. The plan worked just as intended, only perhaps too well for, as soon as Alan started the engine, the chief technician ran in front of the aircraft and began to draw his hand across his throat in a frantic gesture to indicate that the engine should be closed down immediately. When he'd done this Alan climbed out of the cockpit to join the others who were gazing gloomily at a pool of pink hydraulic fluid under one of the Phantom's wings. "The problem's in there somewhere, sir," said the chief technician pointing vaguely in the direction of the port engine, "above the wing and adjacent to the engine."

Victor and Phantom after inter-tropical storm north of Gan.

"Can we be more specific?"

"Not really, sir. It could be a number of things. The only way is to remove panels to try to pin down the exact source of the leak."

At this, Alan began to help with the necessary panel removal while the chief technician used a torch to peer inside the Phantom. Meanwhile Alan's navigator, Flight Lieutenant Bob Woodward, hastened to Butterworth's wing operations set-up to co-ordinate the next day's plan. XV420, after take-off from Butterworth, was due to rendezvous with another Phantom accompanied by a Victor tanker. The three aircraft would then transit to RAF Masirah, a British base on a small island off the east coast of Oman, for an overnight stop before an onward flight to RAF Coningsby.

The engineers took several hours to discover the source of the hydraulic leak – a split pipe awkwardly placed behind a vertical fuselage frame and next to the engine. The engine, under normal circumstances, would be removed to allow access but there was no equipment at Butterworth for this. Clearly, another plan was required. "I can improvise with a locally available pipe," the chief technician told Alan, "but we'll have to route the pipe outside the fuselage."

"*Outside* the fuselage? Will that be strong enough?"

The chief technician shrugged. "We'll do our best," he said with a grin.

"And will it be in time for tomorrow's flight?"

"We're quite good at fixing the impossible," said the chief technician, "it's only miracles that take a little longer."

"Well, well," said Alan, "a Meccano model of a Phantom. Some miracle!" At this the chief technician and his colleagues, while hardly struck with an irrepressible bout of joie de vivre, nevertheless chortled to each other with amusement.

Meantime, as Bob Woodward spoke with the duty officer in the Butterworth wing operations unit, he was told that telephone communication with Singapore was poor. But positioned in Singapore were the other Phantom and the Victor tanker involved in tomorrow's rendezvous. "We'll need to talk with the crews tomorrow morning," said Bob. "Accurate timing and precise navigation will be crucial or the rendezvous might go seriously pear-shaped."

"Telephone contact with Singapore is usually subject to delay," said the duty officer mournfully.

"How much delay?"

The duty officer shifted uneasily on his feet. His oriental eyes half-closed behind steel-rimmed glasses as he prepared to deliver a bombshell. "There's often a delay of several hours," he mumbled.

"*Several hours?*"

"I'm afraid so. There's a booking system; we have to join a queue. I'm sorry, but we're stuck with it."

Bob let out a low whistle of astonishment. "No way," he said, clicking his tongue in disapproval. "We'll have to think of something else or the planned RV will never work."

"The best alternative is the telefax signals system."

"Okay…okay. Is that subject to delay, too?"

"It's not ideal but hopefully a 'priority' classification should give us timely information."

So it was that, with a Heath Robinson-like communications system, a Meccano-like Phantom, and an exuberant-ish spirit of faith, hope and charity, Alan and his team prepared for their mother of all plans to be executed on Monday 15 December 1969. The day dawned hot and wet. A signal from Singapore stipulated the take-off time after which the rendezvous, over the northern part of Sumatra, would be achieved by use of airborne radar and the Phantom's air-to-air tactical navigation system (Tacan).

Alan and Bob's take-off proceeded satisfactorily but during the climb-out from Butterworth Alan noticed that XV420's right-hand engine's temperature was high, as were the engine revolutions. Then, as the climb continued, he began to notice strange noises from the rear cockpit. "Are you okay back there, Bob?" he asked.

"Not really," said Bob, "the radar's playing up." Alan heard further thumps and expletives from the rear cockpit until Bob said: "It's no good. I've tried every trick in the book but I just cannot get this sodding radar to work."

"What is it about this aircraft?"

"Perhaps it ingested water during that storm."

"We'll have to rely on Tacan."

By this stage cloud had started to build up although, on the left side, Alan was able to see occasional views of the elongated land-mass of Sumatra. With the Strait of Malacca below, he anticipated glimpses of the Andaman Islands ahead. By now, he reckoned, the Tacan should be providing useful information to facilitate the rendezvous but the instrument's bearing needle had begun to go around and around in a circle as if lost.

"Any joy with the Tacan, Bob?" he asked.

"No. Not a sausage."

After a pause, Alan went on: "Let me get this straight. We have no radar, no Tacan, and the radio's not working too well. Is that a correct summation of the situation?" It was.

On the basis that the more you look, the more you see, and in the absence of any form of electronic or technological enlightenment, Alan and Bob now, to the best of their abilities, had to search visually for signs of their colleagues. With calculations whirling through their heads, both men began to work out the action to take if, as looked likely, the rendezvous failed. "We'll have to divert to Singapore," said Bob. "We'll have enough fuel for that."

"I guess so," said Alan, "although…standby…"

"Can you see something?"

"Yes…I think so…" Alan hesitated as he stared ahead. "In our ten o'clock position I think I can see a couple of semi-persistent contrails emerging…one thick, one thin."

"The thick one could be the Victor, the thin one the Phantom."

Before long, as Alan increased airspeed to follow the line of contrails, he became more convinced that, as much by chance as design, the rendezvous would work out after all. His attempts to make radio contact with the Victor tanker's captain eventually succeeded at which point he was cleared to join the formation to commence refuelling. "At last," he muttered to his navigator, "things seem to be going well for a change."

"Don't count your chickens and all that..." said Bob, a remark that proved prophetic when they saw the other Phantom begin to draw away from the refuelling basket prematurely. "What's up with him?" went on Bob. The answer came quite quickly. "We've had a generator failure," said the pilot of the other Phantom.

"Roger," sighed the Victor captain, "can you continue?"

"Negative. We'll have to return to Singapore."

Heavy sighs all round could be imagined, if not heard. "Understood," said the Victor captain, "turning starboard through one eighty degrees." With Christmas looming in just over a week's time, all of the aircrew cursed inwardly, no doubt, as the formation headed back towards Singapore.

After landing at RAF Tengah in the western part of Singapore, Alan and Bob were more than a little curious to see if the botched Butterworth repair had remained intact. "It looks okay to me, sir," said an engineer who came up to inspect XV420, "best left as it is, I reckon, then a proper repair can be done when you get back to Coningsby. Any other problems with this kite?"

"The starboard engine," said Alan, "is running a bit hot."

"We'll tweak the top RPM down a bit."

*　　*　　*

Matters were less straightforward for the other Phantom, however, which took longer than anticipated to rectify. As a result two days elapsed before, finally, the formation was ready to depart from Tengah. All were eager to proceed; none realised the perils ahead.

The take-off from Tengah was not good. Alan realised straightaway that the engineers' 'tweaking' of the starboard engine had not improved matters. In a non-standard procedure, he cancelled that engine's reheat immediately after take-off and throttled back to keep the temperature within required limits. This had implications for in-flight refuelling as, with one engine pegged back, the other engine ran out of power when the fuel tanks began to fill up. To keep the Phantom's refuelling probe in contact with the refuelling basket, therefore, Alan needed to apply brief bursts of reheat on the good engine. This, though, meant that XV420 consumed more fuel than planned. The conundrum, fortunately, was resolved when the Victor crew calculated that they could give away additional fuel before handing over to Victor colleagues from RAF Gan in the Maldive Islands.

The rendezvous with the Victor tanker from Gan worked as planned, the Phantoms took on more fuel, then the formation turned onto a north- westerly heading for Masirah. It was at this point that further trouble threatened. In the upper atmosphere ahead a thin haze started to appear while streaky clouds like vapour trails heralded the main body of cloud. As if a noted artist had been let loose with a colossal paintbrush, the skies began to look dishevelled

Shackleton, Canberra, F-4 and C-130 on the pan at Butterworth.

and livid. Nature offered a vivid depiction of an inter-tropical front, the area formed by the convergence of air masses originating from the earth's two hemispheres. The aircrew had been warned, they knew what to expect but any hope of circumventing trouble was thwarted by the size of the storm's stretch.

At first there was no rain. Then as the formation flew towards the initial layers of cumulonimbus, a few drops pattered politely against the windscreen. Quite quickly after that the rain grew stronger, the turbulence wilder. "Standby, Bob!" Alan warned his navigator. Bursts of wind erupted erratically but even this proved to be something of a foretaste for when the full force of the storm struck the sky darkened and suddenly it felt as if time had stopped. The windscreen, pounded by powerful gusts, was engulfed by rainwater that seethed and surged against the Phantom. Like rockets in a firework display, streaks of lightning careened across the sky. At times almost blinded by the frantic leaps and quivers of light, Alan struggled to control his aircraft which was hurled violently up, down, from side to side. The boom of thunder, the waves of rainwater, the surreal hissing sounds emitted by St Elmo's fire that skittered from one side of the windshield to the other all added to an eerie cacophony of sound.

Filled with a sense of impotence as if grappling with an invisible adversary, Alan battled on. His throat felt dry; his heartbeat raced. Painfully aware of the imperative need to keep the Victor in sight, he had to fly uncomfortably close to the tanker's wing. At times he felt as if he could reach out to touch the red lines painted on the wing's underside. He heard some garbled talk on the aircraft radio but he was unable to make out what was said. This was unfortunate for suddenly, from within the security of its pod, the refuelling basket began to deploy to a trail position: storm or no storm, the next refuelling bracket had been reached. The basket smacked against the Phantom's windscreen then Alan followed the device as he eased back in a co-ordinated move.

Now, as he prepared to refuel, Alan faced new hazards. While he struggled to line up the Phantom's refuelling probe, the basket cavorted as if in reaction to a series of sharp kicks. His efforts were frustrated by the remorseless level of turbulence – again and again he'd try, encouraged by his navigator's calm commentary: "Just missed...ten o'clock position...ease right..." Within the layers of cloud, the electrically-charged atmosphere continued to discharge flickers of lightning. Thunder boomed; the Phantom shook; the refuelling basket refused to settle. When, finally, he heard his navigator's cry: "Contact!" Alan reckoned that his success was due as much to luck as judgement. The pilot in the other Phantom, who had similar difficulties but managed to make contact at about the same time, later agreed with this sentiment.

The problems, though, were not over yet. Having connected probe and basket, Alan now had to maintain contact. The combination of bad visibility, extreme turbulence and the urgent need to take on fuel all tested his flying skills to the limit. Furthermore, with XV420's right engine still restricted and, consequently, the ongoing need for occasional bursts of reheat on the left engine, he started to over-control the left throttle. If he pulled back too far, the flow of fuel from the Victor stopped. When he engaged reheat, the Phantom shot forward causing kinks in the refuelling hose which threatened to snap off the tip of the Phantom's refuelling probe. Despite the pitfalls, slowly the fuel gauge indicators started to creep in the right direction until, after twenty-seven minutes, the Victor's pod lights indicated that the Phantom's tanks were full.

The sensation of relief was impossible to ignore. As Alan withdrew the refuelling probe, it wasn't jubilation that he felt – he was too tired and numb – so much as a sense of hope that welled up from deep inside. Virtually unaware that he was drenched in perspiration, he routinely went through the post-refuelling drills. When he flicked a switch to retract the refuelling probe into its housing, another switch, this one controlled by nature, appeared to be flicked simultaneously; the formation had reached the far edge of the frontal zone. The three aircraft were rocked, as if the sky's unsettled giant wished to make a final point, but it was a last-gasp effort for suddenly an uncanny silence settled upon the scene, an awesome stillness. The effect was stunning. The sun now shone with a fierce, contained brilliance. The sea sparkled in a dancing play of light that extended without limits to the far horizon. From the storm's tight confines, now the volume of air was confounding. They had escaped pandemonium; ahead lay utopia.

It did not seem long before the formation landed at Masirah after which the three aircraft were directed to the visiting aircraft section. When Alan had closed down XV420 and he and Bob had climbed out of their respective cockpits, the two men exchanged glances as their feet touched the ground. They said nothing but walked back to inspect the left side of their Phantom where they could see at once that the Butterworth bodge had held fast. The hydraulic pipe had survived the storm, testimony, indeed, to the skills of the engineering team. Alan gave a thumbs up sign to Bob as the two of them now set off for the engineering line hut. As they walked and as they pondered they listened to the wind sighing gently through the airfield buildings.

CHAPTER 10
MAKING WAVES

ROLAND 'ROLY' TOMLIN ON 92 SQUADRON

Yes, it was an interesting day. Flight Lieutenant Roland 'Roly' Tomlin, as a pilot with 92 (East India) Squadron based at RAF Wildenrath in Germany, was on duty one Sunday together with his navigator and the other duty crew. The four men sat and chatted as they waited in Wildenrath's quick reaction set-up, known locally as 'Battle Flight'. Nearby, in a specially designed hardened shelter, their Phantom XV435 was fully armed and fuelled ready for the crews to react in the event of a call to action.

As they waited, conversation centred on the issues of the day especially those of some 8,000 miles away where, less than a couple of weeks previously, an Argentine scrap metal dealer had raised the Argentine flag in South Georgia, Falkland Islands. Perhaps, at the time, that event may have seemed of distant significance, though what was to follow turned out to be far from insignificant. For this was 1982, and the raising of that flag on 18 March would herald momentous repercussions. Her Majesty's forces were alerted to the very real prospect of war and by the end of the month, as Roly and his colleagues held their Battle Flight duties in Germany, they realised that, despite strenuous diplomatic efforts by the Americans and others, war could flare up within a matter of days. At that point, with many unanswered questions, the sense of uncertainty added to an air of anxiety. Few current personnel had experience of war and individuals naturally worried about the way in which peacetime lives would change. Military training offered preparation to an extent, nonetheless minds speculated about the realities of war, the effects of brutalisation, the way an individual's plans could be cauterised and closed.

Suddenly the men's conversations were interrupted by a voice from a small 'squawk' box set up in one corner of the room: *"Battle Flight alert one Phantom..."* At once, all stopped what they were doing and began to run to the two Phantoms. While the aircrew hastened up steps for cockpit access, the engineers turned on electrical power, opened the shelter doors and manned fire extinguishers ready for engine start. The four aircrew, meantime, swiftly checked in with the controller who ordered them to maintain cockpit readiness. As he waited, Roly glanced at his surroundings. Equipment, signs and notices on the shelter's walls were daubed with the squadron colours which left the casual onlooker in no doubt that this was a unit whose personnel were proud of their squadron. With a distinguished history, 92 Squadron had been active in both world wars and was noted as the first squadron into action on 15 September 1940, later known as Battle of Britain day. In the early 1960s the squadron was selected as Fighter Command's aerobatic team under the command of Squadron Leader Brian Mercer. With bright blue Hawker Hunters the team had thrilled the crowds as the pilots displayed precision flying which had included looping eighteen aircraft. In 1965 92 Squadron had been reallocated from the United Kingdom to RAF Germany, initially at Geilenkirchen before a transfer to Gütersloh where, equipped with English Electric Lightning aircraft, the squadron was based for a dozen years until reforming with Phantoms at RAF Wildenrath.

As he continued to check around him, Roly noticed one of the ground crewmen stoop down to pick up a small item of 'FOD' (foreign object damage – aviation's term for litter). The thoughtful act prompted a jolly response from his mate who, although he didn't exactly cry out incredulously, wheel about with clenched fists raised in the air, perform three steps of a polka dance just for the hell of it (actions which may have prompted the wrath of the observing chief technician), all present, Roly observed, were moved nonetheless to enjoy this moment of light relief. With the tense atmosphere eased, he watched the relaxed, professional manner in which the ground crew interacted and worked together, and he felt glad to be part of an organisation which was anything but mundane.

It was during such machinations that the controller suddenly piped up again: *"Battle Flight...one Phantom...head zero nine zero...climb to eight thousand feet to intercept an unidentified target...scramble, scramble, scramble...acknowledge."*

Roly's multifunctional capabilities now sprang into action as, almost simultaneously, he acknowledged the controller's orders, signalled the ground crew and initiated the Phantom's scramble start procedure. When satisfied with engine and other checks, Roly gave the signal for wheel chocks to be removed. Two members of ground crew then dashed beneath the Phantom to tug the chocks clear. Now, as he eased the twin throttles forward, Roly began to taxi the Phantom at a fast pace towards the runway. Quickly cleared by air traffic control, he moved directly to the take-off point where, without stopping, he altered the throttles to the full cold power position. He paused for a second or two before pushing the throttles further forward to select maximum reheat. Soon, when the Rolls-Royce Speys reacted and when the Phantom leapt ahead as if yearning to hurry, the two aircrew both felt a familiar punch in the back as the reheats engaged.

When airborne, and as he turned onto the commanded heading, Roly checked in with the fighter controller for additional instructions and information. "Battle Flight Zero One," said the controller, "your target's flying at low airspeed on an erratic but generally northerly course. There's been no radio contact but we've been tracking this aircraft since the pilot took off from a local racecourse. Maintain your current height and heading."

Below, the German countryside was swathed in early evening light. As he levelled the Phantom at a height of 8,000 feet, behind him Roly could discern the established layout of RAF Wildenrath. Sited close to the German/Dutch border, the airfield's single runway, orientated east-west, was flanked by five dispersal areas, including 'Bravo' dispersal which he had just left. In a different area he could see 'Delta' dispersal which was used by his squadron. Constructed parallel to the main runway, the taxiway was wide enough to be used in emergency. Ahead was the River Rhine with, beyond that, the River Lippe running east-west towards the line of the Teutoburger Wald hills. He could spot the colourful patchwork of German countryside, a mix of farmland and large tracts of forest – a stark contrast to the great industrial areas surrounding towns such as Duisburg and Essen.

Before long, as the Phantom flew south of the city of Hanover, the border between East Germany and West Germany loomed. "Your target's still on a generally northerly heading," said the controller, "turn left onto zero four five to intercept."

"Copied," replied Roly, who then said to his navigator: "The visibility's okay, Alistair. We'll get a visual sighting of this bogey quite soon."

"Roger to that. I'm still searching on radar. And we'll be flying very near to the border."

"Yup," said Roly. He'd flown close to the border on previous scrambles, nevertheless the sinister sight of seemingly interminable acres of barbed wire, dog runs, minefields, anti-vehicle ditches, booby traps, automatic alarms, watchtowers manned by a total of some 50,000 armed guards, carefully-combed sandy strips designed to highlight foot-prints...all of these measures, together with other pernicious acts, tended to induce an involuntary shudder in even the hardiest of souls. The border's abrupt closure by East German authorities in the early 1950s, Roly reflected, had created bizarre and cruel predicaments – the residents in one town, for instance, who could no longer gain access to the shallow end of their swimming pool; footballers in a village where the border ran just behind the goal posts thus putting the goalkeeper at risk of being shot by border guards; a house that was divided by the border; endless other cases of homes, businesses, industrial sites, farmland literally split in two.

Roly and Alistair knew that their every move in the vicinity of the border would be observed by the malicious, intrusive eyes of the border guards staring through bin-oculars. "Turn left ten degrees onto zero three five," Alistair interjected, "there's a possible radar contact."

"Zero three five," said Roly. He had every confidence in his navigator whose calm, courteous manner complemented his talents as an experienced and skilled weap-ons-system's operator.

"Hold that heading..." Alistair paused, then: "standby...I think I have radar contact with a slow moving target. He's currently heading about zero one zero. Maintain your heading for now...I'll turn you further left shortly."

Roly peered ahead as he tried to spot the target visually. He kept a wary eye, too, on the border which was gradually closing up on the Phantom's starboard side.

"Turn left onto the target's heading of zero one zero," said Alistair, "this'll put us in his six o'clock position. I estimate that his airspeed is around one hundred knots so we'll catch up quite rapidly." Roly now spoke to the controller who ordered him to shadow the target. "We'll have to set up a racetrack pattern," said Roly to his navigator. "I'll fly at 180 knots – our minimum practical airspeed at this weight and configuration."

"Okay," said Alistair who knew he'd have to employ creative skills to guide his pilot. "Turn left through ninety degrees initially," he instructed.

"Rolling out on two eight zero," said Roly as he completed the turn.

"Hold it...now turn further left through 180 degrees..." and in this way, by trial and error techniques, Alistair worked out an effective method to manage the disparity in airspeed between Phantom and target. Below, Roly identified the area of Luneburg Heath with, beyond and to the left, the town of Luneburg with the sprawling metropolis of Hamburg further ahead. While focused on his navigator's instructions, Roly could still glimpse scenes of normal life below with traffic on the roads, farmers at work in the fields. To his right, however, he knew that life was far from normal in the area of the border and into East Germany itself.

At this point, the controller came up with new instructions: "Battle Flight Zero One, carry out a VID on this target." Roly acknowledged but, as anticipated, he soon found that the VID (visual identification) proved problematic with the Phantom's high overtake speed. "We're about to overtake on his starboard side," said Roly to his navigator, "but I've got good visual contact and can confirm it's a light aircraft...standby..." When he flew by the target Roly identified a Cessna 182 Skylane, an American four-seat, single-engined aircraft popular with private fliers. As he overtook, Roly noted that, interestingly, the Cessna's wingspan was similar to that of the Phantom which, at a little more than thirty-eight feet, exceeded the Cessna's by just over two feet. Other statistics, however, revealed significant contrasts. The Cessna's length, for example, at twenty-nine feet was almost half that of the Phantom, and the latter's maximum take-off weight of 56,000 lbs was nearly (but not quite) twenty times more than the Cessna's. But it was the difference in airspeeds which was about to prove the main issue for Roly. While the Cessna's stall speed was a mere 49 knots, Roly had to fly at over three times that amount to avoid stalling the Phantom.

Meanwhile, Roly passed the Cessna's identification (D-EKWR) to the controller who said: "Battle Flight Zero One, you're to shepherd the Cessna into Hamburg airport. Acknowledge."

Roly duly acknowledged before he said to his navigator: "How the hell are we supposed to do that, Alistair?"

"With difficulty!"

"Okay. For starters I'll lower our flaps and undercarriage. Then we'll fly past his starboard side and I'll 'waggle' our wings."

"You could give him a quick flash of the reheats as you pass."

"Good plan. When clear, I'll turn towards the airport so hopefully he'll get the message."

*   *   *

Roly felt a sense of trepidation. Even though the Cessna pilot was, in all probability, an amateur flyer who'd be willing – more than willing – to comply with the Phantom's obvious signals, this was not guaranteed. For a brief period the Phantom would be flying, in effect, in formation with an un-briefed amateur, male or female, who could well be of a timorous disposition, or perhaps over-excitable, or with a medical condition, or…well, the possibilities were limitless. Roly, therefore, had to deal with an unknown quantity, and the appearance of a fully armed Phantom flying unannounced close to another aircraft was enough to make any pilot feel anxious. And the actions of an anxious pilot, Roly knew, could be unpredictable and hazardous, especially a pilot who'd been observed following an 'erratic course' close to the border.

The controller's instructions were clear, however, and there was no time to waste. "Standby, Alistair," said Roly to his navigator, "let's implement Plan 'A'."

Maintaining 180 knots, Roly lined up the Phantom while Alistair continued to monitor his radar picture as he called out range and other information. "I can see that the Cessna's still on a generally northerly course," said Alistair, "here's hoping he doesn't have a sudden desire to turn to starboard."

But Roly manoeuvred judiciously and when he flew past the Cessna, overtaking as rapidly as last time, he engaged the Phantom's reheats for a second or two before he turned gently towards Hamburg airport. Soon well clear of the Cessna, he executed a steep turn through 360 degrees for another run, that time to check on the pilot's reaction. This proved that the plan had worked as intended for the Cessna pilot (perhaps frightened out of his or her wits) had evidently made a panicky call on the emergency frequency which, at last, gave air traffic control the opportunity to establish radio contact. The pilot's reaction could be imagined: the eyes refocusing, the jaw twitching, maybe one or two other events inclined to afflict the seriously startled. But the pilot, now in the shadowy clutches of air traffic control, would have to face a few realities and learn a thing or two about aeronautical procedures.

However, for Roly and Alistair their task had been accomplished, their services were no longer needed. "Thanks for your help, Battle Flight Zero One," said the controller, "you can return to Wildenrath."

By the time Roly landed the Phantom, a small group of squadron members had congregated to see what all the fuss was about. Roly and Alistair climbed out of their cockpits to be handed mugs of industrial-strength coffee. There seemed, they reckoned, to be a buzz of excitement within the Battle Flight set-up. There were forms to fill in, questions to answer, telephone calls to make but both men felt the sense of satisfaction from a job well done.

Eight months later

Fields had been harvested and large round hay bales wrapped in black polythene lay among the stubble in the vicinity of RAF Wildenrath. Much had occurred in the intervening months since Roly's springtime Battle Flight experience, including the dramatic events of the Falklands War which began on 2 April 1982 and which lasted for seventy-four days. In that time nearly 1,000 lives were lost, including 649 Argentine military personnel, 255 British military personnel and three Falkland Islanders.

With the unsuitability of the runway at Stanley, Phantoms had not been able to operate there although a detachment of three Phantoms had been deployed to Ascension Island to provide air cover for aircraft flying to and from the war zone. After the conflict, the runway was reconstructed and Phantoms were sent there for air defence of the islands.

While the Phantom squadrons in RAF Germany were not affected directly, the war's ramifications were felt there nonetheless. The psychological and other impacts of war, reaching into remote corners, could be profound and the recent lessons learnt in the South Atlantic were applied elsewhere in various ways, including to the regular exercises held at stations in RAF Germany, especially the so-called Taceval (tactical evaluation) exercises.

The initial call-to-duty for these came in the form of a loud siren triggered, more often than not, in the middle of the night by the Taceval team leader. As personnel tumbled out of bed in reaction to the racket, none would have any idea about how long the exercise would last or where they might end up, especially tough if you had a wife who was equally in the dark.

So it was that RAF Wildenrath's personnel were summonsed in October 1982 by the alert siren which required everyone to scurry here and there while the Taceval team members observed proceedings, clutched at clipboards, scribbled down notes, said little but looked impressively inquisitive. Within 92 Squadron's operations room, activity became notably hectic as schedules were organised, maps prepared, programme boards checked, weather conditions scrutinised, aircrew briefed. For Roly and his navigator this meant a morning flight in a low-flying area across Germany. They were briefed to fly as number two in a two-ship formation with a Taceval observer in the lead aircraft.

Meantime, as they waited for the engineers to generate serviceable aircraft, the aircrew were given further briefings which included safety issues following an infamous episode some six months earlier during another of RAF Germany's relentless series of exercises. The first phase of that exercise had required the squadron Phantoms to be armed and ready for flight within six hours. After that, normal practice should have involved downloading the live weapons to replace them with harmless replicas. However, on this occasion the station commander had decided that, for the exercise's flying phase, the live weapons should remain on the aircraft. Routine precautions should have included red warning tape placed across the pilot's master arm switch, although on the day in question 92 Squadron, regretfully, amazingly, had run out of red warning tape.

As appeared to be the case in rather too many aircraft accidents, the consequences of one seemingly trivial factor in a series of events would prove dire indeed.

In a flurry of urgent activity, Phantom XV422 was scrambled to intercept any 'trade' that might have come the crew's way. With the absence of red warning tape and hampered, no doubt, by a general state of harassment, shortly after take-off the pilot carried out the standard procedure for training flights at the time: he selected XV422's master arm switch 'on'. The scene was set.

Towards the end of the sortie, a sortie which had lacked any trade, the Phantom crew, perhaps harbouring a sense of frustration, decided to carry out a simulated attack against a Jaguar aircraft preparing to land at RAF Brüggen. In what some might see as imprudent, if not flawed, design, there was just one way in which to film the attack: the Phantom pilot needed to squeeze the firing trigger – also known, in American-speak, as the 'fire committal switch', although this peculiar, discursive gobbledegook was, for once, quite appropriate for the switch *did* connect, the committed AIM-9 Sidewinder missile did fire and...bingo...Her Majesty's Royal Air Force was suddenly minus one Jaguar aircraft. Fortunately, the Jaguar pilot ejected safely. The two members of the Phantom crew, though, faced a court martial where both pilot and navigator were evidently found wanting and punished with loss of all seniority in their current ranks.

Just now, with 92 Squadron's supplies of red warning tape no doubt replenished for the Taceval, Roly and his navigator chatted with colleagues as they continued to wait for their planned flight in Phantom XV465. Suddenly, a squadron leader appeared in the crewroom doorway and beckoned Roly: "Time to get going," said the man known as 'Bear'. Anxious to fly, Roly and his navigator Keith nodded gladly and stood up to join Bear and the Taceval observer as the four men collected their lifejackets, bone dome flying helmets and other equipment before walking out to their waiting Phantoms. "The latest forecast for LFA2 looks okay," said Bear as they walked. LFA2 (low-flying area 2), situated in the vicinity of the city of Münster in north-west Germany, covered mainly agricultural land with low population density. The area was reasonably flat and obstruction free which allowed the Phantoms tactical flexibility to engage targets.

Roly and Bear made for the engineering line hut while their respective navigators went directly to their allocated Phantoms. Within the line hut, a Taceval team member complete with clipboard watched the procedure as the two pilots scrupulously scrutinised the technical logbooks of their respective aircraft. "Wonderful!" said Roly as he scribbled a signature.

"Yes, sir," said the attendant chief technician, "excellent kite this one." Avoiding the Taceval man's gaze the 'chiefie' winked and pulled a face.

Outside, Roly sensed a distinct chill in the autumn air as he and Bear strode towards their Phantoms. The Taceval observer, Roly noted, was still being assisted by a senior member of the ground crew team while Roly's navigator, already ensconced, was concentrating on cockpit checks. Before long, with external checks and engine start-up procedures completed, Bear called for clearance from air traffic control: "...Phantom formation...taxi."

"Clear to taxi for runway zero nine...surface wind one zero zero at ten knots." While the two Phantoms moved at a steady pace along the taxiway, the crews spotted mobile surface-to-air missile units manned by RAF Regiment personnel in NBC (nuclear, biological, chemical) kit as part of the Taceval exercise.

Soon, with clearance from the controller to line up and take off, Bear moved smartly to the far side of the runway while Roly manoeuvred to take up an echelon starboard position.

Now, with Bear's signal to increase engine power, Roly advanced his aircraft's twin throttles and glanced at XV465's engine instruments; the readings were normal without any indication of the problems to come. Bear now gave a firm nod of his head at which both pilots released their brakes and the Phantoms, still in close formation, accelerated along the runway.

When airborne, Roly moved swiftly to a wide battle formation position to facilitate manoeuvrability and tactical efficiency, key facets for fighter aircraft searching for hostile targets. Soon, as they flew within the low-flying area, Roly and Keith's training and experience proved beneficial during the complex turns needed to help the crews to spot enemy intruders. It was during one of these turns, however, that they were suddenly faced with the first sign of trouble. A warning came from Bear's radio call: "Have you just engaged reheat?" he asked tersely.

"Negative," said Roly, surprised by the brusqueness of the call.

"In that case, you're on fire!" said Bear as, more or less simultaneously, a fire warning light appeared in XV465's cockpit. At once Roly, monitored by Keith, carried out the prescribed drills before announcing on the emergency 'guard' frequency:

"PAN...PAN...PAN...Mike Lima...Phantom aircraft...low level in LFA2 with left engine fire warning!"

Almost immediately the emergency controller responded: "Mike Lima PAN acknowledged. State your intentions."

"Mike Lima...request immediate diversion to Laarbruch." Situated on the border between Germany and Holland, RAF Laarbruch was the nearest suitable diversion airfield.

"Copied Mike Lima...steer two zero zero for Laarbruch."

While Roly turned as directed, it was not long before the cockpit fire warning light began to fade then go out altogether. "Mike Lima..." Roly spoke to the controller again, "...fire warning now out. We'll continue to Laarbruch for priority landing."

"Acknowledged Mike Lima. Your present heading is good."

"Request direct approach from the east and we'll take the cable."

"Standby, Mike Lima..." The emergency controller now liaised with Laarbruch's controller to clear Roly's approach which would be against the flow of other traffic.

"Mike Lima...?" he continued eventually.

"Go ahead."

"That approach has been approved. Remain on this frequency."

"Copied – thanks."

And so the professional flow of procedures smoothed the way for Roly to land as rapidly as possible in case the fire flared up again. Roly's skill was evident to the small group of onlookers that watched his landing, accurately executed on the spot needed for the Phantom's tail-hook to catch the emergency cable stretched across Laarbruch's runway. As the cable system of steel wires attached to hydraulic dampers brought the Phantom to an abrupt stop, Roly closed down both engines, checked around his cockpit and opened his canopy. Glancing to the side, he was a little surprised, even impressed, to see that his navigator had already evacuated the Phantom's rear cockpit and legged it to the grass verge where he was lighting a cigarette. Roly did not take long to join him.

Meanwhile, firemen positioned their fire trucks in a way that fire trucks should be positioned after which, when given a thumbs up signal, Roly and Keith joined a local engineering officer to examine the

XV465: damage caused by fire in left-hand engine.

Phantom. They gazed at the port tailpipe, scarred by fire marks, and at the fuselage plating which, in the vicinity of the tail-hook, bulged outwards at a grotesque angle. The engineering officer shook his head: "I'm a Buccaneer man, me – not qualified on these Yankee Doodle things," he said as, torch in hand, he inspected the damage closely, "but it looks as if this Spey engine has suffered a bypass duct failure which seems to have sheared the fuel lines."

"That explains the fire, then," said Roly.

"Indeed. Bit of a job to fix, I'm afraid." The engineering officer let out a long sigh, then lapsed into silence for a moment before he went on: "Now tell me, young man," he said to Roly, "this fire was controlled, but in my opinion it was a close thing. I wonder...if the warning had persisted...?" But Roly did not reply. There was no need. The engineering officer had spotted Roly's expression and worked out the answer.

CHAPTER 11

CLOSE ENCOUNTERS

DICK NORTHCOTE RECALLS

The party dissipated from its rowdy social centre into various peripheries. Someone picked up drinks and carried them across to a group; a hand waved idly nearby; faces took shape then dissolved within the watery light of the officers' mess at RAF Wattisham in Suffolk. It was October 1986 and from a darkened corner of the mess anteroom an improvised disco boomed out Chris de Burgh's *The Lady in Red* and Madonna's latest hit *True Blue*. As with any good farewell party, Wing Commander Dick Northcote was moved by the generous and spontaneous remarks made by individuals who came up to bid him goodbye as commanding officer of 74 (F) Squadron. "Thanks for everything, boss." "Good luck with your next posting, boss." "Don't forget to keep in touch." "Send us a postcard from the Falklands."

The scene, he reflected later, was rather different from just a few days earlier when he reckoned to have come closer to meeting his creator, as they say, than at any other time in his life.

But now it was time to move on, time for a change and time, with an accumulation of over 2,500 flying hours on the Phantom, to face the inevitable ground tour. The past may have been another place but even so, he mused, the memories lived on – and what memories, including those from a dozen or so years ago when he was serving an exchange tour with the 4501st Tactical Fighter Squadron of the United States Air Force at MacDill, Florida. MacDill back then offered him exciting opportunities with good flying in good weather. It was a place, also, with an interesting past; he learnt about this when he first arrived. Dick was briefed that the base was named after Colonel Leslie MacDill, a World War One aviator who had commanded an aerial gunnery school in France. Construction of the base was started in the autumn of 1939, a year after Colonel MacDill's death in a flying accident. In World War Two the primary mission of MacDill air base, known as MacDill Field, was the training of bombardment units. The bomber theme continued after the war into the 1950s and early 1960s at which point the base converted to Tactical Air Command operating the F-84 Thunderstreak fighter for a short period until the arrival of Phantoms.

Before his posting to MacDill, Dick Northcote had been a member of 54 Squadron based at RAF Coningsby. He had joined the 4501st, therefore, with a reasonable amount of experience as a Phantom pilot. So it was that, one summer's day in 1975, he was authorised to carry out a full air test on a Phantom F-4E. It was high summer and the sun shone full onto the landscape of Florida, that prominent peninsular which formed the most south-eastern state in the United States. With over 1,300 miles of coastline, bordered by the Atlantic Ocean on one side, the Gulf of Mexico on the other side, this was an appropriate location to conduct an air test which included a period of supersonic flight.

As he headed for the engineering set-up to inspect and sign the F-4E's technical log, Dick reflected on his good fortune to be posted to the 'Sunshine State'. There were many advantages but he was conscious, nonetheless, that this US state could suffer problems too. Central Florida, for example, was known as the lightning capital of the United States. Then there was the hurricane issue, in particular between the months of August and October when category four or higher storms could strike with deadly results. Massive thunderstorms in late spring until, on average, early autumn were known to produce some of the highest precipitation levels in the entire USA. Dick was aware of a tragic case some ten years previously when, in extreme turbulence, a North-west Airlines Boeing 720 had broken up and plunged into the Everglades.

"All the stuff's here for you, sir," said the large USAF chief master sergeant as Dick walked up to a desk with the technical log laid out. In the background a radio played The Carpenter's version of Please Mister Postman, number one in the charts at the beginning of 1975. Nearby, a group of airmen were in animated discussion about the mass evacuation of Americans following the fall of Saigon to communist forces some three months ago. The unconditional surrender of South Vietnam and the ending of the Vietnam War were now the cause of much debate and soul-searching across the USA.

When he'd signed the technical log, Dick strode towards the waiting F-4E. He was aware that, with over 1,300 F-4Es built by McDonnell Douglas, this was the most numerous of the Phantom variants. The elongated nose, which contained the AN/APQ-120 radar with a smaller cross-section to accommodate the M61 Vulcan cannon, gave the aircraft a distinctive outline which hardly helped to assuage the Phantom's reputation as 'double ugly'. Other sobriquets, including 'rhino', 'old smokey', 'lead sled', 'elephant' and one or two others, seemed to him equally unjustified for such a sound, effective machine.

Before long, after completion of his external checks, Dick was helped by a member of the ground crew to strap in. Having carefully checked the seat straps and verified removal of the ejection seat safety pins, the ground crewman gave a thumbs up sign before he climbed down the cockpit access steps. Dick now spoke briefly to his back-seater: "Everything okay?" "Sure. I've got the air test forms. Let's go!"

Soon, with both engines started and with clearance from air traffic control, Dick taxied the F-4E towards the runway entry point where he was given permission to move directly onto the runway for take-off. When in position, he applied the aircraft brakes before he began to read out cockpit instrument readings for his back-seater to record. With the necessary figures noted, he had a last glance around his cockpit. All seemed satisfactory. Now, with cockpit indications still normal, he released the Phantom's brakes, eased the twin throttles forward and concentrated in front as the aircraft accelerated during take-off.

When airborne, Dick followed local air traffic procedures as he flew the Phantom in a westerly direction towards the Gulf of Mexico. To the north, curved around Tampa Bay, he had a fine view of the city of Tampa, so named, he'd been told, after a native American tribe's word for 'sticks of fire' – a reference to the area's large number of lightning strikes. Behind him he could make out the flat expanse of Florida; with much of the state at or near sea level and with a high point of just 345 feet, this was the lowest peak of any US state. Apart from the severe weather periods, Florida offered generally hazard-free conditions for flyers, including the state's large number of private operators. In the distance he glimpsed the sprawling city of Orlando, known as the theme park capital of the world, with, beyond that, the area containing the John F. Kennedy Space Center adjacent to Cape Canaveral Air Force Station. In the good visibility of that day he could identify the famous site which, he'd been told, was visited twice by President Kennedy himself in 1962 – the year when construction started – and again the following year just a week before the tragedy of the president's assassination. Dick was aware that in a recent test project, coincident with the last Apollo mission, an American Apollo and a Soviet Soyuz had docked in orbit, the first such link-up between spacecraft from the two nations.

As Dick flew the F-4E to high altitude, he continued to call out instrument readings for his back-seater to record. Eventually, the back-seater said: "When you're ready, we can carry out the supersonic run – we're well clear of land."

"Okay," said Dick, "engaging afterburner." He eased the Phantom's twin throttles forward and checked the engine instruments as the aircraft accelerated from subsonic, through transonic to supersonic airspeed. At high altitude in a cloudless sky there were no outside reference points but the machmeter displayed the aircraft's increasing airspeed: *Mach 1.1...Mach 1.2...Mach 1.3...* Dick monitored the fuel gauges carefully for the afterburner system, by injecting additional fuel into the engines' jet pipes downstream of the turbine, had begun to consume the Phantom's reserves at an alarming rate. *Mach 1.4...Mach 1.5...Mach 1.6...* at this, Dick reached his highest airspeed to date in a Phantom, but with full afterburner still selected the machmeter continued towards Mach 2.0, the manufacturer's published maximum limit. And it was not long before Dick said to his back-seater: "Standby for readings...just reaching Mach 2.0..." when suddenly, with the F-4E now pointing away from Tampa at a distance of over 100 miles, the left-hand fire warning light illuminated. At once, he carried out the necessary drills before he transmitted a Mayday call on the aircraft radio.

"Steer zero eight zero for MacDill," said the emergency controller. Dick acknowledged the order, turned as instructed and with the twin throttles eased back he monitored the altimeter as the F-4E began a slow descent. Before long, however, the fire warning light began to fade, then extinguish. He informed the controller, but in view of the considerable distance to MacDill and with low fuel reserves following the supersonic run, Dick decided not to downgrade the emergency status.

When, at length, the outline of MacDill Field came into view, Dick asked for a straight-in approach and landing, which was duly approved. As he landed and brought the aircraft to a halt, a number of large (very large) fire wagons drove up to surround the F-4E. Fortunately, the fire trucks were not needed and when Dick and his back-seater had evacuated their cockpits, the two men were driven to the engineering line office. As they entered, Dick walked up to the USAF chief master sergeant to debrief him. "Welcome back, sir!" said the American, who, thought Dick, seemed rather relaxed. Despite this, Dick went over the incident in detail after which the chief master sergeant said in a low voice: "Happens every time, sir. Goddam fire warning always comes on just then. Goes out eventually, though." He grinned. "So what's not to like?"

Dick stared at him. He thought: happens every time? Every time? But of course...*of course!* And what, indeed, was not to like? He'd try to remember that for next time.

*   *   *

Not long after this experience, by which point Dick was a qualified instructor with the USAF 4501st Tactical Fighter Squadron (part of the 56th Tactical Fighter Wing whose duties included the training of Phantom pilots and weapons systems officers), he was programmed one day for a combat training flight with his student. The flight would involve a well-briefed exercise with one of the USAF aggressor squadrons, units designed to teach students the difficult art of air combat between dissimilar aircraft types. As the use of actual enemy aircraft and equipment was impractical, surrogate aircraft were disguised to emulate potential adversaries.

As part of his introductory briefings, Dick had learnt that the first formal use of the aggressor squadron system had been instigated seven years previously, in 1968, by the US Navy Fighter Weapons School, informally known as 'Top Gun'. This unit, he'd been briefed, had used Douglas A-4 Skyhawk aircraft simulating the performance of the Mikoyan-Gurevich MiG-17 (NATO code-name 'Fresco'), both of which aircraft had performed key roles in the Vietnam War. The USAF had followed suit with their first aggressor squadron at Nellis Air Force Base, Nevada, equipped with the Northrop T-38 Talon – the same aircraft which, after the OPEC oil embargo of two years previously, had been adopted by the USAF Thunderbirds aerobatic team in place of fuel-hungry Phantoms.

For that day's exercise, Dick and his student would be pitted against the pilot of a Northrop F-5 Freedom Fighter. This single-seat, twin-engine aircraft was renowned as a rugged, high performance machine which had won the International Fighter Aircraft competition five years ago, in 1970. For the planned mission, the aggressor squadron F-5, painted to resemble a Soviet MiG-21, NATO code-name 'Fishbed' (a single-seat, single-engine fighter of approximately the same dimensions as the F-5), would take off in company with Dick and his student's F-4E. After take-off, the two aircraft would fly in a loose formation to the stipulated exercise area.

Following a comprehensive brief, the three pilots walked together to check the technical logs before manning their aircraft. While his student carried out external checks, Dick strapped into the F-4E's rear cockpit. He knew that his restricted view from that cockpit would create difficulties, but he had been trained to cope with this.

Presently, after engine start and air traffic control clearance, Dick's student taxied the F-4E in company with the F-5 for take-off. Maintaining the briefed loose formation and with the F-5 in the lead, the two aircraft set off down the runway. When safely airborne, they turned due west to head for the designated air combat training area over the sea. Dick knew that his student would make this an interesting flight, the more so, perhaps, as the sortie would be a visual one without the benefit of guidance from an airborne radar operator. And the student would be rigorous in his approach: why do it this way? Why not try that way? His enquiring mind would not like to be fobbed off. With broad principles laid down in manuals, the student knew that, more than manuals, training and experience were the keys to success. Luck, to an extent, played a part but many of the air combat aces of the past had become experts in tactical detail – a certain emphasis here, a minor procedural change there, the fine judgement required when executing a particular manoeuvre.

Then there were local aspects to consider. The bright Florida sun could be helpful in some respects, but if an opponent was positioned directly into the sun – the classic 'Hun in the sun' of World War Two – detection could be difficult. With the high closing velocity, Dick would begin to worry if time seemed to be running out. He'd screw up his eyes, staring towards the sun. If there was still no contact, he'd wonder if the F-5 was already about to manoeuvre into the Phantom's 'six o'clock' position. If so, at any second he could expect a call of 'Fox 2' with a theoretical missile heading his way. In a real situation, if within cannon-firing range there'd be sudden signs of tracer as dozens of bright points streamed like red droplets towards the Phantom. At this, the Phantom pilot would over-bank until the aircraft was virtually inverted, then pull positive G to the maximum limit as he struggled to escape.

In briefings, Dick had emphasised the importance of learning about an opponent's capabilities, his aircraft types, radar and missile systems, methods of operating. 'Know thy enemy', the famed, centuries-old mantra from the Chinese military strategist Sun Tzu's book *The Art of War,* was as true today as ever. Together with his student, Dick had studied comparisons between the F-4 and the MiG-21. Common adversaries in the Vietnam War, Dick had highlighted significant differences – the F-4, for example, weighed some twenty tons, almost twice that of the MiG-21 which, consequently, was agile in turns and its silhouette was difficult to acquire at any great distance. The MiG-21 was typically armed with missiles such as the AA-2 Atoll, a short-range infrared homing missile similar to the F-4's AIM-9 Sidewinder, but the F-4, on the other hand, could be armed with up to eight missiles – four times the number fitted to the MiG-21.

By now about to enter the air combat training area, Dick said to his student: "Ready for the fray?" "Sure." Both men double-checked their anti-G suit connections, ensured there were no loose articles in the cockpits, adjusted their seat harnesses. Dick continued to monitor the aggressor squadron F-5, still in position on his starboard side at a range of some 100 yards line abreast. "Standby…" the F-5 pilot called on the aircraft radio, "… outward turn for combat…GO!" At this, the pilots of both machines applied bank to turn away from each other. Dick pressed his stopwatch. He aimed to calculate separation of approximately twenty miles when he'd expect the F-5 pilot's call: "inwards turn!" From that moment, the battle could commence.

In reality, however, this did not happen. The first sign of trouble was when Dick, at the same time as his peripheral vision glimpsed another aircraft, grabbed the Phantom's stick and hauled it back. "What the…" but there was no time for explanation: the F-5 shot past just a few feet away. Instinctively, Dick ducked down within his cockpit. His student continued to take evasive action then, as he eased the control stick forward again, he muttered some inaudible comment. For some moments, a stunned silence dominated the Phantom's cockpits. Meantime, a glance at the G meter revealed the worst: the aircraft, over-stressed by the violent evasive manoeuvre, was now unserviceable. "We'll have to head back for base," said Dick flatly.

It did not take long for the student to fly to MacDill where, after landing, he taxied to the 4501st parking area. Still baffled by what had happened, the two men spoke with engineers who confirmed that the aircraft would be taken out of action for investigation. Dick and his student then went to the debriefing room to meet up with the F-5 pilot who, as soon as he saw them, looked abashed. "Sorry, about that guys," he said, "it was all my fault."

"What went wrong?" said Dick after a pause.

"Remember we briefed that I should turn starboard at my 'outward turn' call? Well, I didn't," said the aggressor squadron man. "I turned port instead."

With sudden understanding, Dick and his student glanced at each other and shrugged.

A philosophical, *c'est la vie* reaction seemed appropriate, they reckoned, and there was little more to be said on the matter.

*   *   *

It was almost a dozen years later when Dick recalled this episode for, while not exactly a case of history repeating itself, he would still see a curious connection between the incident at MacDill and an experience during one of his last flights in a Phantom. For some time he'd been worried about this flight; final flights were notorious for tempting fate.

In October 1986, by which time he'd served for two years as the commanding officer of 74 Squadron, he was due to hand over to a new CO. When, in 1984, Dick had taken command, the squadron had just reformed as a Phantom unit at RAF Wattisham. Before that, it had been equipped with the English Electric Lightning and based in the Far East until disbandment in August 1971.

Phantoms earmarked for the re-equipment programme were ex-US Navy/Marine F-4J versions, designated in RAF service as the F-4J (UK). The prospect of a so-called super Phantom, a joint venture initiated between the US companies Boeing and Pratt & Whitney, had raised interest but plans were cancelled early in development. The F-4Js bought by the RAF were intended as a stopgap to replace the 23 Squadron Phantoms sent to the Falkland Islands after the war there. The aircraft, in a fetching shade of light grey, were ferried from the USA to Wattisham in groups accompanied by VC10 in-flight refuelling tankers and Dick's job had been to build up a new unit from scratch. This, he'd felt, had seemed appropriate for a squadron with a history of introducing new aircraft into service, such as the Lightning, and a unit renowned for the development of tactics such as those of the 74 Squadron fighter ace Sailor Malan who, in World War Two, had devised a set of straightforward rules for new fighter pilots – 'Ten of my rules for air fighting'.

A few days before handing over as CO, Dick was programmed for a sortie of supersonic practice interceptions. Together with another Phantom, the crews of the two aircraft would alternate as fighter and target. After a detailed sortie briefing, and as the four aircrew walked out to their waiting Phantoms, Dick was conscious that this could be one of his last flights in a Phantom – although not, he reckoned, the contentious 'final flight' itself. While he walked, a breeze blew from the Suffolk countryside across the airfield. Autumn colours were vivid and in the distance a flock of wild geese, in the shape of a 'V', flapped noisily due north. His time at Wattisham, Dick reflected, had been challenging, nonetheless he'd be sorry to leave the place. Two years ago he had few illusions about the hurdles involved with reforming a squadron from scratch and these had, indeed, turned out to be many and various. With good humour and flexibility, however, most of the problems had been resolved and for his efforts he had been hon-

Group shot of 74 Squadron RAF Wattisham. Dick Northcote in the middle of the front row.

oured with the award of an OBE (Order of the British Empire).

Before long, with the two Phantoms manned and ready to proceed, Dick called air traffic control for clearance to lead them for take-off and climb out. Proceedings went routinely and soon, when airborne, the aircraft crossed the Suffolk coast to head for airspace above the North Sea. When directed by the fighter controller, the target flew a stipulated heading while the fighter set up for the interception. As airspeeds of around Mach 1.5 were reached, high fuel consumption meant that just a few such runs could be practised before a return to Wattisham. On the last run, for which Dick and his navigator acted as the fighter, the interception went as planned until, suddenly, the crews sensed that something was wrong. They couldn't pinpoint the exact problem, nevertheless a vertigo of confusion, a tingling of the nerves induced, maybe, by some strange sixth sense, suggested danger.

"We'll abort this run," Dick said to his navigator. With a closing speed in excess of Mach 2.0, there was no room for doubt. But now, just as he was about to press the radio transmit button, his peripheral vision picked up a flash from another aircraft. Then, abruptly, a Phantom shot past his aircraft. The two aircraft passed head-on separated by a matter of feet. He glimpsed two heads in the cockpit. He heard someone utter a brief profanity on the aircraft radio before...silence. For a good thirty seconds an eerie hush dominated the airwaves. When, eventually, this was broken it was by Dick himself who called off the sortie and ordered his number two to rejoin in formation for a return to Wattisham.

After landing, and with all four crew members feeling more than a little chastened, a sortie debrief tried to establish what had gone wrong. There was a suggestion that another Phantom had somehow become mixed-up with the interception, but this was not proved. Eventually, unable to determine the cause of the problem, with reluctance they accepted that the mystery would persist. But the unsatisfactory conclusion haunted Dick for years. He had no doubt in his mind that luck alone had prevented a head-on collision. When looking back, he had no doubt, either, that in some twenty-five years of flying the incident was the closest he'd come to an untimely meeting with his creator. For his own peace of mind he was anxious to resolve the puzzle. On the other hand, he realised that sometimes, in certain situations, perhaps it was better not to know.

CHAPTER 12

PROXY PILOT

ALAN WINKLES STRUGGLES WITH NATURE

If aircrew medical check-ups are an accepted necessity, sometimes situations could arise to remind us that even the toughest of tests may prove inadequate. Take, for example, the matter of eyesight checks. These are of particular significance for unless an individual can meet rigorous minimum standards he will not be allowed to fly. It was somehow ironic, therefore, that one time when Flight Lieutenant Alan Winkles, a Phantom pilot on 17 Squadron, was forced to fly as if with his eyes closed, and when all the careful optician's testing parameters – 'read the letters on the bottom line'…'cover one eye and read the letters backwards'…'which is brighter, the left circle or the right?'…when all of that obligatory, if tiresome, procedure, not to mention the amazing, expensive and sophisticated optical testing equipment designed to check this and that, proved to be a complete waste of time, the reason would have to be a good one indeed.

It was one night in June 1971 when Alan and his navigator, Flight Lieutenant Bob Woodward, were briefed to carry out a night-time mission in a Phantom FGR2 based at RAF Brüggen in Germany. Brüggen at that time was a major base for Phantoms, including 17 Squadron which had reformed in the autumn of 1970. The multi-role capability of the Phantom included the capacity to carry nuclear weapons with all the attendant risks, a point emphasised, incidentally, over a dozen years in the future, in the spring of 1984, when a nuclear device stored at Brüggen turned out to be poorly secured when moved in a special truck. Gasps of horror ensued when the device, eight times more powerful than the bomb dropped on Hiroshima in 1945, fell to the ground. In frantic, heart-stopping scenes tests were carried out but these eventually showed that the device remained sound – a testament to the inherent strength of nuclear weapons' casings.

Other roles practised by the 17 Squadron Phantoms included attack with conventional weapons, also air defence using AIM-7 Sparrow missiles, AIM-9 Sidewinder missiles and 20-mm Gatling guns. Alan and his fellow aircrew were required to maintain proficiency in these various roles and for the night flight in question he and his navigator were briefed to carry out a radar navigation and bombing mission. As this was Bob's first flight for over a month following eye injuries caused by a bird strike, the flight would be an opportunity for him to settle back into the routine of flying. To achieve a realistic training environment they had to wait for the summer sun to set fully.

While they waited, and as the hours ticked by, conversation covered a number of issues including a recent accident involving a United States Marine Corps Phantom. It was just a few days ago when this Phantom, flying at around 15,000 feet near the city of Duarte in the northern fringes of Los Angeles, was heading for the marine corps base at El Toro. The time was around six pm and as he wanted to check for any other air traffic in the vicinity, the Phantom pilot performed an aileron roll through 360 degrees. Meanwhile, his radar operator in the F-4's back cockpit was looking down at his radar which had been giving problems. However, when, by chance, the radar operator glanced up, his peripheral vision spotted an aircraft. He shouted a warning to his pilot who attempted an evasive roll but it was too late, the aircraft collided with an airliner and both machines plunged down to the mountains below. Shocked witnesses reported that they'd heard a loud noise and seen two burning objects fall from the sky. Out of a total of fifty-two souls, including fifty passengers and crew on board the airliner, a Hughes Airwest Douglas DC-9, the only survivor was the F-4's radar operator who managed to eject.

This tragedy was of particular significance to Alan and his colleagues because it was fairly common procedure for the 17 Squadron Phantoms, always anxious to make the most of training opportunities, to intercept passing airliners. Such intercepts were under the control of a ground radar unit and thus were well regulated and legal. Furthermore, as the airline passengers and crew were unaware of what was happening behind them, and with the pressing need for Phantom crews to hone their air defence skills, the intercepts provided a pragmatic solution to the problem of limited training resources. "Look upon it as a necessary evil," said Alan.

"Hardly," laughed his navigator.

"But come the day…"

"The day?"

"When the Soviets decide to invade…"

"True – we'll need all the practice we can get."

"Which brings us back to the question we talked about recently. Do we concentrate on being bombers or fighters?"

"We're Jack of all trades, I suppose."

"And you know what they say about poor old Jack."

This point, Alan reflected, continued to be one of contention for, despite the ongoing fuel crisis at the time with consequent flying restrictions, operational demands were still high, the required roles remained diverse, the technology was relatively basic. The Phantom fleet was not equipped with the terrain-following radar planned for the Panavia Tornado, and night-time strike missions could prove especially challenging. With forward-looking radar selected to 'mapping mode', a skilled navigator, by twiddling knobs that controlled gain, contrast and scanner angle, could achieve a readable picture of the terrain ahead but hardly with the level of accuracy needed for delivery of modern weapons with great destructive power. As for navigational information, the F-4's Ferranti elec-tro-mechanical inertial system could, with luck, determine the aircraft's position within a mile or two, but again this was not the pinpoint precision necessary for the delivery of contemporary weapons. With such equipment limitations, it was not safe or practical for Alan and his colleagues to fly night missions at ground-hugging, enemy radar-avoiding heights. Instead, these missions were generally flown at several hundred feet above ground level, but even this was far from hazard free. Alan and Bob were about to find this out. They would discover, too, that the Phantom fleet's widely-used and encouraged term 'good crew co-operation' would assume a whole new significance.

Fortunately, by prudent navigational planning of routes over the plains of northern Germany, crews could bypass hilly areas. On the evening in question, as the time drew near for the flight Alan decided to walk to the squadron operations set-up to check the latest meteorological information. He studied various charts and long-winded meteor-ological sheets the 'ifs' and 'buts' of which seemed to reflect the universal vagaries of weather forecasting. "You should be generally okay," said the duty operations officer, "the weather man reckons there'll be some heavy showers in the area with associated cumulonimbus, otherwise the weather looks good." Alan and Bob now went to collect their life jackets, bone dome headsets, flying gloves, maps and other paraphernalia needed before the two men walked out to their Phantom.

Soon, with the flight authorisation sheet signed and the aircraft technical log checked, they went through the start-up procedures before Alan requested taxi clearance from the air traffic controller. "Standby one," said the controller, and for a brief moment while he waited Alan glanced at the slither of moon which had risen high but which cast little light across the German countryside. Behind the Phantom lay the airfield boundary fence and beyond that, not too far away, was the German-Dutch border. In between, he could almost make out the shapes of pine trees that stood out in contrast to the area's flat farmland. "You're clear to taxi, now..." said the controller who went on to confirm the runway in use and the wind direction and speed.

While he taxied at a moderate pace, Alan could identify the line of the runway ahead flanked by twin rows of bright lights. Inside his cockpit he was grateful to feel the warmth of the aircraft heating system for the night air was cold. The weather man was right, he reckoned, it looks like a clear night and these showers, he thought, had brought out the odour of the ground for even through the cockpit air-conditioning system he could smell the tang of fresh rain.

"There's no other air traffic," the controller interjected. "You're cleared to line up and take off." He sounded impatient, reckoned Alan, as if anxious for the Phantom to leave.

With the pre-take-off checks completed, Alan moved judiciously along the last stretch of taxiway, turned onto the runway and used the white centreline to guide him as he lined up the Phantom. He advanced both throttles to around eighty per cent power.

After a last check of the instruments, he released the aircraft brakes and felt the potent Rolls-Royce Speys accelerate the aircraft as he pushed the throttles forward. With the engines' reheats engaged, observers on the ground saw the night sky lit up by an elongated flame emerging from the jet pipes as the Phantom was propelled ever faster down the runway.

Airborne within moments, Alan levelled the aircraft at a height of 1,000 feet and turned onto the first leg of the navigational route. With the Phantom soon at an airspeed of 420 knots, he concentrated on visual 'lookout' while Bob used a combination of information from the Westinghouse AN/AWG radar and the Ferranti inertial system to keep the aircraft on track. At intervals, however, Bob had to demand a heading change to steer away from storm cells revealed on his radar. As a safety measure, Alan adjusted the 'bug' on his radio altimeter so that a red warning light would shine if the aircraft descended below 900 feet.

The navigational route that night was planned to take just less than an hour. As he flew along, Alan observed how the vault of the night sky, studded with stars, made a spectacular backdrop above. Below, however, most of the notable features of north Germany were concealed within the veil of night. Dark stretches of pine forests blended into the pale expanse of agricultural land, though in places the glitter of lights from towns and villages stood out conspicuously. Conspicuous, too, was the sight of moving car headlights that pierced the inky surrounds.

For the final stages the route passed above sparsely populated areas. When, eventually, the Phantom approached the Nordhorn bombing range close to the German-Dutch border, Alan prepared to accelerate to 500 knots and descend to 600 feet for the bombing run. He noted that the range area appeared unusually dark. At a distance of ten miles from weapon release, he and his navigator were required to carry out a formal 'command and response' check. This part of the flight held particular challenges. When flying at 500 knots, Alan found that the Phantom's flight controls were especially sensitive. Concentrating 'head down' in the cockpit, he had to follow exact instructions from Bob. Meantime, Bob had his own difficulties as he worked to identify faint target markers on his radar screen. These would show up provided that the Phantom was precisely on track.

For that night's 'toss' attack, Alan had to follow punctilious procedures. When instructed by Bob, he pulled back the stick while carefully monitoring the Phantom's G meter. He needed to pull exactly 4.5 G. The manoeuvre was slick, nonetheless a rapid increase in height was inevitable. On Bob's command 'pickle', Alan pressed the pickle button on his stick. As soon as the weapon was released, he rolled the Phantom inverted, pulled to the horizon, then rolled upright again to escape any point defences near the target.

Now, as he took up a heading for Brüggen, Alan eased the Phantom to the right. Meanwhile, to search for hazards ahead Bob raised his scanner upwards – then immediately ordered a hard turn through forty degrees: "There's a storm cell showing on radar," he yelled, "...a big bugger – and it's within a couple of miles." At once, Alan increased the angle of bank to veer away but drops of heavy rain began to strike the Phantom's windshield. A sudden flash of lightning revealed an adjacent tower of cumulonimbus which was far from still. Near the base of it, lighter streaks of layered cloudbanks were hustled along as if under the orders of a meteorological policeman. In the surrounding pandemonium, mounting levels of turbulence hinted at the trouble about to strike. Alan tried to peer in front but he saw only rain driven against his windshield in horizontal sheets, like marauding waves of black liquid. A shiver of angst went through him. The Phantom, now close to the base of the cumulonimbus, started to leap violently upwards, downwards, sideways in the soaring levels of turbulence. Alan and Bob both tugged at their seat straps to secure themselves as firmly as possible to their Martin-Baker ejection seats. Adding to a general cacophony of sound, the racket of rain persisted to hammer against the Phantom's windshield. Occasional crackles from lightning clashed with booms of thunder which reverberated as if from a great bass drum.

The reducing visibility now forced Alan to fly by reference to his flight instruments. In other circumstances, he pondered, nature's paradoxical blend of violence and splendour could offer a thrilling spectacle, but at that moment it was more like a hostile and confining barrier. He felt an odd sense of loneliness, a feeling which could grip the mind and lead to misjudgement. If he glanced up to try to force his eyes to see what lay between the cloud layers there was nothing, just blackness apart from disconcerting reflections from the Phantom's navigation lights. One time, a shape seemed to loom out of the shadows. He returned his gaze to the flight instruments but an inner alarm seemed to be prompted by an arcane sixth sense. He looked up again and it was then, at that chance moment of distraction, that something happened. He was aware of an explosive *craaaack* and a brilliant flash as the lightning struck.

Alan knew at once that his vision was affected. As though he'd stared directly into the sun before entering a darkened room, the pupils in his eyes were overwhelmed. Instinctively he pulled back the stick and advanced the Phantom's throttles to climb to a safe height. "Bob – I can't see the flight instruments," he cried, "the lightning dazzle has blinded my eyes."

Bob immediately checked the rudimentary instruments in the rear cockpit. In a deliberately calm voice he began a running commentary to guide his pilot: "the right wing is low," he said, focusing on his small attitude indicator, "ease left a bit...push the stick forward to check the climb..." as if flying by proxy, Bob helped Alan in the struggle to retain control of the Phantom... "don't over-correct the bank...ease the stick to the right again...and watch that pitch angle!...it's increased to ten degrees nose-up...push the stick forward..." In small, cautious control movements Alan continued to react to his navigator's commentary.

Alan's peripheral vision was the first part of his eyesight to recover. When it did so, he glanced around the cockpit – and saw warning lights on the emergencies panel: "We've had a genny failure with bus-tie open," he cried to Bob. With a failed generator and the electrical 'bus' (distribution bar) open, the Phantom had lost a number of electrical services.

"My radar picture's gone blank," said Alan.

"So's mine," said Bob, "that lightning strike must have blown up the radar system."

"I'll try recycling the generator." Alan used his right hand to reach for the generator switch which he selected on and off several times. At length this worked and with some electrical services restored, including one of the aircraft radios, he was able to contact the emergency controller. The controller at once gave a heading to steer for Brüggen which Alan followed as he said to Bob: "I think a slow speed recovery will be a prudent move." He'd discover soon enough that this, indeed, would prove to be more than a little prudent.

Meantime, the emergency services at Brüggen were alerted and Alan flew back to base at a reduced airspeed of 280 knots. As he approached the airfield he was warned of low lying mist in the area. When the runway loomed, he worried about the possibility of latent impairment to his eyes; it occurred to him that if his navigator was expected to control a landing by proxy this, for sure, would be quite a big 'ask'. Shortly before touchdown, Alan tried not to stare at the bright runway lights on either side which, ringed with haze, began to flash past in pairs. He concentrated instead on the 'big picture' in front while he carried out the landing for which his years of experience as a pilot paid dividends when he touched down safely and brought the Phantom to a controlled stop.

Cleared by air traffic control to taxi to the 17 Squadron dispersal area, Alan and Bob were anxious to inspect their aircraft for damage. After shut-down, they climbed impatiently out of their cockpits only to be surprised, even a bit frustrated, that a perfunctory check of the airframe showed no obvious signs of damage. From the outside there was little evidence of a lightning strike, although careful examination revealed two pin-prick-sized holes with sooty surrounds which marked the entry and exit points of the lightning. However, when engineers swung open the Phantom's nose radome, that rugged device designed to protect the Westinghouse radar antenna, a different story was revealed. The inner layer of composite material had unravelled like a cardboard coil thereby reducing the normally robust radome material to wafer-thin strength. Alan shuddered. The engineers looked stunned. All shook their heads and muttered expletives. If the radome had detached in flight, debris would have entered the engine air intakes before being drawn into the engines themselves, a scenario that had led to the loss of an English Electric Lightning aircraft some four years earlier in January 1967.

Later, when Alan and Bob discussed the incident, anxiety seemed to have drained the colour from their faces. Both were keenly conscious that a flight back to base at normal airspeeds could have resulted in a so-called 'Martin-Baker let-down' – use of their Martin-Baker ejection seats. Modern technology would have managed to reduce their aircraft from a pedigree racer to a great pile of smoking wreckage. Lightning, according to some, doesn't strike twice. Maybe, maybe not, mused Alan, but in this case once was more than enough.

CHAPTER 13
MIXED MESSAGES
JOHN MEGARRY AND THE NEED TO WATCH ONE'S BACK

In the crush, a hand plucked at his sleeve: "John...you're wanted over here..." The debriefing room was crowded with people, more so than normal, but then, thought Flight Lieutenant John Megarry, the situation they faced was far from normal. In an atmosphere of high excitement, earnest conversations took place within various groups. "Hogwash!" someone muttered. "Now, now," came the riposte, "calm down. We'll get to the bottom of it." The room, flavoured with the dusty odour of cigarette smoke, had a disorderly ambience which John found faintly obnoxious. Retrospective judgements were all very well, he reckoned, but it was he and his navigator as well as the other two crews who'd had to deal with the potential disaster at the time. He was certain of one thing: since joining the Phantom force three years ago in 1980 he'd not seen anything like this before. It was not as if there'd been any form of warning; the event itself and the subsequent heated discussions could not have been predicted even in his wildest dreams. Neither could he have anticipated any of this when he was selected for the qualified weapons' instructor (QWI) course, a course which he'd started quite recently. The course was known to be complex and onerous although not quite in the way, John ruminated, that he'd just experienced.

It had begun with the need for a test firing of a Skyflash air-to-air missile. The Skyflash, manufactured by the British Aerospace Company, was a medium-range, semi-active radar homing missile derived from the United States' AIM-7 Sparrow. Brought into service on some marks of Phantom from the late 1970s, the Skyflash, unlike some earlier generations of air-to-air missile, could function successfully in hostile electronic-countermeasure environments. The missile was nothing if not flexible: it could be launched from as low as 300 feet against a high altitude target, or from high altitude against a target as low as 200 feet. Such flexibility was revolutionary, perhaps a little too revolutionary as John would discover.

115

Skyflash air-to-air missile testing.

With his QWI course well underway, John and his navigator were tasked one day to carry out a Skyflash test firing with a difference. This firing, for which their Phantom would operate from the Strike Command Air-to-Air Missile Establishment at RAF Valley in Anglesey, was designed to test the missile's backup, manually-sighted mode. The target, an unmanned Jindivik Mark 2 drone towing a radar reflector, was powered by an Armstrong Siddeley Viper turbojet engine similar to the type used in the British Aircraft Company's Jet Provost training aircraft. The Jindivik could achieve airspeeds of nearly 500 knots and offered, therefore, a suitably challenging target for the likes of Phantoms. A not-altogether uncommon problem was for the missile to ignore the towed reflector and to shoot down the expensive Jindivik instead. For John's experimental test firing that day, the Skyflash warhead had been removed and replaced with a telemetry package to allow sundry scientists to see how well the missile guidance system performed in its backup mode.

Before the flight itself, John had received detailed briefings. He was, in any case, used to these for there'd been much to learn on the QWI course. Sometimes he would stay up long into the night to study notes, bone up on technical manuals, and absorb details on operating procedures. If fatigue caused the light to swim before his eyes, he'd remind himself that standards were high and that there'd be no shortcuts if he wanted to pass the course. Perhaps, therefore, his head was brimming with new-found knowledge that day when, together with his navigator, he walked out to his Skyflash-armed Phantom. Unusually, they were accompanied by two other Phantom crews; arrangements had been made to deploy two aircraft as photo-chase machines tasked to record the day's special firing. Thus, with six members of aircrew, there were plenty of well-qualified observers even though not one of them realised the peril about to be faced.

As John performed the routine of a pre-flight walk-around to check his Phantom, he was aware of British Aerospace Hawk training aircraft in the airfield circuit. These aircraft had first arrived at Valley in 1976, the year that he had joined the Royal Air Force, and it was here that he had been a student on the Hawk as part of his advanced training.

Before long, with start-up procedures completed and with all three Phantoms ready to proceed, the local air traffic controller ordered the Hawks in the circuit to hold clear while the revered Phantoms lined up and took off. Procedures were slick, however, and the three Phantoms soon roared down the runway before assuming a loose 'vic' formation after take-off as they headed east towards the Menai Straits.

When instructed, the three Phantoms changed radio frequency to speak with the radar controller at RAF Aberporth, a military base north of Fishguard. This controller now gave instructions to John as he manoeuvred to intercept the Jindivik which had taken off from Llanbedr, a Royal Air Force station north of Aberystwyth on the coast of Cardigan Bay. "Maintain your altitude and turn onto a heading of one seven five degrees," said the controller in his lilting Welsh accent. On John's right side, the Llyn Peninsular, which formed the northern boundary of Cardigan Bay, stood out clearly. Inland, he could spot various lakes including Lake Bala which, at four miles long, was a distinctive navigational feature for aircraft. "The target's at low level crossing left to right," said the controller, "maintain your present heading."

John glanced around his cockpit...engine instruments...fuel...oxygen...weapons switches... his experienced eye took no more than a second or so to check the indications. The controller's calm voice continued the countdown: "Target still on your left, currently approaching ten miles range."

"Okay, you can call Judy," said John's navigator. This call, which John now made to the ground radar controller, indicated that his navigator would assume control of the intercept. "Turn right ten onto one eight five degrees," said the navigator after a pause. John searched visually but the small Jindivik was hard to make out, especially at low level.

"Target's now at seven miles on your left side, standby for starboard turn," said the navigator.

John swiftly verified that the other two Phantoms were in position. Then he applied a high angle of bank at his navigator's next call: "Target's range is five miles, turn hard right onto two eight zero degrees." As he turned, John noticed the roughened surface of the slate-grey sea below then, suddenly, his peripheral vision picked up movement above the sea's surface. "I have visual contact with the Jindivik!" he cried to his navigator.

"Okay. Check manual mode selected."

"Manual mode confirmed. Missile live."

"Standby to fire!" yelled the navigator. Heart thumping, John had a final check of cockpit switches. The navigator's next call soon came: "We're in range...when ready...*fire!*"

John's finger clasped the firing trigger. Maybe some last second thoughts flashed through his mind...*this has to be right....I've double-checked the switchery...the photo-shoot aircraft are in position...there are no surface vessels visible...*

As John squeezed the firing trigger he was aware of a slight thump as the Skyflash left its housing. Then he saw a streak of flame followed by a line of smoke as the missile accelerated away from the Phantom. Adjacent to the missile's path, the air seemed to shake visibly, like the mirage above hot desert terrain. Observing the smoke trail, he found it relatively easy to see that the Skyflash was guiding correctly for he could identify a series of small flight path corrections. If a radar-guided missile such as the Skyflash malfunctioned it was likely to dive towards Mother Earth. That day, however, the missile tracking looked good and John could discern a very close miss with the Jindivik which, in a real situation, would have been destroyed as the warhead detonated.

Satisfied that the test firing had been a success, John initiated a gentle climb with the other two Phantoms still in loose formation. Perhaps lulled into a state of complacency by the smooth progress of planned events, he looked forward to a routine recovery to Valley before a gratifying debrief where admiring boffins would be anxious to express their high esteem for the skill and dedication displayed by the Phantom aircrews. It must have felt all the more shocking, therefore, when, suddenly, John realised that something was amiss. The ground radar controller's voice sounded unusually high-pitched and panicky when he exclaimed on the aircraft radio: "It's coming back!" For a moment or two, this peculiar, non-standard call caused a stunned silence to dominate the airwaves. A large thought bubble might have appeared above the cockpits of John and his navigator. A swift, tense conversation ensued:

"Coming back? What's coming back?"

"He must mean the Jindivik."

"But the Jindivik hasn't turned."

"Maybe it's about to…"

John now pressed his radio transmit button to speak with the controller: "Aberporth, repeat your last call, please." The controller, his voice now even more high-pitched and progressively more panic-stricken, cried: "It's coming back...the missile's coming back!"

John's mind went into overdrive. If random thoughts fled through his head these were brief for he understood only too well the need to focus urgently on immediate issues. With insufficient time to regain sight of the missile, he figured that the best chance lay in the 'big sky' theory: with plenty of open space above, the three Phantoms would present a relatively small object in the sky. Then John remembered something else: his aircraft's continuous waveform (CW) transmitter was sending out a non-stop missile illumination signal – an ideal homing aid for the Skyflash. With adrenalin charging through his system, at once he reached for the CW transmitter switch, flicked it off and simultaneously applied a high angle of bank in an attempt to throw off the missile and to escape the likely impact area. Even without a warhead the Skyflash made a potent weapon as its twelve-feet-long body, 425-pound weight was hurtled through the sky at airspeeds up to Mach 4.0 by the solid propellant Rocketdyne motor.

Now, as the other two Phantoms followed, the crews' anti-G suits inflated to maximum while the aircraft were hauled round in a series of aggressive turns and climbs. In the helter-skelter of movement, the navigators, thrown around in the back cockpits, had to rely on the pilots' commentaries to warn them of the next violent manoeuvre. In an instinctive, if futile, reaction, John tried to duck down inside his cockpit. With his mind still filled with many thoughts, he may have experienced heightened awareness of surrounding detail...marks on the Phantom's windshield...scattered clouds that chased each other in a whirl of different shades...*light then dark then light then dark*...the sea below that appeared blurred and hostile, the aircraft radio that seemed to produce an unfamiliar hissing sound as if disturbed by a nest of angry snakes...

Suddenly, as if jerking him back to reality, John was aware of the controller's voice: "*Skyflash down*...the missile's hit the sea..."

"Confirm missile down?" said John.

"Affirmative. You're clear to return to base."

And with that, as if at the flick of another cockpit switch, the crews' ordeal was over. The sense of relief was great. Further explanations just at that moment seemed superfluous so John, his tone subdued, merely acknowledged the information as he turned towards Valley and initiated a descent to lead the others back for a much-anticipated debrief.

Within the small debriefing room, now crowded with specialists who were shocked and bemused by what had occurred, intense conversations persisted until the commanding officer stood up to speak. He explained that investigations were ongoing, however initial information suggested that the Skyflash had performed as designed: when at its closest point to the target, a maximum control input was demanded so that the warhead was placed as close as possible to the target. Because the missile had passed directly under the Jindivik, the control demand had caused the missile to pull sharply upwards, almost to the vertical. The Skyflash had zoomed up to a height of some 20,000 feet before turning back to plunge down to the sea, impacting the water just behind the Phantoms. "May I ask, sir, how far behind the Phantoms?" interjected John.

"Oh...not too far," the commanding officer said hesitatingly. He paused before he went on: "We reckon that the missile missed you by around half-a-mile. In other words," he looked anxiously at the faces around the room, "at the airspeeds you were flying, the Skyflash was less than five seconds from your position."

Two Davids and a Goliath
No doubt feeling a bit older and wiser after such an experience, John Megarry successfully completed his QWI course to be posted in 1984 to 43 (F) Squadron at RAF Leuchars.

The following year he transferred to the United States Naval Air Station at Oceana in Virginia Beach, Virginia, as a member of staff on the VF-101 training unit where he flew the Grumman F-14 Tomcat. Three years later, in 1988, he was posted back to Phantoms as commander, in the rank of squadron leader, of the F-4 QWI School of 228 Operational Conversion Unit. This job involved regular deployments to the Italian air force base at Decimomannu, Sardinia, where NATO air forces used a nearby range for dissimilar-type air-to-air combat training.

It was on one of these deployments that John, with the benefit of experience gained at Oceana, decided to set up an unusual training session with his single F-4 pitted against two BAE Systems Hawk aircraft. If this appeared initially as something of a mismatch contest, examination of a statistic or two revealed some interesting points. For example, the Hawk's length at just over forty feet was dwarfed by the Phantom's near-sixty feet which made the larger aircraft easier for an opponent to see. The Hawk's maximum take-off weight of 20,000 lbs may have seemed somewhat meagre compared to the Phantom's figure of nearly three times that amount, but from the Hawk pilot's point of view this offered him the bonus of greater agility. However, as a subsonic aircraft powered by a single Rolls-Royce Adour turbofan engine, the Hawk's performance was positively puny compared to that produced by the mightiness of the Phantom's twin Rolls-Royce Speys which could accelerate the F-4 to around Mach 2.0. On the key issue of armament, each Hawk was equipped with AIM-9 Sidewinder missiles which, as heat seekers, had to be fired at a target's rear. The Phantom's four Sidewinders were subject to similar constraints, however in addition to the Sidewinders the F-4 was fitted with four AIM-7 Sparrow missiles which could be fired head-on. Another key aspect, the F-4's airborne radar, was lacked by the Hawks. To take advantage of this, the Phantom needed the expertise of a first-rate navigator and in this respect John had one of the best.

In summary, to win the contest canniness was needed with tactics that would make the best use of strong points while exploiting the opponents' weak points. In this way, John planned extra training benefit for the Hawk pilots as well as for the experienced F-4 fighter crew. Keen to apply some of the ideas he'd learnt at Oceana, he stipulated that the Hawks, when 'shot down', should be treated as if reincarnated after thirty seconds. This would offer the F-4 crew a greater number of targets and therefore more training value. The Phantom, on the other hand, would remain 'shot down' if struck by a Hawk AIM-9 missile in which case the exercise would be over. To add further realism, John and his navigator were authorised for their F-4 to carry an operational flare dispenser, a device which, when used, would disrupt the flight path of a Sidewinder missile.

John and his navigator decided on a straightforward plan: to carry out high-speed attacks which should avoid the classic Battle of Britain-type dogfight scenario with aircraft struggling to out-turn each other.

After detailed briefings, it was time for action. An atmosphere of anticipation was evident in the aircrew bus as an Italian airman drove the aircrew to the flight-line. While the bus trundled along, John noticed beyond the airfield perimeter fence how the land-scape, a mixture of scrub, rocks, cork trees and olive trees, was dominated by the Sulcis mountain range to the west with Monte Linas rising to some 3,500 feet. When not required for flying, from time to time he'd take opportunities to explore the local area on foot. To the north-west of Decimomannu, a village built by the Fascist government of the 1920s, made an intriguing place to visit. Originally named Villaggio Mussolini, this was upgraded to Mussolinia di Sardegna before the residents, after World War Two, settled for Arborea. When flying to the range due west of Decimomannu, the transit flight passed above other villages with ignoble pasts following the activities of Mussolini's fascist blackshirts. Now, though, all of that was history and these days the Italian air force seemed efficient with the set-up at Decimomannu providing an impressive facility.

Before long, as the aircrew bus drew up at the flight-line, John and his navigator together with the two Hawk pilots bade their driver *arrivederci* before they walked towards their respective aircraft. Tension was in the air now as the aircrew carried out their briefed plan – the Hawks would take off ahead of the F-4 after which, when air-borne, the radar-less Hawks would rely on directions from the ground controller. John and his navigator, however, would have no such guidance, relying instead on their Phantom's Westinghouse AN/AWG radar.

With start-up and take-off procedures completed and with the flight soon underway, John headed due west for the range while his navigator began a commentary. "Nothing seen yet, but maintain this heading for now."

"Copied, Geoff. Weather conditions in the range look okay – the visibility's good."

"Understood...I should pick up the Hawks on radar quite quickly."

As he flew towards the west coast of Sardinia, John kept a wary eye on Monte Linas to his right. Below, he could picture the natural scene as birds like the Sardinian warbler flitted above rough grasses and wild flowers. However, it was as he glanced down to check his cockpit instruments that Geoff suddenly cried: "Contact! Two targets just appearing on our right side range forty miles. Turn right through twenty degrees. And when over the sea accelerate to Mach 1.3." Soon clear of the coast and entering the range, John eased his twin throttles forwards and outboards to select reheat on the twin Rolls-Royce Speys. The machmeter reacted as the Phantom accelerated from subsonic to supersonic airspeeds.

"Approaching Mach 1.3," said John.

"Okay. Hold that for now," said Geoff aware that too high an airspeed would create excessive heat on the F-4's airframe which would facilitate the Hawks' missile lock-on. "Turn right a further twenty degrees," went on Geoff, "the targets are presently range thirty-five miles."

As he followed his navigator's instructions, John ran swiftly through the cockpit checks...guns/missiles circuit breaker...radar function...CW radar switch...interlock switch...missiles/guns selector...selected lights on steady...master arm...ready lights...

By this stage, with the radar automatically tracking the Hawks, John anticipated possible evasive manoeuvres by the Hawk pilots. "Target's range now thirty miles," called Geoff.

As the range counted down the pace seemed to increase exponentially at such high airspeeds.

"Target's range approaching twenty miles," said Geoff before long.

"Still good contact?"

"Affirmative. The radar's behaving well."

"Good aircraft, this – one of the best on the deployment."

"Standby," said Geoff, "targets' now down to fifteen miles." John's second finger loosely clasped the firing trigger. His navigator would call when to fire; the Sparrow's ideal firing range depended on various factors, including the F-4's launch speed and the relative velocity of the target. In head-on attacks such as this, the launch range could be as high as twenty miles, though much less for stern attacks.

"Targets' just passing ten miles," called Geoff, excitement mounting in his tone.

John peered anxiously ahead as he tried to spot the Hawks visually. With moist air directly above the surface of the Mediterranean Sea and with heat from the sun hovering above, visibility could be patchy in places. That day, however, with generally good conditions, John was not affected by poor visibility. By now with his heart beating like a merry drum, he was just about to identify the Hawks when Geoff cried breathlessly: "Standby to fire!" Within seconds, the next call was unambiguous and terse: *"FIRE!"*

John squeezed the trigger. After a slight pause, he called on the aircraft radio: "Fox 1!" – the code for a successful head-on missile firing. Moments later, Geoff confirmed radar lock-on to the second Hawk and it was not long before John was able to repeat his 'Fox 1' call. Now, with both of the Hawks 'shot down' and with the exercise rules giving the F-4 crew thirty seconds before they 'came alive' again, John needed to reposition urgently. Still flying at Mach 1.3 and guided by his navigator, he held the Phantom's heading until well beyond the reach of the Hawks' Sidewinders. Then he applied a high angle of bank to haul the F-4 through 180 degrees to take up a reciprocal heading. "Contact!" cried Geoff as, with speed and dexterity, he worked his radar controls to lock-on to the Hawks again.

So it was that the F-4's high-speed tactics proved successful. Another split was arranged with similar results, but on a third split the Phantom's extension was mistimed: John and his navigator found themselves threatened by a Hawk closing up to within Sidewinder firing range. With the F-4 still at supersonic airspeed, John, intending to deny the shot, turned and pulled vigorously towards the Hawk. Simultaneously he triggered several flares as decoys against the heat-seeking Sidewinders.

At that point, with over sixty degrees of bank applied, the F-4, as if standing on one wing, was close to limits when a loud bang and an ominous thump reverberated through the airframe. The twenty-odd-ton Phantom seemed to be pushed sideways. The machine shuddered as John struggled with the controls, his mind racing as he tried to work out what had happened. His initial reaction – engine fire – was soon discounted, as was the possibility of collision with one of the Hawks for both of those aircraft flew on unaffected. "What the hell was that?" John asked his navigator.

"Bugger knows," said Geoff.

"*Stop...stop...stop...*" cried John on the aircraft radio using a pre-arranged call to terminate the exercise immediately.

"We could get the Hawks to inspect our airframe?" suggested Geoff.

"They're too far away now," said John, "we'd better recover to base without delay." With that, John took up a heading for Decimomannu and adjusted his throttles to fly at an appropriate airspeed. The controller at Decimomannu confirmed that the F-4 had priority for landing and before long John was able to fly a straight-in approach for the landing.

When clear of the runway, he considered closing down the aircraft there and then, but as the F-4's handling appeared to be normal he decided to taxi back to the flight-line. News of the incident had apparently spread for a small crowd of onlookers watched as the Phantom approached. John noticed that they pointed at the fuselage and tail-plane area. When he and his navigator climbed out of their cockpits, they were astonished to see the extent of the damage. They gazed, horrified, at a large blackened area that covered the left stabiliser, along the leading edge and onto the fuselage. As if enemy machines had attacked with missiles emitting orange fire and long plumes of black smoke, the aircraft could have just returned from a war zone. Later analysis, however, showed something less drastic. Evidently the defensive manoeuvre at supersonic airspeeds had deflected the flares from their usual trajectory; instead of traversing down and away from the aircraft, the flares had detonated on impact with the tail. Fortunately, the Phantom had suffered no serious damage, further proof, perhaps, that the Phantom, as they say, was a tough old bird.

Cypriot shock

He could be stern-faced, but a good man nevertheless – and extremely keen. As an officer in the Royal Air Force Regiment, he held his body straight and his handshake was powerful enough to make someone wince. When asked if he could help out with a particular task planned for a families' open day, his answer was unequivocal: of course he would help, delighted to do so, he'd make sure that the day went with a bang. Quite how much of a bang was not realised at the time.

For this event, John Megarry was scheduled to fly one of a pair of Phantoms in a series of fly-pasts followed by a firepower demonstration. Detached from his home base, John, along with other members of his squadron, was now on the island of Cyprus for the squadron's annual armament practice camp. Based at RAF Akrotiri on the island's southern tip, the squadron's Phantom crews would hone their skills at cannon firing against a banner target towed by brave souls who crewed an English Electric Canberra aircraft.

After his long in-flight refuelling transit from the United Kingdom, when John landed at Akrotiri he was struck by the high level of security at the base. He and his colleagues were briefed that the reason for this went back some two years to when the United States had launched retaliatory attacks against Libya after the country's leader, Muammar Gaddafi, had been implicated in terrorist attacks against US military bases. The US bombers, whose missions were staged from the UK, had planned to employ RAF Akrotiri as an emergency diversion if needed – a facility, as it turned out, that was used by at least one aircraft. Libya, though, had threatened to respond against locations connected to the bombing attacks, a threat which was carried out against Akrotiri in early August 1986 with an assault by insurgents armed with mortars, rocket-propelled grenades and small arms. The assaults, widely assumed to have been commissioned by Libya and conducted by a Palestinian group, caused negligible damage although three British dependants were wounded.

John and his colleagues were briefed, also, that in the 1970s Akrotiri had played a significant part as a base for United States U-2 aircraft tasked to monitor the Egyptian-Israeli Suez Canal fighting and ceasefire, as well as monitoring events during the 1973 Yom Kippur War. The following year, when Cyprus had been invaded by Turkish forces after a Greek-sponsored coup, the effect on Akrotiri had been profound. The Royal Air Force had evacuated most of its aircraft squadrons apart from a search and rescue helicopter unit and 34 Squadron RAF Regiment. The latter's alliterative motto 'Feu de Fer' (Fire from Iron) seemed somewhat apposite – and apposite, too, was 34 Squadron's change of role from low-level air defence to counter-terrorist duties.

It was against this background that the families' open day at Akrotiri, despite the needs of high security, would continue as an event designed to boost morale and to demonstrate to everyone present the type of work carried out by the station personnel. A posting to Cyprus was regarded by most as highly desirable with off-duty opportunities to enjoy sandy beaches and to swim in clear, warm waters, but to add to these advantages, the open day was still seen as a useful means to build a cohesive team spirit around the station.

*   *   *

Once the Phantom crews had settled into the routines at Akrotiri, duty days often involved an early-morning start in efforts to complete the planned flying programme before the noonday heat became suffocatingly intense. The early starts could bring other benefits too. Sometimes, from outside the squadron buildings John would look up into the sky and listen. Birdsong was ubiquitous and along with the birdsong he would hear the faint pounding of sea upon beach. The sweet smell of Cypriot orange blossom was pungent and the surrounding atmosphere could provoke a sense of wistfulness. By midday the summer sun would bear down on peoples' necks, shoulders, backs with such ferocity that service shirts offered scant protection. The high temperatures would soften the tar so that everyone had to step carefully when walking outside. The runway's black surface, a dark scar set between sandy-coloured grasses, would glimmer in the heat and on some days a haze would hang like a vapour over the airfield.

For the families' day itself, held on a Saturday, an early start was not required. Instead, the two F-4 crews involved in the flying received a mid-morning brief on the plans for the day. The Phantoms' participation, as agreed earlier, would comprise two elements: firstly, both F-4s would conduct a few fly-pasts after which one aircraft would peel away while the other carried out the firepower demonstration. As John was still ground-attack qualified, he and his navigator were selected for the latter. The duty controller in air traffic control would give a special signal to indicate when the firepower demonstration should commence. A target – a small white car – had been carefully pre-positioned so as to be visible to spectators yet sufficiently distant for safety reasons. At the controller's signal, John would pull up before rolling-in for a strafe pass against the car. For added amusement, the commentator would declare that the car was illegally parked and had to be dealt with, therefore, the 'Akrotiri way'. Meanwhile, for even greater amusement, a Royal Air Force Regiment officer had agreed enthusiastically to set off a small explosion inside the car to signify a successful attack.

The weather was of typical Cypriot brilliance when John and the other three members of the aircrew walked out to their aircraft. Soon, as the men started up the two Phantoms, the racket of Rolls-Royce Speys stimulated an atmosphere of excitement among the spectators. When cleared, John led the formation to the runway for take-off as a pair before flying due north for a period until permitted by air traffic control to return for the fly-pasts. These went as planned while the two pilots, no doubt enjoying the exercise, turned steeply, climbed, and descended in a series of manoeuvres within the airfield boundary. From some angles the aircrew could discern observers gazing up at the formation then, turning inland, they were aware of a mix of hues – pale yellows, dark greens and purples – in the foothills leading up to Mount Olympus. The roar of engines in reheat and the tight manoeuvres caused the air to quiver like the shimmer coming off the local roads in the day's heat. From time to time, with the F-4s pointing towards the sea, the aircrews could glimpse a particular phosphorescence reflected from the water's surface.

Eventually, with the fly-pasts concluded, John began to position for the firepower demonstration. It was not long before he received the agreed signal at which spectators gasped when they saw the Phantom swoop out of the clear sky, descending towards the white car. John felt an adrenalin rush while he manoeuvred the aircraft down. The airframe started to vibrate as the airspeed accelerated towards 420 knots. Outside, a tapestry of colours flashed by while he adjusted his line of approach. He was vaguely aware of the crowds of spectators, their necks craning to observe the spectacle. In the distance, Mount Olympus appeared aloof, oblivious of the crews' concentrated effort – not exactly a white-knuckle fairground ride, nevertheless the ground seemed to rush towards the Phantom with bewildering rapidity. John, authorised to descend to a height of 100 feet, knew that timing was critical at such low altitudes. Experience, though, was key when, at precisely the right moment, he started to pull back hard on the stick. His cockpit G meter registered six times gravity (6 G) while he carried out the standard recovery action. Less than standard, however, was what happened next.

Suddenly, a huge fireball appeared directly ahead of the F-4. A concentrated mass of flame and smoke seemed about to devour the Phantom. The white car, as if demolished by a giant oxy-acetylene torch, vanished within an incandescent blast. John, unable to avoid debris, was forced to fly through scattered fragments of white-hot metal shards. In the struggle to recover he was caught off-guard by his navigator's yell: "Did you see that?"

"Er...no...what, Ned?"

"I thought we were about to collide with another aircraft."

"*What?*"

"So you didn't see anything fly past us?"

"No!" and with that John turned the Phantom downwind to set up for a safe approach and landing.

It was later, after landing, that John confirmed that he'd operated his gun camera during the split-second episode. This was as well for now there was a chance to work out exactly what had occurred. "Whatever it was you reckon you saw," he muttered to his navigator, "the camera will tell all." The two of them started to run through the camera sequence, examining the results frame by frame. As they did so, an RAF Regiment officer, the one who had 'fixed' the white car, entered the room. A lovely bloke, thought John, but – oh, man! – excessively keen. "Good show you put on there," said John.

"Thanks," grinned the officer, "thought you'd like it." With friends like this, mused John, who needs...

"Purely out of interest, what exactly did you do to 'fix' that car?"

"Ah well, I used a normal amount of composition C-4 plastic explosive – marvellous stuff, you know...can be moulded like modelling clay – then I added my own special recipe."

"And may one ask what that was?"

"Why not? It's easy enough. Just take a hundred condoms, fill them with petrol, and... Bingo!"

"A hundred petrol-filled condoms?" said John whose jaw dropped with shock.

"Was there a problem?"

"Have a look," said John who pointed at the gun cine frames which, played in slow motion, revealed scattered car remnants, including a complete bonnet, flash past the Phantom's windshield at a distance of a few feet. "And by the way," went on John, "we were flying at 420 knots at the time."

"At least we achieved the desired result!" came the reply.

CHAPTER 14

ITALIAN JOB

ARCHIE LIGGAT'S UNCONVENTIONAL TACTICAL CHECK

There was, thought Flight Lieutenant Archie Liggat, a look of relief on the face of his navigator. Maybe he was only too glad that it was all over. Certainly, the sortie from which they'd just returned had proved more difficult than planned...in fact, a great deal more difficult. Then again, pondered Archie, perhaps even that understated the case; some might go so far as to say that events had bordered on the disastrous, although this, felt Archie, exaggerated the matter. It was not as if the navigator, who'd been briefed to conduct Archie's tactical check, had displayed gratitude for a safe landing – he hadn't burst into song, or cried out: 'Thank you! Thank you! Thank you!' or, worse still, broken into applause as can happen (so one has been told) on bucket-holiday-type flights, but no, although a little subdued, Archie's 'checker' had remained, on the whole, calm and objective during the debrief.

Proceedings for the sortie, reflected Archie, had proceeded badly from the start. The sortie's master plan, intended as a four-ship escort provided by 111 (F) Squadron Phantoms for Panavia Tornado bomber aircraft, had begun to go awry as various setbacks cropped up left, right and centre. Despite stalwart efforts by the 111 Squadron engineers, radar and other unserviceabilities had resulted in the original Phantom four-ship downgrading to a three-ship, then to a two-ship after which further problems reduced the master plan to a less-than-masterful single-ship. Fortunately, thought Archie, his own aircraft had not let him down and it was with relief mixed with agitation that he and his checker had managed to get airborne on that early summer's day in 1988 – even if they were a little late. Actually, more than a little late, mused Archie, for he knew that, in truth, the lateness issue added a further unfortunate twist to the growing saga: timing was tight if the pre-briefed plan was to work out.

At least he was reasonably familiar with the local area, for not long after he and his 111 Squadron colleagues had arrived for a week-long detachment hosted by the Italian air force (Aeronautica Militare) at their base at Istrana in northern Italy, the resident squadron commander, at the controls of his Lockheed F-104 Starfighter, had led the F-4 crews on a sector reconnaissance flight. To the south and east of Istrana, an intricate network of channels formed a wide delta which, highly distinctive when viewed from an aircraft, marked where the rivers Piave and Po, the latter forming Italy's longest river, projected into the Adriatic Sea near Venice. To the north, the Dolomite mountain range provided a spectacular backdrop to Italy's northern reaches. As the F-104 led the 111 Squadron guests enthusiastically along deep valleys then up and around jagged pinnacles covered in snow, Archie was reminded that a lack of 'hot and high' performance left the Phantoms with limited room for manoeuvre.

After this flight, and in deference to Archie's position as a qualified flying instructor, his opposite number on the Italian squadron invited him on a further sector reconnaissance flight, this time to be flown in a two-seat Aermacchi MB-326 training aircraft. Following a cursory brief, and when the two of them had strapped into the Aermacchi for their flight, Archie felt in no position to criticise when the single Bristol Siddeley Viper turbojet engine failed to start. Unlike the 111 Squadron ground crews, however, the Italians had few qualms about giving the machine's fuselage a sharp slap or two as if goading some recalcitrant child to behave. With a few more slaps the engine eventually came to life and *hey presto!* the Aermacchi was underway. After take-off, the flight headed towards the Dolomites to discover that – surprise, surprise – the Italian pilot's family just happened to be in the hills where, in addition to enjoying a picnic, enthralled family members were treated to an impromptu flying display.

On return, a rather different matter arose when it was announced that a joint Anglo/Italian exercise involving a large number of aircraft would take place the next day. As well as an opportune time for NATO allies to practise mutual procedures, the exercise would be a suitable occasion to conduct Archie's tactical check, an annual evaluation to verify his status as an operational squadron pilot.

When crews were gathered the next day for a pre-flight briefing, Archie stood up to deliver a brief from the 111 Squadron perspective, after which an Italian officer took to the podium. Archie and his colleagues were a little taken aback by this officer's informal approach. His main emphasis appeared to be on the need for flexibility. Archie's efforts seemed, somehow, to have come to nothing which left him with a sense of anguish, although in the interests of diplomacy he tried not to show it. "That all seems a bit casual," a squadron colleague muttered to Archie, "what with this dodgy-sounding rendezvous with the Tornados...meet up at 'around' lunchtime...be there or be square, he said. What sort of briefing is that, for goodness sake?"

"What can one say? The Battle of Britain pilots didn't have the endless briefings of these days before anyone gets airborne. Air defence is meant to be a reactive force, is it not?" There was something of a willed resolve in the briskness of Archie's words as he spoke. It was only later, with the benefit of hindsight, that he might have modified this opinion.

A total of fourteen aircraft were detailed for the formation, hardly Battle of Britain-like numbers, nonetheless the eight Tornado bombers from the nearby Italian base at Ghedi would represent the largest single group of Tornados to have taken off from that airfield. The intention was for four 111 Squadron Phantoms to escort the Tornados while the bombers carried out their task to attack a bombing range on Italy's east coast. The formation would be joined by two F-104s from the Aeronautica Militaire whose pilots, with their experience of local topography, would provide navigational guidance. When approaching the range, the remainder of the Phantom detachment would intercept the bombers. That, as they say, was the plan.

But following the start-up delays and with the escort now down to just a single Phantom, Archie had to rush to make up for lost time. He'd anticipated a take-off in company with the two F-104s, but as he began to taxi from the dispersal area he was surprised to see both of them about to set off down the runway for take-off. "Maybe they're not too bothered about pre-flight routines," he said to his checker who sat quietly in the F-4's rear cockpit. And this mentality, Archie thought to himself, of kick the tyres, light the fires and the last one airborne is a sissy, was hardly ideal for a check ride. As the Phantom sped along the taxiway trying to catch up, Archie was painfully conscious that the sortie so far had revealed a lamentable lack of the unflustered, measured demonstration of drills normally expected on check rides. Not only was he in a hurry but he was hot and stressed and his mind was in a state of preoccupation. Obliged to rattle through the pre-take-off procedures, he needed cockpit canopies to be closed as swiftly as possible while he stuffed maps in various nooks and crannies around the cockpit as, in gung-ho fashion, he

Archie Liggat prepares for the sortie.

continued to race along the taxiway. Ahead, he was alarmed to see plumes of dirty exhaust smoke rise from the F-104s' tailpipes as their pilots prepared to take off. Even at a distance Archie could hear the peculiar howl associated with Starfighter engines, then he suddenly realised that the two pilots had released their brakes to zoom off down the runway – evidently without so much as a second thought for their F-4 guest. With the urgent need to keep them in sight, it was with ever greater haste that Archie hurtled round the taxi-way bend to the runway, watched fretfully for the green Aldis light to signify take-off clearance, rocked both throttles forward and outboard, and monitored his engine gauges to confirm reheat light-up as the Phantom accelerated down the runway.

Soon airborne and grateful for it, the hot and hassled Archie glanced at the river delta to the east and the mountains to the north, then concentrated ahead as he struggled to retain visual contact with the F-104s. By now mere dots on the horizon, the F-104s hugged the terrain as they flew at low level to the west. Of the various sobriquets used by operators of the F-104, the Italian 'hatpin', reckoned Archie, was pretty apposite at present; the Pakistani *Badmash* ('hooligan') or the German *Fliegender Sarg* (flying coffin) were well known, though just at that moment the most relevant of all was probably 'missile with a man in it'. The Starfighter's short, stubby wings attached to a long, thin fuselage made the aircraft hard to see at the best of times, but viewed at a distance from the rear, Archie's task was extra hard. He was helped, however, by the General Electric J-79 turbojet engine whose sooty output formed dark scars against the lighter background of Italy's Padan Plain which stretched for some 400 miles in an east-west direction.

Before long, though, the Starfighter pilots seemed to throttle back which caused the engine smoke to reduce and the aircraft effectively to vanish from Archie's sight. Even flying at very low level he found that visual contact was sporadic, although his navigator managed to obtain a few radar glimpses on pulse mode and, on pulse-Doppler mode, intermittent velocity modulation signals. It was on these tenuous variables that Archie managed to continue. A brief radio call could have alerted the F-104 pilots to his plight but radio silence had been ordered for the duration of the exercise. With little alternative but to persist with a high-speed dash at very low level, the unfamiliar Italian countryside seemed to flash past at an ever faster rate: roads, railways and towns shot by in a blur of unrecognised features. He tried to follow the route on an aeronautical map but at those speeds and heights use of a map was unrealistic.

Suddenly, to his left, Archie became aware that he was flying close to a major airfield. With a feeling of dread he realised that he must have infringed protected airspace, a grave violation in law let alone from the point of view of passing his tactical check. This is ridiculous, he said to himself – *enough!* – this mad chase has to stop. With that, he eased back on the power and increased altitude slightly to a level where map reading was practicable. Now alone and approximately in charge of his own destiny, Archie experienced a welcome degree of equanimity which allowed him to go back to basics.

While he attempted to rectify the regrettable state of being 'temporarily unsure of position' – a bad idea at any time let alone during a tactical check – he extracted another chart or two from the various cockpit hidey-holes used earlier during the rush to get airborne. He managed to pinpoint his position after which, working on old-fashioned track and timing techniques, it was not too long before a disused airfield loomed ahead. A little to his surprise, he began to realise that this was, indeed, the actual airfield intended as the formation rendezvous site – a point that was confirmed by the welcome sight of the two F-104s circling the area in a combat air patrol.

Now, as they climbed up to around 2,000 feet to join the combat air patrol, he and his navigator assumed the lead: their state-of-the-art equipment, the Phantom's Westinghouse radar, was more advanced than that fitted to Starfighters. From what little he had managed to fathom at the briefing, Archie reckoned that the Tornados would probably avoid a 'loft' attack profile, a bombing technique where the attackers came in low and fast, then pulled up sharply to release their bombs at a pre-determined distance from the target thereby evading point defences. Instead, he figured that the Tornados would overfly the disused airfield then set course for a straightforward bomb drop over the range. In either case, the fighters' job was to intercept, identify then destroy hostile bombers well before the target was reached. As bomber escorts, Archie and the Starfighters' task was to interrupt the fighters' activities so that the bombers were able to complete their mission.

While Archie and his navigator continued to lead the combat air patrol in a racetrack pattern, they concentrated their search to the north, the direction from which the Tornados were expected to approach. At the stage when the Tornados were sighted, Archie planned to manoeuvre to the outside of the bombers' eight-ship formation to take up an efficient escort position while the F-104s, in theory at least, would do the same. Meantime, when he glanced at the ground, Archie was struck by the rugged and attractive nature of the Italian countryside. Surrounded by a mix of subtle greens and yellows, he could identify countless numbers of small villages arranged haphazardly within a patchwork of farmers' fields. 'Not a bad neck of the woods, this' he thought to himself. To the north, however, where the River Po ran through the Padan Plain past the major lakes of Como, Garda and Maggiore, his view was restricted by that day's summer smog – a hazard which added to the difficulty of spotting the Tornado formation. But modern technology, despite its sometimes dubious reputation, was about to come to the rescue when his navigator cried: "I've got numerous pulse-Doppler radar contacts!"

"Coming in from the north?"

"Affirmative. Looks like our Tornado friends."

And so it proved: cruising in relatively clear air at a height of around 500 feet, neat ranks of Tornados started to appear. Spaced in trailing, card-four formations, the aircraft seemed to stretch back a long way. Though not exactly in the same league as the thousand-bomber raids of World War Two, nonetheless the group looked big by modern-day standards and Archie was impressed by the way the formation changed course in relatively stately fashion onto the easterly attack heading towards the intended target. Now, as planned, Archie moved into a defensive position where his navigator was best able to use his radar to scan the skies for air defence fighters.

Despite earlier mutterings that this could be the phase at which everything turned pear-shaped, Archie realised that, in fact, it was proving to be the best part of the exercise so far. With everyone in their correct places and apparently behaving themselves for once, the proceedings seemed to be working out better than anticipated. Indeed, he felt gratified to act as escort for what looked like a well-disciplined, controlled and purposeful attack group. For the first time that day, Archie felt almost able to relax. It could not last.

Fairly soon after the formation had settled, the F-104 pilots appeared to become restless. Ignoring Archie's careful briefing, the two headstrong pilots began to accelerate and descend to low level. Then, regretfully, their example seemed to influence the Tornado pilots who, instead of holding a good steady heading for the bombing run as all good bomber pilots should do, decided that a more interesting idea would be to follow the F-104s. It was not long, therefore, before the entire formation ended up at high speed and low level with aircraft thundering along like legendary bats out of hell almost touching the greenish grasses of the Padan Plain. In the poor visibility, Archie worried about the navigation equipment in the Tornados. Had the crews made due allowance for the precise positioning needed for an accurate target strike? As for his aircraft, his FG1 version of the Phantom was limited to a few random bits of ex-navy equipment which meant, in effect, the need to resort to time-honoured but outmoded map reading.

At about this stage, Archie's navigator warned him that the 'bounce' F-4s were in the vicinity: "I'm getting some pulse-Doppler returns and signals from the radar warning receiver!" he yelled. Archie now had visions of the Tornados reacting in the same way as, for instance, the disciplined (if somewhat staid) crews of the RAF's Buccaneer force whose reputation for sticking to the task – drop bombs on a target, break away and return to base for rearming – was renowned. But no, such ideas seemed to be lost on the Italian Tornado crews. As if honour was at stake and testosterone levels had to be proved, they appeared determined to disregard convention, including golden rule number one for bombers: do not become embroiled in dogfights with fighters.

Like the proverbial bull in a china shop, the lead Tornado pilot must have thought that now was a good time to start charging around like...like a bull in a china shop. With the creature's horns sharpened, head lowered and one foot scraping the floor ahead of a charge, the brute was about to be let loose. As the sole remaining Phantom escort and with his supposedly fellow F-104 escorts nowhere to be seen, Archie faced a dilemma. He was hardly in a position to issue instructions over the radio; the results would be dubious, to put it mildly. So what, exactly, was he supposed to do?

The answer came quite quickly. Selecting his Tornado's swing-wing system fully forward for maximum manoeuvrability, the lead Tornado pilot broke cover, engaged reheat and initiated a hard turn towards the fighters. His colleagues followed in rapid succession. Within moments, a series of individual dogfights ensued, some one-on-one, some two-on-one but in either case any semblance of order was clearly lost to the four winds. Forced to accept that events were now beyond his control, Archie was left with few options. He was, as they say, caught between the devil and the deep blue sea, and decided that he had little choice but to enter the fray.

Pushing his twin throttles forward, Archie engaged reheat on the Rolls-Royce Speys. Simultaneously he pulled the stick hard back, and over to the left. He kicked his left foot against the rudder. The Phantom lurched violently onto its side and changed direction. With blood draining from his head and eyes, Archie strived to avoid blacking out and he was aided by his anti-G suit which inflated fiercely. As if urging the flight controls to co-operate, he moved them rapidly but with finesse; ham-fisted techniques would lead to trouble. His stomach felt in knots; adrenalin surged through his system. In the mayhem all around, he was aware of an aircraft turning in parallel with him before it banked away hard then reversed direction as the pilot attempted to gain advantage. Turning in ever-tighter circles Archie suddenly saw another aircraft wheel around then climb to gain height all the time watching for the best moment to over-bank and descend for engagement. Time seemed to distort. Phantoms, Tornados, Starfighters careered around the sky in urgent, endless manoeuvres. Someone hauled his aircraft upwards, half-rolled, then dived away but his opponent anticipated this by diving with him before, at the last second, pulling out at low level when the ground began to balloon up. His heartbeat racing, Archie mumbled hasty prayers as the Phantom, at the limits of control, juddered viciously during the manoeuvres. He witnessed a number of near collisions. "Break left...break left," his navigator yelled at one stage, "there's an aircraft closing in our six-o'clock!"

The melee must have persisted for around fifteen minutes. Like throngs of boxers circling each other in the ring, everyone struggled for an opening or for the dropping of a guard. As they fought, Starfighters flashed among Phantoms, Tornados turned and twisted between both. In moves that must have looked bizarre to observers on the ground, a number of aircraft displayed the heavy wing-rock symptomatic of an impending stall. With reheats engaged, the racket at ground level must have caused watchers to clamp hands over ears. For crews in the aircraft, the agreed safety frequency was over-whelmed by an excess of excited radio calls, some in Italian – *"c'è un aeromobile dietro di voi"... "attenzione al bastardo sopra"... "guarda a ore sei"... "vai su!"* – some in English ... "there's an aircraft behind you" ... "mind that bastard above" ... "watch your six o'clock" ... "pull up!" ... although the resultant cacophony made little sense to anyone at all.

But it could not go on. One by one, as time, energy, testosterone levels, fuel reserves and a few other things besides began to diminish, individual aircraft disengaged to fly to the range before returning to base. When Archie decided that it was time for him, too, to disengage, his head was reeling. He struggled to make sense of what had occurred. As if reading Archie's mind his navigator said flatly: "suggest an initial heading of zero-eight-zero for Istrana." Conversation with his navigator, however, was generally minimal, perhaps in part because Archie was convinced that his tactical check was, in the terms of the poker-faced poker player, a busted flush. How could it be anything else?

Now flying alone as he took up his navigator's suggested heading, Archie found that the ensuing period of relative calm seemed quite strange. It also allowed his mind to dwell on a number of matters. He pondered, for example, the time when the Italians were the enemy and today's activities would have been fought in much the same way, only with live weapons. The affair, he ruminated, was probably the closest he'd come to the experiences of the Spitfire and Hurricane pilots in the Battle of Britain. In some ways, reckoned Archie, that battle felt like centuries in the past although, within the scheme of things, it was not so very long ago. Unlike the present day, however, when crews were highly trained and tested – tests which included annual tactical checks – the Spitfire and Hurricane pilots had been required to cope with drastic demands despite a woeful lack of training and experience. Archie tried to picture the scene. He surmised that his predecessors, as they waited for the call to action, would have been sitting outside in the balmy weather of that summer in 1940. Perhaps a wireless played hit songs of the day. A surreal atmosphere might have transported the minds of those young men away from the violence that was just a telephone call away. Some, no doubt, tried to gain snatches of sleep – probably fitful and full of extreme dreams. Others would play cards or try to read. All would check watches with apprehensive, over-frequent glances. When the scramble bell was rung, when the pilots jumped up to race out to their aircraft, they faced daunting odds. Yet it never seemed to occur to most that the Royal Air Force might not win the battle. Archie had heard how the ground crews, often years older than the pilots, would help the young men to strap in to cockpits, then a quick tap on the shoulder and a final word – "You be careful now, sir. There ain't no sense in being careless" – would send the pilots on their way.

Once airborne, the aircraft would fly in formation as the squadron gained altitude to meet the attackers. When the enemy bombers were sighted and when the fighter leader called "echelon starboard go" shortly followed by "going down now!" the fighters, one after the other, would peel off to enter a power dive. However, unlike today, reflected Archie, air-to-air missiles were not available back then. The Spitfire and Hurricane pilots would aim to have an enemy machine stabilised in the gun-sight by around 300 yards before closing up to some 200 yards for a three or four-second burst of machine-gun fire. An every-man-for-himself melee rapidly developed with, just as happened today thought Archie, a chaotic scene of frenetic, mind-boggling activity.

Then an odd thing would happen. Archie had been told how Battle of Britain pilots later talked about the way bedlam in the sky had suddenly seemed to evaporate. As if by divine intervention, evidently the skies emptied so that, with not another aircraft in sight, a poignant, chilling atmosphere prevailed such that an individual's feelings of confusion and isolation were great. His experiences today, mused Archie, had not been so different…

"Let's avoid that active airfield we infringed last time," his navigator's voice cut through Archie's revery. "Turn left twenty degrees," went on the navigator. Archie felt a pang of despondency when he was reminded of another reason why he should fail his tactical check. At least, he assumed, from now on events should progress smoothly and easily for the remainder of the sortie. If nothing else, at least the last part of the test should create a favourable impression. How wrong he was!

*　　*　　*

As he approached Istrana airfield, Archie calculated that, although not particularly short of fuel just yet, the Phantom was not exactly flush with the stuff. As long as he could be assured of a timely approach and landing there'd be no problem. When he called Istrana air traffic control, however, it was with a sinking feeling that he absorbed the news of landing delays. "Hold a-clear of the airfield to the east," said the controller in a strongly accented Italian voice. Like an airliner in a landing queue, Archie was forced to go round in circles while he waited for clearance to proceed. Regular, anxious glances at his fuel gauges became progressively more regular and anxious. From time to time he reached down to change his radio selector to tower frequency so that he could monitor what was happening. The messages were not good. It seemed that various pilots, critically short of fuel, had declared emergencies to allow them to jump the landing queue.

Archie checked his fuel state again. Although not quite at the stage of declaring an emergency, he informed air traffic control that he'd have to divert to another airfield if Istrana was not available soon. "That is no problem," said the controller unctuously, "we'll have you down soon. Maintain the hold." Far be it from me, thought Archie, to accuse you of spouting hot air, but this is getting silly. He spoke again to the controller but the answer was the same. Archie tried once more, insistence in his voice as he strived to convey a degree of urgency and this time the controller appeared to sit up and take note. Apart from anything else, to add to Archie's problems local visibility had started to reduce which meant that he'd probably need ground radar to guide him during the approach. Furthermore, despite the controller's encouraging noises, Archie still awaited clearance. He was just at the point of requesting a diversion when the controller finally declared: "You are a-cleared to commence an approach."

"Copied," sighed Archie. Action at last, he thought, as he took up a radar heading towards Istrana airfield. Nursing the throttles to eke out slender reserves, Archie flew accurate headings guided by surveillance radar as he prepared to descend. He knew that the aircraft would be just below stipulated fuel minima on landing but that, he judged, should be no particular problem as long as he landed without further complications. Before long, when instructed to commence descent, he flew the Phantom smoothly, steadily down the correct approach path just as any top fighter pilot should do. The visibility, he noticed, was deteriorating progressively as he neared the touchdown point. A thick haze covered the airfield, but he was not too worried: the controller's voice remained calm, the approach seemed to be going well, all appeared fine...but here lay the problem. As if by telepathy, he knew that it couldn't last.

By late finals the approach still seemed fine: the Phantom was on course, the fuel state remained manageable, Archie had pegged the correct heading, airspeed and rate of descent. He expected to see the touchdown point start to loom out of the mist at any second. He was confident of his ability to carry out a safe landing. He was an experienced pilot; he was used to coping with challenges; the landing conditions that day were not ideal but he had known much worse. Ahead, like a 'welcome home' sign, the line of the runway lights began to shine through the mist. Archie continued down. The Phantom passed the airfield boundary. The runway threshold was now a matter of metres away. Archie started to ease the stick back and he adjusted the twin throttles.

The bombshell, when it came, was explosive. It came in the form of a voice; the air traffic controller's voice. The tone of the voice was one of panic. In a thick Italian accent, the voice shrieked two words: *"Overshoot! Overshoot!"* There was no call sign, no explanation, no hint of any further advice. Notional question marks must have popped up above cockpits across the area. In Archie's case, his line of thought was at once logical and swift...*in about two seconds I'll touch down on the runway...I'm too short of fuel to overshoot... the runway ahead looks clear as far as I can see...who is this plonker calling for overshoot anyway...it could be any old...*

Archie landed firmly then operated the Phantom's tail parachute. He felt an immediate tug from behind as the 'chute deployed. The aircraft began to slow. The runway lights flicked past at a decreasing rate. When he glanced sideways, he noticed that the airfield grass was covered in a thin layer of damp formed by a fusillade of drops where the mist had settled. He looked ahead again. The runway was still clear. He anticipated a turn-off soon – and not before time, he thought to himself. This had been a flight from hell – for sure, a tactical test with a difference. However, at least he could now consider himself past the point of another bombshell. How wrong can one be!

The next bombshell, as it struck, was even more explosive than the last. Suddenly, out of the mists, a shadowy shape began to materialise. The shape was travelling fast. Within seconds Archie was able to identify the shape as a Tornado. A Tornado that was in the process of landing in the opposite direction. Landing? In the wrong direction? Impossible! Archie's tortured mind raced. Like it or not, the Tornado pilot, for some reason best known to himself, had evidently elected to land downwind. Archie's options were limited – absurdly limited. As if attempting to squeeze past traffic in a busy street, he decided to manoeuvre the Phantom to one side of the runway. But which side? He was in Italy. Drivers drive on the right in Italy. Typical! He forced the aircraft over to the right...as far as he dared before the undercarriage wheels touched the grass and began to dig in. This was known to distort the airframe and disable the ejection system. In urgent, short sentences he conferred with his navigator. Should they eject before striking the grass? It was a possibility but one with attendant risks. Even so, under the circumstances it might be the best thing to do. Archie was on the verge of yelling: *"Eject! Eject!"* when he spotted something. A surge of black smoke had appeared from the Tornado's jet pipe area. Then he saw the Tornado's nose rise from the runway. These signs convinced Archie that the Tornado pilot had initiated a 'rejected landing' procedure. He decided, therefore, not to proceed with the ejection plan. Instead, by hugging the right-hand edge of the runway he hoped and prayed to avoid a collision. As it turned out, the decision was justified – but only just for when the Tornado lifted from the runway surface, the aircraft shot past at a distance of a few metres before disappearing into the misty void.

By now the Phantom had slowed to a taxiing speed. When he turned off the runway to head for the squadron's allotted parking area, Archie found himself progressing at an unusually pedestrian and thoughtful pace. Indeed, he felt shaky with shock. He tried to speak with the air traffic controller but the controller did not reply. Perhaps, thought Archie, the fellow had passed out or gone on strike or decided to take a timely lunch break. Maybe he was struck dumb with shock.

With the parking area in sight Archie noticed that a reception party had gathered nearby. 'Oh no,' he thought, 'here comes another bombshell.' He followed the marshaller's signals, stopped when instructed and applied the Phantom's brakes. As he closed down the engines, the whine of the Rolls-Royce Speys faded to the quiet tinkling sound of rotating compressors. Archie glanced at the glum faces lined up below, unstrapped his seat harness and climbed stiffly out of his cockpit. Time to face the music, he thought, as he and his navigator pulled off their bone dome headsets whose insides, drenched in perspiration, did not make pretty sights.

The commanding officer of the Starfighter squadron stepped forward. Here it comes, thought Archie: a mega-blast Italian style; no doubt he'll let rip about that airspace violation as well as quite a lot else besides. To Archie's surprise, however, this didn't happen. Instead, the Italian officer was full of apologies...Tornado very short of fuel... appeared on short finals at the last minute...went for the downwind runway by mistake... air traffic control didn't notice until very late...the Tornado pilot suddenly realised his error...he overshot to carry out a quick circuit...he landed safely...there would be an enquiry, of course.

Archie Liggat strapping into his F-4 after joining 74 Squadron at Wattisham.

If Archie felt a sense of relief, it was surely understandable. However, another hurdle remained, that of the debrief for his tactical check. Having signed the technical log and the flight authorisation sheet, Archie, together with his checker, walked down a corridor, opened the door to a briefing room and entered. As they sat down, Archie glanced out of a window to observe some F-104s manoeuvring across the hard-standing. Engineers scurried about; the bright colours of a nearby windsock showed up even through the mists. He gazed at his checker, focusing on the narrow gleam of light that shone in his eyes. There was a tension between them as if each was waiting for the other to speak first. When he did speak, the checker's full and objective remarks, reckoned Archie, were thoroughly justified.

Later that night, when Archie went to his room in the officers' mess, the day's events continued to whirl through his mind. He felt his head throb with different emotions. It was as if his mind had been opened up by other people's actions and he had no way of shutting off his sense of frustration. Some nationalities did things differently; perhaps there was something too narrow in his understanding of the world. Archie lay on his back, staring upwards into the darkness. What a day, he reflected, but at least he'd passed his tactical check.

CHAPTER 15

FOUR-SECOND SOLO

JON 'HERBIE' HANCOCK'S UNSCHEDULED EXPERIENCE

As the aircrew minibus left the 111 (F) Squadron head-quarters at RAF Leuchars, Flying Officer Jon Hancock glanced at one of his fellow navigators and quipped: "Is there time for me to shoot back to the officers' mess to check my life insurance?" His colleague grinned by way of reply and it was not long before the bus drew up alongside Phantom FG1 XT861 'Alpha Charlie' which had been allocated to Jon and his pilot on that September day in 1987. The aircraft, painted in tactical grey/green camouflage, portrayed the black and white chequers of 43 (F) Squadron which had loaned the air-craft to 111 Squadron.

Jon felt proud to be a member of 111 Squadron, a famous unit which had recently celebrated its seventieth anniversary. This was the squadron which, under the leadership of Squadron Leader R. L. Topp, had looped twenty-two 'Black Arrows' Hawker Hunter aircraft at the 1958 Farnborough air show (a record which stands to this day). For the seventieth anniversary celebrations at Leuchars in 1987, a diamond-nine formation of Phantoms had made several fly-pasts across the airfield, and by September of that year it was decided to continue the Black Arrows theme for the annual RAF Leuchars Battle of Britain At Home Day. To ensure that experience was distributed around the squadron, the planned five-ship would contain crews who had not flown in the diamond nine. This included Jon. Delighted to be selected, he and his pilot were allotted the 'Black Two' position and as a twenty-two-year-old navigator still in his first year on a front-line squadron Jon was living a boyhood dream.

On Monday 7 September 1987 there was an early morning report for duty at the squadron's pilots' briefing facility (PBF) where, mugs of tea or coffee in hand, those involved congregated for a detailed briefing. For Jon, having never experienced anything more complicated than close formation pairs work, this heralded a whole new world. He followed the formation leader's brief intently. The sortie itself was straightforward: five of the Phantoms would conduct practice interceptions while the formation leader rehearsed timing runs over the airfield. After this, the formation would join up to practise various close formation positions while a sixth Phantom would act as a 'whipper-in'. The sortie would end with a run across the airfield with five of the Phantoms in a card five formation called the St Andrew's Cross. For the latter, Jon's aircraft would fly line abreast on the leader's right-hand side. Black Four was allocated the central position, briefed to fly at the same height as Black One and Black Two. Black Three and Black Five would occupy the rear station but stepped down in height. At this point in the briefing, Jon's attentiveness spiked when he was given responsibility for collision avoidance between his Phantom and Black Four. He was to advise his pilot if he thought they were too close. That gave him his first sense of misgiving but – hey! – he was surrounded by experienced crews who had done this before, the proposed formation had been approved by headquarter's staff officers, it had been planned and briefed in detail so nothing, surely, could go wrong, right? Right!

So it was that, after take-off at 0915 on that bright Monday morning, and on completion of the practice interception phase, the formation joined up at a height of 5,000 feet in loose echelon with Black Six whipping-in from above. In the rear cockpit of Black Two, excitement levels rose when the leader called the formation into St Andrew's Cross. Jon's Phantom was the first into position, his pilot gently manoeuvring into loose line abreast, level with and to the right of Black One. So far so good. Now Black Four moved into a close level echelon with the lead Phantom. Jon suddenly made eye

Diamond nine formation celebrating 111 Squadron's anniversary.

contact with Black Four's navigator and was reminded of his earlier throwaway comment about life insurance. Moments later, as the two rear aircraft slid into place, Jon's pilot tightened up his line abreast position on Black Four. This completed the formation and gave the first opportunity to capture the visual formation references.

As the whipper-in radioed a few adjustments, the formation descended towards 2,000 feet to allow the whip to manoeuvre below a thin layer of broken cloud. Additionally, this allowed the pilots to use more representative engine power settings. When all were happy, the leader commenced a 360-degree turn to the left at an angle of bank of forty-five degrees. Jon was aware of some minor jockeying for position but with the overall formation remaining fairly steady he was reluctant to say anything that could cause an over-compensation of any corrections; this might unsettle the formation further back. Nonetheless, he found that his right hand was slowly crushing the navigator's radar hand controller. He looked for something equally comforting to grip with his left hand. His attention was focused by the aerodynamic noise levels which varied while the formation adjusted position, and his anxiety was exacerbated by the unfamiliar image of another Phantom immediately to his left in line abreast.

On completion of the first 360-degree turn the leader steadied, then initiated a turn to the right. This felt uncomfortable and Jon's youthful exuberance began to drain away when the formation was reversed into a climbing turn to the left. It felt wrong. Black Four appeared to ease out slightly to the right while Jon's aircraft was in the process of moving back with a slight amount of over-bank. Suddenly, enthusiasm exhausted and conscious of looking into Black Four's starboard engine intake, Jon decided that it was time to offer some useful advice to his pilot: "We're going to hit!" he cried with an oath. Simultaneously he turned his head, closed his eyes and ducked in a vain attempt at self-preservation. Immediately he was aware of a deep, sickening shudder through the airframe. A second later, a loud 'dusssh' noise reverberated in his eardrums. He wrongly interpreted this as an engine surge, although having never before experienced one this seemed the next logical step in the unfolding disaster.

When he opened his eyes, Jon looked up to be confronted with a cockpit full of smoke and debris. Then he realised something else. Without the courtesy of telling him, the pilot had ejected. Jon was alone in the Phantom.

Now the seconds started to tick by slowly.

One second – Jon sat there shocked and bewildered. His world was literally turning upside down.

Two seconds – his brain attempted to assess whether he could ride this one out. However, a glance out of the left-hand side of his canopy through the dispersing smoke and dust convinced him otherwise: the North Sea was barrelling rapidly around him with very little sky visible.

Three seconds – so, the ejection decision was made. He realised that it was going to

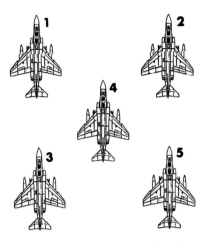

Diagram showing the relevant positions of Blacks One to Five in formation.

be painful. Just nine months earlier after another rush of youthful exuberance he had fallen from a height of some fifteen feet during the Station Commander's Cup assault course competition. He'd suffered spinal compression fractures to his lower vertebrae and his spine really did not need an ejection.

Four seconds – clearly this was going to hurt badly. He tried to follow his ejection seat training but first he pushed the camera bag by his right thigh onto the cockpit floor. He tugged at his lap straps to tighten them as much as possible. He forced the base of his spine into the rear of the seat. He straightened his back, locked his head against the headrest and closed his eyes. Applying the approved technique of one hand clasping the opposite wrist he pulled the seat pan handle with all of his might.

But nothing happened...

If the mind can play tricks when confronted with a life-or-death situation, in this case time didn't just slow down but appeared to freeze. Convinced that his seat had failed to fire, Jon began to curse his bad luck when, in a sudden explosion of smoke and noise, he was thrown forwards as the ejection seat fired. The action was sufficiently violent to cause his upper and lower jaws to crunch together so that his upper teeth took a sizeable bite from his bottom lip. He managed to keep his eyes firmly shut and he remained conscious. He felt the blast of wind smash into him; he was aware of uncontrolled tumbling; he heard the sound of whirrs and clicks as the Martin-Baker mechanisms automatically separated him from the seat. Then, with a great snap, the parachute blossomed above him, forcing Jon's eyes open. The ejection seat handle was ripped painfully from his fingers. He glanced up to see the rear silhouettes of four Phantoms, black exhaust smoke trailing behind them as, widening out from close formation, they flew towards the horizon. Conscious that the roar of the Rolls-Royce Speys was receding gradually, suddenly his attention was drawn to a white flash below. It was XT861 as the Phantom struck the surface of the North Sea. He saw a cloud of spray start to spread above a white circle of froth which expanded swiftly to form a stark contrast to the dark colour of the sea. He realised that, despite initial optimism, he would not have been able to 'ride it out'. Now, his warm, comfortable environment of just a few seconds ago had been shredded beyond recognition to begin a long, slow descent to the seabed.

Still in a state of shock, Jon hadn't been aware that while he was claiming solo flight time, XT861 had continued to pitch up while it barrelled over the formation. As it turned out, his timing had been fortunate: an earlier ejection would have increased the chances of his seat colliding with one of the other Phantoms. His ejection had coincided with XT861's final dive, the rate of descent causing him to lose about 600 feet during the ejection sequence. He'd spent the next few seconds shouting in wild despair even though he knew that no-one could hear him. This, however, had seemed to jolt him back to reality and now every other emotion was subjugated to an overwhelming instinct to survive.

Regular training rapidly took over as he checked that his parachute was fully deployed and that the rigging lines were untwisted. When he attempted to release his oxygen mask's quick-release toggle, however, Jon realised that it had been torn off and was hanging limply from the chain assembly. Then he noticed that his bone dome headset visor was spattered with blood. Looking down, he saw a stream of crimson drops falling to the water below. He decided, though, that there were other, more pressing, priorities; he'd worry about the blood later. With one hand, he felt for his lifejacket's operating toggle and tugged at it sharply. A reassuring hiss was accompanied by a yellow stole inflating around his neck and chest, although his head was thrust forward uncomfortably. Working down, he located two Martin-Baker quick release clips and a further clip that connected him to his personal survival pack. Mindful of past mistakes made by other aircrew, carefully he grasped his survival pack with one hand while operating a release clip with the other hand. Then he released the pack, relieved when its fall was arrested by a lanyard to settle about fifteen feet below him.

On completion of the immediate drills, Jon had a few moments to assess his situation. Suspended below a fully deployed parachute, he anticipated the descent to the sea would take about ninety seconds. It was during this time that the violence of the ejection began to give way to an eerie sense of serenity. In the far distance he could still see the other Phantoms, now as remote specks on the horizon, but he could no longer hear their engine noise. This had been replaced by the rhythmic creakings of his parachute harness and personal survival pack lanyard. Clear blue skies that reflected onto the sea's surface added to the backdrop of picture-perfect cumulus cloud creating a dissonant sense of inner well-being. Gradually, though, as the coastline of eastern Scotland disappeared below the western horizon, Jon began to feel rather lonely. For the first time, he became aware of pain. Remembering the blood that he'd seen earlier, he spat out the bloody saliva produced by his cut lip. He prodded his face gently to find the source of the steady blood stream into the sea. He discovered a gash on his chin which had been caused when his head was thrust onto the lifejacket breastplate during the ejection process. He noticed that both ankle pockets on his anti-G suit had been torn off. His right flying boot was torn. Before long, he found it harder to discern where XT861 had crashed: the circle of foam had suffused gradually to leave just a slick of oil. He became very concerned about the fate of his pilot; the restrictive neck stole of Jon's lifejacket meant that he could not see the other parachute that was, in fact, above and behind him. In a

series of random thoughts, Jon mentally rehearsed the telephone call that he would
have to make to his parents.

*   *   *

Meanwhile, as Jon descended in his parachute towards the sea, Black Four moved away
from the rest of the formation to head back to Leuchars. Simultaneously, Black One
and Black Five transmitted Mayday calls on their in-use frequency. The intensity of
radio calls, however, meant that Black Four had to switch to the emergency 'Guard'
frequency to transmit a Mayday call. Approaching the visual circuit at Leuchars, Black
Four carried out a slow-speed handling check which was monitored by another aircraft
before the damaged Phantom's pilot executed a successful landing and engagement of
the approach end runway cable.

Jon's ejection had taken place at about 0958 hours. Two minutes later, the off-going
helicopter search and rescue crew, members of B Flight 22 Squadron, were in the
handover process to the oncoming crew. When the telephone rang, the crews stopped
speaking. The telephone message stated that a Phantom was down approximately fifty-five miles east of the city of Dundee. Two parachutes had been seen. Without
hesitation, both crews ran to the two Westland Wessex helicopters at readiness outside.
Within minutes the pilots of the bright yellow helicopters took off in the mid-morning
sunshine to head towards the reported crash site.

*   *   *

Now very close to the water, Jon braced himself for a sea dip. He could hear the gentle
slap of waves below when, hastily, he felt for the serrated grip on the parachute harness
quick-release box. He rotated the grip through ninety degrees. Then, just as his personal
survival pack touched the water's surface, he thumped the quick-release box hard. This
was a mistake: as he entered the water with a great splash, he assumed, incorrectly, that
he'd separated from his parachute.

The shock of plunging into the sea caused him to inhale an involuntary, sharp intake
of breath as he dived below the surface. His lifejacket, though, brought him back up
rapidly where he experienced another overwhelming urge to survive. The water, he
reckoned, didn't seem especially cold (it was 13°C) which was fortunate for he was wearing
the basic summer aircrew kit rather than an uncomfortable immersion suit. He grabbed
the survival pack lanyard to pull the pack towards him and as he did so he was aware of
being dragged through the water: he was still attached to the parachute. He banged the
quick-release box again. Another mistake: the box was full of water and thumping the
device was likely to be even less successful than before. Recalling the correct drills, he

Westland Wessex, the renowned SAR helicopter.

placed his fingers behind the quick-release box and squeezed the top with both thumbs. At this, the parachute released and he was able to wriggle free from the harness. Now, as he retrieved the personal survival pack, he gave the operating handle a sharp pull. The pack, as advertised, began to inflate at once. Without waiting for full inflation, Jon flipped the dinghy the right way up, grabbed the boarding handles and started to haul himself aboard as, in a single deft movement, he rotated himself to a sitting position.

Over and over again Jon kept telling himself that having survived the collision and ejection, he wasn't going to die now. Short of breath, he'd been helped, no doubt, by the effect of adrenalin as, in a matter of seconds, he went through the procedures. Now, as he looked skywards, he was aware of a pair of Phantoms circling above. This was good news: the crews would radio his position to the rescue services. Glancing down again he noticed his parachute floating below the dinghy – a useful location aid, he thought, until he realised with dismay that the nose of the dinghy was sinking. The parachute rigging lines, entangled around his legs and still attached to the submerged parachute, were dragging the dinghy down. Withdrawing his aircrew knife from its scabbard, he slashed through the lines with a few strokes.

Safely in his dinghy, Jon proceeded with the rest of the survival drills. He hauled the personal survival pack on board and closed the canopy around him. He used the Velcro-lined sides to seal himself from the elements. He fired a couple of mini-flares: 'That'll tell my mates circling above that I'm okay,' he thought. Using the baling device, he started to work away to drain as much water as possible. He continued to worry about his pilot unaware that the pilot had boarded his own dinghy downwind of Jon's position.

The sea swell, greater than it appeared during the parachute descent, made Jon decide to search for the survival pack's supply of seasickness tablets. It was just as he'd found these tablets that he began to pick up a faint but unmistakeable sound wavering in the distance. Convinced that he could hear the thud of helicopter rotor blades, he burst open the dinghy's canopy to discover, heading straight towards him, what was surely one of the finest, most welcome, most beautiful sights in the whole wide world: a resplendent, yellow-painted Westland Wessex. Jon fired a mini-flare at once, then waited until the helicopter was about a mile away before he set off a smoke device to give the pilot an accurate wind check.

Soon, the distinct form of a helicopter crewman emerged from the cabin door and started to wave instructions to the winch operator. Jon's own arms flashed around as he struggled to unravel the survival pack lanyard from around his feet and as he tried to locate the Martin-Baker clip that still connected him to the dinghy. Gradually manoeuvring towards the dinghy, the helicopter's down-wash produced prodigious amounts of spray. The crewman dipped a static line into the water then started to cycle his legs as if walking on the surface. Now colliding with the dinghy, the crewman was accompanied by a surge of water as he thrust a 'grabbit' hook through Jon's lifejacket beckets. "Been in the wars, have we?" yelled the crewman above the racket of the helicopter. Jon, made aware of his condition, nonetheless realised that never before had he felt this delighted to be so close to a middle-aged flight sergeant crewman.

The flight sergeant slickly placed a strop around Jon, then signalled 'ready to lift' to the winch operator. During the ascent, the crewman cut away the remaining parachute rigging lines, undid a Martin-Baker clip and let the dinghy fall away, its job done. Spinning gently on the winch line as he ascended, Jon glanced up to see the helicopter pilot sitting high in the Wessex cockpit, smiling at him from under his moustache. 'That's George!' thought Jon as he recognised the ex-Army Air Corps pilot with whom he'd shared a couple of beers a few weeks ago. Jon held the search and rescue crews in high esteem, especially the way that they placed their own lives in jeopardy in order to save others. Within moments, as Jon was gently but firmly manhandled through the helicopter door and into the security of the cabin, he was made to lie down on a stretcher while a neck brace was applied. As the helicopter accelerated towards land, he learned with a great sense of relief that his pilot had been rescued by the other helicopter. The time was now around 1035; Jon and his pilot had been in their dinghies for about thirty minutes before rescue.

Jon was flown directly to Ninewells Hospital in Dundee where the local media took photographs when the helicopter had landed. Following profuse thanks to the helicopter crew, he was transferred to the accident and emergency department. Manoeuvred on a wheeled stretcher through a labyrinth of corridors, he was eventually pushed into a small waiting room. It was here that he was reunited with his pilot. The two shook hands and grinned, both equally relieved to see that the other was largely unhurt apart from identical chin gashes. Separated again, Jon was attended by a doctor who, clearly unfamiliar with treating an ejectee, struggled to wrestle off the flying kit until a nurse suggested a large pair of scissors. At length, with every piece of flying kit sliced away, a cold and shivering Jon was given a hospital smock to help preserve his dignity.

By now Jon found that every part of his body had started to ache. X-rays of his spine and right thigh were taken, and the gash on his chin was stitched up after which he was taken to a hospital ward and left to warm up. Before long, as he lay on the hospital bed, a familiar figure in the form of a squadron flight commander walked into the ward, grinned when he spotted Jon then used his nickname as he called out: "Hello Herbie! Good to see you. You look a sight!" At this, the flight commander left the ward to return shortly afterwards: "I've had a word with the doc. He says you're fine. We can go!" In no mood to stay a moment longer, Jon swung himself off the bed and, wearing no more than the hospital smock, walked out of the building. The time was 1350.

As Jon was driven back to Leuchars, he was briefed by the flight commander. Squadron flying had been cancelled for the rest of the day. After a quick visit to the officers' mess for a change of clothing, Jon would be taken to the squadron crewroom to say hello to his colleagues before a visit to the station medical centre for another check-up. At 1700 hours sharp, the officers' mess bar would open.

At the squadron crewroom, Jon was met with handshakes and (unwelcome) backslaps. Over a mug of tea, he recounted the morning's dramatic events and, reunited with Black Four's crew, he listened to details of the accident from their perspective. Apparently the left stabilator of Jon's Phantom had collided with the starboard underside of Black Four's nose cone. The stabilator then scraped along the forward fuselage into the right-hand engine intake ramp. When the two aircraft separated, Jon's Phantom pitched up violently. His pilot attempted corrective inputs but as these were unsuccessful the pilot ejected. At the time of his ejection the aircraft height was 2,000 feet. In view of the risk of collision with the pilot's canopy if the navigator ejected first, this action followed the standard operating procedures for the FG1 version of the Phantom which lacked a command ejection system.

When examined at the station medical centre, Jon's mid-thoracic backache was noted and he was told that, compared to the last periodic medical examination, he was now four centimetres shorter. This was perhaps mentioned when, later that evening in the officers' mess bar (for which the entire complement of his squadron turned up), Jon recounted his experiences to colleagues keenly interested in events. He did his best to appear nonchalant but the facial cuts and bruises must have told their own story. By about ten o'clock, suddenly overtaken by fatigue and not having eaten since breakfast, he decided that it was time to leave even though the bar was still packed. Just before he did so, one of his colleagues, a senior navigator on his squadron, sought him out to offer a word of advice. This man had survived a dramatic accident in an English Electric Canberra aircraft nine years earlier in 1978. "Before you go to sleep," he said, "write everything down." Another squadron navigator then walked Jon back to his room to make sure that he didn't have a further accident en route.

It was the end of a long day. Jon thanked his colleague and closed the door. He sat down at his desk and started to write.

*   *   *

The next morning, when staring at his face in the mirror, Jon slowly took in the swollen lips, the neatly stitched but heavily bruised chin, the black shadows of bruising under his eyes. Covering both shoulders and thighs he had symmetrical bruising patterns caused by the Phantom's seat harness. Bruising around his calves matched the position of the leg restraint garters. His head ached but that was caused in part, perhaps, by the morning-after-the-night-before syndrome. He decided to head for the mess dining room for breakfast, his first food in twenty-four hours.

After breakfast, Jon went to his squadron where he was told that a Board of Inquiry had been convened. The board members were on their way from headquarters and wished to speak with him that afternoon. So it was that, notebook in hand, Jon tried to recount as much detail as possible to the board president, a wing commander, and the board members. They smiled sympathetically as Jon spoke and at the session's conclusion, when he left the interview office, he thought to himself: 'There! That wasn't too bad.'

Following an early start the next day, Jon and his pilot were driven to Edinburgh Airport for a flight to London where, met by another service driver, they were taken to the RAF Hospital at Halton in Buckinghamshire. At the hospital, isotope injections were applied before bone scans were taken. After two or so hours, a senior non-commissioned officer came up to them: "You're both fine," he said, "except that…" he glanced at Jon, "…you have a couple of hot spots. Nothing to write home about, though, so you're clear to leave." As they left for the journey home, Jon and his pilot both thought that the proceedings had seemed remarkably low key. Meantime, Jon was wondering why his back hurt so much.

The next day, Thursday 10 September 1987, Jon had to give formal evidence to the Board of Inquiry. This seemed an altogether more sober affair and having sworn his oath before giving evidence, Jon noticed the stenographer responsible for recording verbatim every word spoken. He answered questions patiently, adding detail when he thought it would be helpful. He spoke about his difficulties with the parachute quick-release box, his problems with the rigging lines and he commented on the inadequacies of the survival pack's day/night flare arrangement. At the end of the session, as Jon rose to leave, the board president asked: "Who was briefed to maintain collision avoidance between your aircraft and Black Four?" Jon stared at the president for a moment then said: "I was, sir." "Thank you. That will be all."

As Jon closed the door behind him, he felt the weight of the world crash down on his shoulders. The accident had been his fault!

With a sense of gloom, Jon walked to the officers' mess, worry writ across his sad, bruised face. At the mess he collected a small parcel which had just arrived and as, impatiently, he opened the package his mood lifted slightly when he took out a dark blue tie emblazoned with small red triangles. The signatory to the covering letter congratulated Jon on his successful ejection and invited him to become a member of the exclusive Martin-Baker Caterpillar Club. Jon was amazed to learn that he was the 2,081st aviator to eject successfully from a Phantom using a Martin-Baker seat.

Events took a strange turn the following evening. Jon's bruising had begun to fade and he could speak without chewing his bottom lip. In the officers' mess, a few pints of beer helped to assuage the still-present aches. As tended to happen, a group of young officers ordered taxis for the drive to St Andrews and a visit to a local curry house. While tucking in to his main course, Jon noticed the manager take another telephone order, although this one turned out to be something other than an order for curry with poppadom and all the trimmings. The manager walked across to Jon's group: "The station duty officer from RAF Leuchars called," he said, "is there anyone here called Hancock?"

"Yes, me," said Jon.

"In that case, sir, you should lie down on the floor until the ambulance comes!"

'Sod that', thought Jon and carried on eating his curry. Presently, a couple of medics arrived and, having conceded defeat trying to weave a stretcher through the crowded restaurant, allowed Jon to walk to the ambulance then lie on the stretcher inside. He now learned that, following a medical reassessment of the fractures around his dorsi-lumbar region, he would be transferred back to the RAF Hospital at Halton.

A period of boredom and soul-searching followed as Jon was confined to a side ward at Halton Hospital for sixteen days of bed rest. No longer available was the support he'd received from his colleagues at Leuchars. As the days dragged by his sense of introspection became almost overwhelming. Visitors were few, stimulating conversation rare (the ward cleaner and the dinner lady didn't seem to want to say much) and the other patients in the orthopaedic ward were out of earshot. An unannounced psychiatric assessment took a cursory ten minutes after which Jon was declared fine. Discharged from Halton Hospital at the end of September 1987, he left with a downgraded medical category and three months off flying ejection-seat-equipped aircraft.

Back at Leuchars, Jon felt that he had some debts to repay. He bought supplies from the officers' mess then toured the station with cans of beer and bottles of wine to reward those, he reckoned, who deserved his gratitude – the helicopter crew, the safety equipment fitters, the young lady who had packed his parachute, the ejection seat specialists. A personal thanks, he felt, was the very least he could offer.

Meantime, he assisted the squadron adjutant with various duties and he self-studied to keep up the necessary thorough understanding of encyclopaedic manuals and classified weapons' supplements. He volunteered for frequent sessions in the Phantom flight

Phantom FG1s spelling out 111 Squadron formation, 1 August 1987.

simulator in order to maintain the high standard required of his radar handling skills, intercept techniques, emergency procedures. Just a few days before his ejection he had completed the demanding quick-reaction alert/phase 111 visual identification check, and he was conscious that, even during the short time that he'd been a member of the squadron, two navigators had failed to make the grade and consequently had been posted elsewhere. During his three months off flying, Jon was allowed to join the squadron for a five-week deployment to Cyprus, a period that worked wonders for his morale.

The three months passed quite quickly. Shortly before Christmas 1987 he returned to Halton Hospital and from there, still suffering from backache and stiffness of the lower spine, he was referred to the Defence Services Medical Rehabilitation Unit at RAF Headley Court in Surrey. Starting his treatment there in late January 1988, he underwent two weeks of intensive aerobic training, spinal education and occupational therapy classes, hydrotherapy sessions and circuit training. Describing his treatment as 'superb' he left Headley Court stronger and fitter than ever before, and almost ready to return to the cockpit.

At Leuchars, changes to the squadron had occurred, experienced aircrew had departed, new members had arrived including another commanding officer. The new boss took exceptional efforts to monitor Jon's recovery and to plan his return to flying. On 11 February 1988 Jon reported to Halton Hospital for the last time and he was signed off as fit to return to full flying duties. Four days later, having completed a pre-flight briefing, he donned his immersion suit, snapped on brand new leg restraint garters and walked out from squadron headquarters together with a United States Marine Corps exchange pilot. As the two of them walked towards their allocated aircraft, Phantom XT865 'Bravo Uniform', Jon caught the tang of sea air. He breathed in deeply. He cast an admiring glance at the menacing profile of their Phantom, its mean and purposeful look painted in air defence grey, the way that the 111 Squadron black and gold lightning flash reflected the morning sun. Within minutes, XT865 was blasting off from RAF Leuchars to head west into the low-flying system. It was 1000 hours on a bright Monday morning and he was back.

*   *   *

Soon after Jon's return to flying, the findings of the Board of Inquiry were published. These concluded formally, if predictably, that the accident occurred because the two pilots flew their Phantoms in close formation with neither monitoring the other's aircraft. The board members also stated that they were of the opinion that, given the responsibilities briefed before take-off, a collision was almost inevitable. To his disappointment, Jon received some minor criticism for his actions when struggling with the quick-release box of his parachute harness, and it was noted that he'd been wearing non-approved flying gloves. When his CO showed him the report's critical paragraphs, Jon felt that he'd been given gentle admonishment but that it would not be held against him in the future.

Looking back, Jon had no doubt that the events of 7 September 1987 had made a deep and lasting impression on his life. At the time young and fairly resilient, the accident occurred within the first 180 hours of a fast-jet career that eventually amassed over 3,200 air defence flying hours. Outwardly he seemed to bounce back fairly quickly and he was never diagnosed with post-traumatic stress disorder. Within himself, however, he realised in subsequent years that he may have exhibited some of the traits of that disorder. Never again did he enjoy close formation flying in a Phantom, although this changed when he converted to the Panavia Tornado F3. For a long time the day's events remained close to the front of his mind. The memories did not fade. Over the years he would retreat from a crowded situation on the seventh day of September for moments of quiet reflection. He would give thanks for another year of life lived. To this day, a loud 'crack' or the smell of spent fireworks on a November evening will take him back to the moment of ejection.

In re-calibrating life's priorities, issues that once were pressing no longer seemed so urgent to Jon. In just four seconds his youthful naivety had disappeared. He became acutely aware of his own mortality, a consciousness heightened when, in the sixteen months after his own case, five colleagues were lost in accidents when flying Leuchars-based Phantoms. As an aviator he became more likely to challenge supervisory aspects of a sortie. As a person, ambition became less significant. He learned the need to make the most of the here and now, the immediate time and place. And that notion, even if acquired in a mere four seconds, should surely count as one of life's valuable lessons.

CHAPTER 16

GOLDEN SILENCE

PHIL OWEN RECOLLECTS A TROUBLESOME FLIGHT

At the hour of six in the morning the airfield at RAF Coningsby was shrouded in grey. Dawn was coming but was slow and pale. Squadron Leader Philip Owen, a member of staff at the Phantom Operational Conversion Unit, had an early flight scheduled. As a flying instructor he was used to concocting practice emergency situations designed to challenge his students, but soon he would need all of his skills in a real-life emergency.

As he walked towards the engineering line hut on that morning in March 1981 he spotted Phantom FGR2 XT910 parked nearby. This was the aircraft he had been detailed to fly: following a major servicing, an air test was required.

After signing the technical log, Phil left the line hut to pace briskly towards XT910 where his navigator for the flight, Flight Lieutenant Mike Pugh, was strapping in to the rear cockpit. Phil glanced up at the sky. The weatherman's forecast of cloud between 2,000 and 5,000 feet should present no problems, he thought, although the planned flight-test profile might be affected by the crosswind factor – twenty-five knots across the Coningsby runway. While manageable under normal circumstances, he was not to know, of course, that events on that day were about to prove far from normal.

As he continued to walk towards XT910, Phil noticed that other Phantoms were being towed to the line from nearby hangars. Over a dozen years had elapsed since the first Phantom's arrival at Coningsby, and since that time, he mused, the air base had become the United Kingdom's fount of Phantom-ly wisdom. For such a complex aircraft with many thousands built in the United States of America, perhaps it was inevitable that numerous variants would emerge, including the British Phantoms. The engines for the latter, he knew, had been a particular issue for, by installing the Rolls-Royce Spey turbofan instead of the American General Electric J79 turbojet, the engine air intakes and the rear fuselage had been modified. Although the Spey-engined version had a number of advantages, including a shorter take-off distance and a faster climb, he knew that, with increased drag caused by the fuselage modifications,

performance was reduced at higher altitudes. "Morning, sir," said the ground crewman cheerily when Phil walked up to XT910.

"Morning," said Phil. As he commenced his external walk-around checks, he had a
sense of admiration for the purposeful, potent aura exuded by the Phantom. Dubbed
'double ugly' by some, this was unjustified in his opinion, although with dihedral on
the wings' outer section and anhedral on the tailplane's stabilators, the aircraft could,
he had to concede, look a bit peculiar. The appeal of the aircraft's outline was inclined,
apparently, to 'grow on one' as if affected by a sort of aeronautical fungus. The control
surfaces on the wings were unconventional, too, with an up-going spoiler co-ordinated
with a down-going aileron on the opposite wing. Then there was the boundary layer
control system. This blew high pressure air over the upper surfaces of the wings when
the flaps were down, but if the system was faulty all hell was let loose. The flight reference cards mentioned a long list of potential indications including possible fumes in
the cockpit and/or control stick transients and/or mild thumps and bangs and/or
hydraulic failure and/or generator failure and/or fire warnings and/or stiff throttles
and/or popping this, flashing that – the list was really quite amazing.

"Slight problem with the ground crew intercom system, this morning, sir," interjected
the ground crewman, "we'll have to use hand signals."

By now at the starboard side of XT910, Phil stooped low to check the condition of
the tyres and the undercarriage assembly. The main wheels relied on a single tyre, unlike
the nose wheel's double-tyre arrangement. Phil recalled how the nose-wheel assembly
in another Phantom had been the centre of attention recently when the steering system,
operated by a small switch on the pilot's control stick, had caused problems. It was just
the month before last when the aircraft in question had left the runway during take-off
as a result of which the navigator ejected although the pilot chose to continue his take-
off run – which consequently qualified as the first ever soft ground take-off in a Phantom.
The machine's stabilators had carved gouges along the airfield grass, proof indeed of
the narrowness of the pilot's escape.

Continuing his walk-around inspection, at the aircraft's rear Phil carefully checked
the condition of the jet pipe area and the tail-hook. The latter device, unlike the dainty
tail-hook fitted to the likes of the English Electric Lightning, was exceptionally rugged
in order to cope with aircraft carrier operations. Between them, the carrier's cable
set-up and the Phantom's tail-hook had to retard a twenty-or-so-ton machine from an
airspeed of some 145 knots to zero in a distance of about 150 feet. At this stage, little
did he realise the significant part the tail-hook would play in his forthcoming flight.

Soon, on completion of his inspection of the Phantom's rear section, Phil moved
down the port side to conclude his checks before climbing the access steps to the cockpit.
Pausing at the top step he ensured that the Martin-Baker ejection seat was safe after

which, as he ensconced himself in the cockpit, he felt for the personal equipment connector (PEC) to one side of the seat. With the PEC connected he could speak with his navigator: "Hear me okay, Mike?"

"Loud and clear."

"Happy with the air test paperwork?"

"Ecstatic!"

"Let's get going then."

Quite quickly, with his cockpit checks complete, Phil signalled for 'engine start' to the ground crewman. With the return signal, Phil reached for a switch to initiate the left engine's start sequence. He listened for the whir of an electric motor designed to spin-up the gas turbine starter and he watched the movement of the engine revolutions gauge. At a reading of eight per cent, he selected the left engine throttle to the idle position. By this point the distinctive howl of a Rolls-Royce Spey engine began to fill the air. Before long, with the process repeated for the other engine, he waved to the ground crewman to remove the wheel chocks after which, with clearance from air traffic control, he was swiftly underway.

While Phil taxied the Phantom, the airfield, he thought, had a deserted look with open expanses of grass interrupted by occasional marker boards, specialist lighting, wind socks and various electronic paraphernalia. To the north, beyond the airfield boundary, was the village of Coningsby screened by trees and hedging. When he passed the air traffic control tower, the duty controller gave a friendly wave. "Ready when you are for the pre-take-offs, Mike," Phil said to his navigator, an instructor on the ground school staff of the operational conversion unit. Mike now read out the pre-take-off checks on a 'challenge-and-response' basis, an established technique which the two men would use regularly during the air test.

Soon, when cleared by the controller, Phil taxied XT910 onto the runway where he applied the aircraft brakes before he began to ease the Phantom's twin throttles forward. Prompted by Mike, at various throttle settings he called out engine instrument readings to be noted on the air-test schedule. Eventually, when Mike said: "That's all the figures I need at this stage," Phil selected eighty per cent engine revolutions on both of the Rolls-Royce Speys. He had a final check of necessary parameters, then he released the Phantom's brakes.

As the aircraft accelerated, Phil called out further figures all of which were normal. When airborne, Phil turned the Phantom to follow local climb-out procedures. He called more facts and figures for Mike to note, but the rate of climb and other details continued to meet required standards. Below, the flat, featureless countryside was dotted with towns and villages set among the Lincolnshire fens. Ahead, the equally flat and featureless coastline between the seaside resorts of Mablethorpe and Skegness was marked by long, tempting stretches of sandy beach, exasperatingly unusable apart from the hardiest of souls.

Before long, when he flew high above the North Sea, Phil levelled the Phantom at the prescribed altitude to carry out more tests. This air test, he thought, was going well. However, towards the sortie's end something unusual happened – the first hint of the troubles ahead. He'd checked with Mike that the schedule had been fully covered, then said: "Thanks, Mike, I'll call for recovery to Coningsby if there's nothing else?"

"Nope, that's it. All done. Let's go home."

Phil then pressed the Phantom's radio transmit button to speak with the controller. The controller, though, failed to respond. Phil had another attempt, but still nothing happened. He stared at the radio box. He moved his hand to the selector, tried a different frequency, fiddled with this, pushed that, turned the other as one does, but all to no avail. "Looks like we've had a main radio failure," he said to Mike eventually. "Wait one...I'll try the standby radio." The standby radio, however, proved to be equally defunct. "That's weird," he muttered to his navigator.

"What's weird?"

"I can't get the standby radio to work either."

"That is weird."

"I'll squawk 7600." This was a special 'radio failure' code which, when set on the aircraft's identification friend or foe (IFF) system, was recognised by the ground controller. Phil now began to follow the stipulated procedure for radio failure, a routine he knew well after regular rehearsals with his students. With Mike's aid, he navigated to a position twenty miles on the active runway's extended centreline, 'Point Foxtrot', from where he could pick up a signal from the airfield's instrument landing system (ILS). This would guide him to the runway touchdown point. However, with the Phantom by then flying in cloud, Phil had to trust that his 7600 code had been identified. There were no guarantees, though, which gave him an uneasy, almost eerie, sensation; with two defective radios, perhaps a common fault could have affected the IFF too; maybe other air traffic in the area, unaware of his plight, had not been warned by the controller.

Trying to ignore his qualms, Phil's eyes focused on the Phantom's ILS indicator. Intensely absorbed, he followed the two bars within the indicator, a vertical bar to show if the aircraft was left or right of the runway's extended centreline, a horizontal bar to indicate above or below the ideal glide-path. But with the benefit of four tours, including two on Lightning squadrons, and with considerable experience as an instructor, his skill as a pilot meant that when, suddenly, the Phantom broke through cloud at a range of ten miles from Coningsby, the aircraft was ideally positioned. The next part of the radio failure procedure, to approach the airfield visually then fly past the air traffic control tower at a height of 500 feet, should have been straightforward. Indeed it was until, having flown past the tower while 'waggling' his wings energetically, Phil turned downwind. It was then, as he rolled out and as he attempted to lower the undercarriage, that an ominous light illuminated on the Phantom's warning panel: 'Utilities Hydraulic Failure'.

On top of existing difficulties, this was not good news. The scenario was not dissimilar to one devised by the two instructors regularly, if not a little gleefully, for their hapless students, although the real-life situation was fraught with real-life hazards. The hydraulics problem meant that a landing at Coningsby should not be attempted because of the crosswind factor, but Phil was in no position to communicate this to the controller. And if he was to divert to another airfield, which one should he select? Moreover, how should he let them know?

Phil decided to climb the Phantom to an altitude of 1,500 feet and to fly an orbital pattern above Coningsby airfield. Mike, meantime, paged through the reference cards which listed procedures for Phantom emergencies. He read out the required drills for emergency operation of the aircraft undercarriage and flaps, and he reminded his pilot to anticipate loss of almost all directional control as well as braking ability on landing. This meant use of the tail-hook.

Fortunately, the emergency procedures for lowering the undercarriage and flaps duly worked and the two men could concentrate on the question of where to land. "Waddington is today's nominated diversion," said Phil, "they have an approach end cable and their runway is more or less into wind. First, we have to think of a way to tell air traffic control what's going on."

The solution conceived by the two of them was simple but effective. Descending from 1,500 feet, Phil flew a wide circuit at 500 feet and lowered his landing hook as he flew past the tower. The controller, luckily, worked out what was happening and rang his colleagues at Waddington to alert them. Phil, meanwhile, climbed to a height of 1,000 feet and turned towards Waddington before he followed the line of the River Witham towards Lincoln; RAF Waddington was some ten miles due north of the city. It was during this transit that the flight's next problem arose – the Phantom was low on fuel. Normally, to ensure priority, he'd declare an emergency but this was not an option without a radio; Phil knew that, as they say, he'd have to take his chances.

Before long, Phil turned the Phantom onto a more northerly heading to avoid overflying the city of Lincoln. As the characteristic towers of Lincoln Cathedral loomed, Phil recalled that the building was renowned, among other reasons, as a distinctive aid to navigation for aircraft, including bomber crews returning from raids over Germany in World War Two. He was aware that RAF Waddington in particular typified the strong links between Bomber Command and the county of Lincolnshire, nicknamed 'Bomber County'. He knew that Waddington was currently home to squadrons operating the Avro Vulcan bomber, and he was conscious, too, that the air base held equipment needed to lay a carpet of foam for emergency use by aircraft committed to a wheels-up landing. Fingers firmly crossed, thought Phil, that we'll not need this facility today, although the way things were going...

"I'm visual with Waddington ahead, Mike," said Phil.

"Okay. Good luck!"

Phil now flew the Phantom at a height of 500 feet and, in view of the aircraft's handling constraints without hydraulics, he held a higher airspeed than normal when he joined the airfield circuit at Waddington. The tail-hook remained down as he flew past the air traffic control tower and he 'waggled' the Phantom's wings before turning downwind to execute, at this Bomber Command-type base, a wide, Bomber Command-type circuit with a slack 'finals' turn. Suddenly the controller in the runway caravan fired a green Verey flare – a 'clearance to land' signal. Tension now rose as Phil aimed for the touchdown point. He noticed a group of individuals gathered to one side of the cable. Perhaps they were technical observers or maybe they were there out of morbid curiosity. Whatever the reason, his focus was on a judicious approach...*hold that airspeed...check your height, Phil...not too low...aim for that precise spot...avoid a rough landing...the tail-hook mustn't bounce over the cable...the cable's clearly visible now...we're crossing the threshold...mind the airspeed...don't let the heading wander...watch out!...THUMP...*

A heavy pause followed the landing; a slight instant of uncertainty as the twenty-ton machine persisted to thunder ahead at some 150 knots. Within moments, however, doubts were dismissed, heartbeats calmed as the Phantom was brought swiftly and certainly under control. 'It's done the trick!' thought Phil. The tail-hook, as it caught

111 Squadron line-up.

the cable, stretched the device to its limits. But the system had worked; they were safe; the machine was still in one piece; it was all over bar the paperwork.

Now, aided by firemen, Phil and Mike extracted themselves from the cockpits of XT910 to be met by a senior engineering officer. "Well, well," he said, "welcome to Waddington!"

"Delighted to be here."

"Phantoms are not exactly within my remit, but an engineering team from Coningsby is on the way. We'll get this thing towed to the visiting aircraft hangar and your guys can work on it there. You may have a long wait, though. I suspect it will take a while to fix – I'm not too sure when you'll be able to fly back to Coningsby."

With these words Phil watched his navigator's eyes widen. Both men had been so engrossed that they'd not had time to think this far ahead. Now, however, they realised that the day had only just begun.

CHAPTER 17

YANKEE PHANTOM FLYER ON THREE CONTINENTS

RG HEAD

This chapter is the story of an American combat fighter pilot who instructed in F-4s, became an air campaign planner, political science professor and military scholar.

Background

All I ever wanted to do was fly! Growing up in Iowa, the army was far away, the sea coasts out of sight, but the sky covered everything. I built model airplanes – lots of them – and four dozen or so flew from my bedroom ceiling. The Supermarine Spitfire was my favourite airplane, and I built a flying model in my basement hobby shop. I even wrote to Supermarine and sent them a picture of the model; I was astounded when the return mail included a beautiful book on the development and combat history of this famous aircraft. But my primary activity was wishing for an airplane ride as I blew out the candles of every birthday cake from age five to fifteen. My biggest regret was that I was born too late to fly in the Battle of Britain. I devoured books on World War One and Two aviation and haunted our local model airplane shop on Saturdays. When I was fifteen, my father invited a company colleague, Chuck Sweeney, who had flown in World War Two, and we drove to the Davenport airport, 80 miles away. There Chuck gave me my first two flight lessons that started a lifelong career in aviation. That summer, I was fortunate to get a job at our local airport – pumping gasoline, sweeping the hangar and cleaning airplanes. I was paid $1 an hour if I wanted it in cash, but $2 if I took it out in flying time. The Aeronca Champion aircraft cost $8 per hour, and the instructor was $2.50. The aircraft was so primitive, the gasoline tank indicator was a wire stuck on top of a cork.

I soloed just after my seventeenth birthday, on a cold January morning wearing my gift of a World War Two wool flying suit, and boy, was I proud. A private pilot's licence followed after about forty hours, and from then on I was free to fly whenever

I wanted. I even took my little brother, age 13, in the back seat, and we flew to a 'Fly-in Pancake Breakfast' in Illinois. That fall, with Jim and me in the front seats, we flew our mom and dad to our grandparents, landing on a grass strip near Kansas City. I'm sure my mother was terrified all the way. In 11th Grade, I applied for admission to the US Air Force Academy. My dad introduced me to a prominent businessman in town, and he got me an interview with our Iowa senator. In 12th Grade, I wrote an article about flying with the British in North Africa, fighting Rommel's Afrika Corps. Low and behold, I was appointed by both senators to the Class of 1960, only the second class to enter the air force academy. By then I had 200 hours flying time and knew I could fly if I could get through the academics.

My introduction to worldwide aviation was the air force academy's junior-summer field trip to France, Germany and Britain. We visited the RAF College Cranwell and had our introduction to formal dinners, wine-soaked rolls and brawny games in the vestibule. The US Congress had not yet appropriated money for pilot training at the academy, so we flew in the Convair T-29 trainer and graduated with navigators' wings. I did all I could to fly and spent endless hours on gliders and sailplanes in those four years. Pilot training followed. Primary pilot training was at Bartow Air Base, Florida, where we flew the T-34 and got about fifty hours in the T-37 jet. Basic pilot training was at Williams AFB, Arizona. We were the last class to fly the T-33 jet, so we got over 300 hours in nine months. I was fortunate to finish first in my class, following which I selected fighters and entered advanced training for the F-100 Super Sabre across Phoenix at Luke AFB. That was the thrill of my life, flying the F-100C model with no flaps and a landing speed of 180 knots – the world's fastest tricycle!

We had all been warned about the dangers of a 'hot cockpit' where the engine would send flaming hot air into the pilot compartment; well, one day I had a 'cold cockpit'. We were on a formation training mission, and the air conditioning system went full COLD. It was throwing snowballs into the cockpit, and I thought I would freeze to death before I got to land and open the canopy. Another memorable flight was a solo with a clean airplane (no external fuel tanks). I was all by myself and wanted to see how high the F-100 would go. I slowly got it up to 57,000 feet, looked out and saw the curvature of the earth and the black of outer space. Down below, I could see the entire Gulf of California spanning south into Mexico. What a remarkable view!

Air-to-air firing on the dart aerial target and air refuelling followed at Nellis AFB, Nevada, where I was awarded the Top Gun prize. My first operational unit was the 31st Tactical Fighter Wing at Homestead AFB, Florida, just in time for the Cuban Missile Crisis in 1962. Homestead was a Strategic Air Command (SAC) base with B-47s. One day we were in the officers' club, and the SAC crews who were on alert came in for coffee. They were all wearing flight jackets with crew positions emblazed on the back: one said 'navigator'; 'co-pilot/radio operators' and one 'aircraft commander'.

Pretty cheesy we thought. So the next night one of our intrepid single-seat fighter pilots came into the club with his own version of a crew jacket. It announced in big letters: 'pilot', 'co-pilot', 'navigator', 'gunner' and 'radio operator'.

After the crisis abated, we continued training in air-to-air and air-to-ground (including nuclear) weapons delivery. The night before my qualification check ride, I walked through a plate glass window at our rented house. My right wrist was cut deeply, and the tendon was severed. The hand went to the full-down position. My roommates rushed me to the base hospital where the flight surgeon on duty sewed the tendon together. That cut healed in four weeks, and the tendon has held together for over fifty years.

I passed my check ride and became combat ready. My favourite event was air-to-air refuelling behind a KC-135 tanker. Then the 306th Tactical Fighter Squadron (TFS) flew to Itazuke AB in Japan, from whence we deployed forward to Korea to stand alert. Six months later, in the 308th TFS we deployed to Izmir, Turkey, flying and standing nuclear alert. At Homestead, I met another pilot from Iowa, Dick Kuiper, with whom I was to have four follow-on assignments.

In October 1964, the air force needed an aide-de-camp in Vietnam, so after some soul-searching, I volunteered and entered A-1 Skyraider training. That was probably the best thing I ever did as I was one of only two fighter pilots in our class that was filled with refugees from B-52 bombers and C-124 and C-47 cargo planes. Now, I occasionally tell young pilots, "if you are going to go to a war, it is best to go early; the enemy has not had much time to increase his defences". That was true both in South and North Vietnam, as the intensity of anti-aircraft fire increased dramatically over the years.

Vietnam
I reported to Bien Hoa air base in January 1965, when there were only 17,000 Americans in the country. That made me recall Shakespeare's words he put in the mouth of Henry V at Agincourt, "If we are mark'd to die, we are enow to do our country loss; and if to live, the fewer men, the greater share of honour . . . ."

Mine was the 602nd Fighter Squadron, flying the venerable A-1E, the two-seat version of the Skyraider, nicknamed the SPAD from World War One fame. Eager to check out, I remember I flew 100 missions in the first ninety days so I could go on rest and recuperation to British Hong Kong. Despite my youth, the wing offered me a job in standardization and evaluation, but I refused. I do not believe in having Stan/Eval in a combat zone; combat itself is the only evaluator. Besides, I wanted to stay in the squadron.

We flew with Vietnamese markings on the aircraft, taught young Vietnamese to fly and dive bomb, but in February 1965 when the Viet Cong (VC) ransacked the American barracks at Pleiku, President Johnson took off the Vietnamese markings and we flew combat as Americans. Summer came and we flew frequently defending Special Forces camps from attack by the VC. Night dive-bombing and strafing was our specialty. In

July, my flight deployed to Udorn in northern Thailand. From there we flew missions over North Vietnam, hunting for downed American pilots, using the call sign 'Sandy'. I'll never forget, one day I flew two five-hour missions over the Black River.

One of my memorable flights resulted in a crash-landing. I had taken off from our forward operating base hundreds of miles north of Bien Hoa at Qui Nhon. My right landing gear had broken and would not retract. I knew if I went back to Qui Nhon the belly landing would tear up the pierced steel planking of the runway, so I dropped my ordnance in the sea and headed down to Bien Hoa, where the runway was concrete. After repeated 'bounces' on the hard runway, the gear still swayed on its mount. The only alternative was to try to get the gear to lock in the 'up' position and belly it in. The airfield officers told the fire department to foam the runway and hoist the approach-end barrier. I pushed the nose over, hard, and the gear locked up. Then I brought the plane in, touching down near the end of the runway, short of the foam. Fire and sparks flew up from the propeller hitting the runway, but as soon as the craft slid into the foam, the fire was extinguished. Still afraid the high octane gasoline would ignite, I shut off the fuel, leapt out of the cockpit and ran off the side of the runway. Unknown to me, USAF photographers had been taking movies of the F-5 'Skoshi Tiger' aircraft landing that day, and I had run right toward one of the cameras. But I was safe, and that was all I cared about. The maintenance crews lifted the aircraft with a huge crane, changed the propeller, and the plane flew the next day.

In November 1965, the war really heated up. The North Vietnamese invaded from Laos and were massing attacks against American units including the First Air Cavalry Division (Airmobile) where my colleague, Dick Kuiper, was a forward air controller/air liaison officer. Being scrambled off ground alert, I led several flights to the Ia Drang Valley, where we conducted close air support. Dick directed one of these missions and says I hold the record for closeness – shooting a sniper out of a tree twenty yards in front of American troops. That battle was made famous by the book and movie, *We were Soldiers Once, and Young.* Finally, in early January 1966, with 325 combat missions under my belt, I left my Australian bush hat on my bedpost and departed for my next assignment, F-4 Phantoms.

En route I was directed on a public relations tour of New York City, where the movie of the crash landing was shown on *The Ed Sullivan Show,* and I was introduced from the audience. Then there was a press conference in the Pentagon, where I was asked about the effectiveness of the A-1 propeller plane as compared to the F-100 and F-4 jets that were then being deployed there. I made the very un-politically correct statement that the A-1 was the perfect airplane for that war because being slow, it had a long loiter time and uncanny accuracy. At that point, a general actually stepped in front of me, took the microphone, and said, "What the captain actually meant to say was that the jets are better but we don't have enough of them!"

Flight of F-4E Phantoms, similar to those crossing the Atlantic, refuelling with a KC-135 en route to Germany. (RG Head)

Instructing in Phantoms

I reported in to the 4453rd Combat Crew Training Wing at Davis Monthan Air Force Base, Tucson, Arizona, in March 1966 and checked out immediately as an instructor. I was very impressed with the power of the Phantom's twin engines. I learned to fly and land from both front and back seats – the latter being a chore I would not wish on my worst enemy as the visibility on final approach is through a small doughnut hole on the left side of the front Martin-Baker ejection seat. That seat is also the hardest of any aircraft I have ever flown.

Tucson was great. We flew almost every day in the bright Southwest sunshine, teaching air-to-air tactics and air-to-ground bombing at the huge Goldwater Gunnery Range. Despite the massive size of the Phantom, it was a fast and powerful aircraft. It was a heady experience to be such a young instructor, and one of the few with combat experience. The F-4 had so much power in its two J-79 engines that I could fly a ground-controlled approach on the glide slope by only moving the throttles one per cent. A highlight of the assignment was to ferry six brand-new, F-4 Phantoms from the depot in Georgia to Spangdahlem Air Base in Germany. One day Colonel Chappy James, the vice wing commander, got all the instructors in a lecture room and gave us a rousing speech to all "volunteer for Vietnam". My colleague, Dick Kuiper, and I were perhaps the only two that didn't stampede into volunteering – we had already been there.

A year later, both Dick and I were assigned to teach in the Political Science department at the air force academy. Dick already had his master's degree, so he went directly there. En route to the academy I had to attend graduate school to obtain a master's degree.

The Origin of the F-4E with the Gun

The department sent me to Syracuse University in Syracuse, New York. There I studied for a master's in public administration and was selected for the doctoral program. I chose to research and write a dissertation on the air force's selection of the A-7 Corsair II as a close air support airplane. In that process I learned that the A-7 program selection had gotten wrapped up with the ongoing Phantom acquisition because the air force wanted nothing more than a gun in the F-4.

Some background is appropriate at this point. The navy had selected the Phantom II as its fighter interceptor in the 1950s. The primary mission of an interceptor is to locate, identify and destroy incoming targets, largely non-manoeuvring bombers. Although the machine gun had been the first true air-to-air weapon, and it had been widely used in World Wars One, Two and Korea, by the 1950s airborne radar and aerial missiles had advanced to the point where the experts thought that in future wars a gun would not be needed on interceptors. Missiles would kill all the targets at long distance ('beyond visual range'), and close-in manoeuvring in traditional gun fights would be a thing of the past. Wrong! What the 'experts' had neglected was the real-world requirement placed on the aircrews by political authorities (the 'rules of engagement') for pilots to visually identify the enemy aircraft as hostile before shooting. The second factor, borne out by combat experience in Vietnam, was the high failure rate of missiles. The air force and navy were both flying Phantoms over North Vietnam, and the radar missile – the Sparrow – was especially prone to not fire, not guide, or otherwise malfunction in the heat of combat. Thus, the air staff was adamant that the air force's top priority was to install a gun in the F-4 before any other acquisition program could divert the funds necessary to make this expensive modification.

At this time in 1965, the Systems Analysis staff of Secretary McNamara's Office of the Secretary of Defense (OSD) wanted the air force to buy the lower cost, Navy A-7 Corsair II for the close air support mission. Pressure for this was also coming from Congress. However, the proposed A-7 program ran straight into the air force requirements for a completely new air superiority airplane and to install a gun in the F-4. The result was the development of two cost-effectiveness studies: the 1964 Bohn Study and the 1965 Fish Study that war-gamed a European war in great detail. The 1965 study was titled, 'The Joint Air Force/OSD FX Effort'. The flavour of the study was later described by Russell Murray, the OSD Systems Analysis representative:

> "The activity that I can remember best is sitting in Harold Brown's [Secretary of the Air Force] conference room, day after day, having these meetings with

generals and DDR&E [Defense Director of Research & Engineering]. We would have these great discussions. Then the air force computer model was just going like mad; it was grinding out pages of data. They built this gigantic model which simulated a whole air war....

"There was a lot of this (discussion) going on, and I didn't feel we were getting to any particular conclusion. Naturally Systems Analysis was pushing for an A-7 or an airplane like that. By pushing I mean we were there to see that it at least got a fair shake. The calculations were not done by us; they were done by the air force. I spent some time running through these pages and pages of data, and I can still recall a couple of things that came out of this war. We had a situation where the F-4 was just shooting down everything in sight. It was wonderful what the F-4 could do."[1]

There were three decisions based on the computer study and the discussions with the Chief of Staff and the Secretary of the Air Force:

1. Immediately begin development of a new air superiority fighter, the F-X (later to be called the F-15 Eagle);

2. Put a larger engine and a gun in the F-4 Phantom; and

3. Purchase 387 A-7 aircraft for close air support.

Secretary McNamara in November 1965 denied the request to begin the F-X program, denied the additions to the F-4 program, and *increased* the buy of the A-7. Eight months later, in July 1966, he approved adding the internal cannon for the Phantom, which became the F-4E. The proposal for the F-X program was never approved by the McNamara administration, but the F-15 program was awarded to McDonnell Douglas in 1969. Fortunately for me, I had already flown the F-4C and would shortly fly the F-4D and E versions.

Meanwhile, Dick taught one of the most popular cadet courses in Political Science, Insurgency Warfare, and built the class up from eighteen to over 200 enrolments. I taught and co-edited a textbook, *American Defense Policy,* and we had the opportunity to produce a week-long stage act for instructors in reserve officer training course colleges how to teach the text. Colorado was wonderful. My kids, cadets and I built a Swiss chalet cabin high up in the mountains near the Breckenridge ski resort and taught all four kids to ski. After two years of teaching, I volunteered again for overseas and got orders for Udorn Royal Thai Air Base, Thailand, in 1973. Back to Phantoms.

---

1. RG Head, 'Doctrinal Innovation and the A-7 Attack Aircraft Decisions' in *American Defense Policy, 3rd ed.,* (The Johns Hopkins University Press: Baltimore, 1973) p. 439.

Thailand and the Greatest Squadron

Udorn air base was the home of the 432nd Tactical Reconnaissance Wing, which had just completed participating in the famous 'Christmas Bombing' of North Vietnam in 1972 that finally brought the North Vietnamese to the negotiating table in Geneva, leading to a peace accord signed on 27 January 1973. The wing had five squadrons: four fighter and one reconnaissance, all flying Phantoms. Unfortunately, about twenty-one new lieutenant colonels arrived when I did, and there was considerable competition for billets in one of the flying squadrons. Before that could be decided, the 1973 Middle East Yom Kippur War broke out in October, and our jet fuel line from the Middle East was interrupted. We did not turn a wheel for about four weeks. With my previous experience over the Black River flying 'Sandys', I applied for and was granted membership of the Red River Valley Fighter Pilots' Association – the 'River Rats'. With my political science background, I put together a talk on the political/military situation in the Middle East and its effect on our operations in Thailand. With the sponsorship of the vice commander, I must have given that pitch a half dozen times to men of the 432nd Wing.

With the peace accord, JP-4 fuel began to flow again, and we resumed flying. I was assigned as the operations officer of the 421st Tactical Fighter Squadron, the 'Black Widows', under the command of Charlie Gulley, one of my colleagues from A-1 days. I was elated, and the first thing the pilots did was to take me down to the Indian tailor for a fitting of my 'party suit'. While we who had been flying in South Vietnam were condemned to wearing our 'goat skin' flame-retardant flight suit or other regulation uniform, these guys in Thailand had invented the 'party suit', which was a squadron-unique, light-weight, short sleeved, one-piece cotton outfit with rank, squadron insignia and aircrew wings sewn onto the fabric. Ours in the 421st was black, head-to-toe with a Chinese-red collar insert and red facing in the split-from-the-knee legs. I tell you; we felt HOT! And we looked hot.

That was the best squadron I have ever been in. It was interesting to me, having been raised a single-seat fighter pilot in F-100s, where *everyone* had been a fighter pilot forever, some from World War Two. The pilots' primary off-duty entertainment was drinking and playing poker or a gambling dice game called '4-5-6'. In 1973 the squadron pilots were mostly from Air Training Command where they had been instructors teaching new students to fly. They were a different group than I had previously experienced, smoother, more mature, less rambunctious and easier to lead. And they were very good pilots. Our basic mission was air-to-air, and the checkout of pilots new to the theatre required flying night 'fighting wing' just as the wing had done during the 'Christmas Bombing' of North Vietnam. Fortunately, by that time the air force had installed 'tape lights' on the Phantom. Tape lights are LED (light-emitting diode) strips about three-feet long, mounted on the wingtips, tail and fuselage of the aircraft. They are adjustable in intensity and made flying formation much easier. Flying close formation in the F-100 or A-1 at night was a real challenge because the pinpoint light bulbs on the wingtip and fuselage were devoid of any pitch reference. The tapes provided an orientation of the aircraft, and you could see when the leader was changing the attitude of the aircraft.

The political concern in late 1973 was that the North Vietnamese might violate the peace treaty and try to reinstate military operations, so we stood air defence alert 24/7 with missile-loaded Phantoms. With live ordnance there is always the danger of ignition, and one night we were awakened to the sound of an air-to-air missile firing off one of the ground alert aircraft. The missile had ignited by static electricity and impacted the side of another F-4 parked across the ramp. Luckily, no one was hurt.

The squadron was fortunate because we were one of the early units to get the F-4E Phantom with the Gatling gun in the nose. I had the opportunity to fly the airplane and use the gun that had been one of the major elements of my dissertation three years earlier.

The squadrons had a mission that was the most effective I have ever participated in. A ground control intercept (GCI) radar station was co-located with the wing at Udorn, and we had aerial tanker support from KC-135s based at Utapao, south of Bangkok. We would plan and conduct air-to-air training missions with flights of four aircraft and brief with the radar controllers. Then we would take off, split up the four aircraft into two flights of two. One flight would be the 'friendly force' and one the 'aggressor' flight. The radar control would direct the 'friendly flight' to the simulated 'enemy' aircraft. We would manoeuvre and hassle for 45 minutes. Then we would rejoin the four aircraft and head for the tanker, refuelling at about 25,000 feet for a full load of gas. (I remember I spotted one of our tankers at 95 miles distant, when I saw a sun flash off his aluminium fuselage.) Then we would hassle for another 45 minutes and head back to the base as a flight of four. The quality of that training is, as far as I am concerned, the best that I have ever witnessed. Before that year's tour ended we started the withdrawal from Thailand, and I was assigned to the 3rd Tactical Fighter Wing, Clark Air Base, Philippines.

The Philippines – Peacetime and Red Flag
Unlike the 1965 and 1973 'remote' tours in Vietnam and Thailand, our families accompanied us to the Philippines, and it was great to give my kids this overseas experience. I likened flying duty at Clark to that of the Royal Flying Corps in northern India in the 1930s – remote, insular, self-contained, but part of the Empire. At first I had the dreaded job of Stan/Eval, but soon got appointed as squadron commander of the 90th Fighter Squadron. The squadron was almost the sole source of entertainment and comradeship. We lived on base, we shopped on base, and our parties were at the Clark officers' club, which bordered a huge rectangular parade ground that had been there since the Spanish-American War. In one such party, our 90th Squadron, which had originated with the US Army Air Service on the Western Front in World War One, put on a skit-by-decades. We highlighted the pilots and aircraft the squadron had flown through the years, with jazz, tango and jitterbug dances, each in its era. My role was as the McDonnell Douglas symbol for the Phantom II, a dwarf in a huge black hat, black cape, eternally holding up two fingers to represent the aircraft evolution.

The flying was good with clear skies until the thunderstorm clouds rose to 40,000 feet around noon. Again we flew both air-to-air and air-to-ground, with a little, tiny gunnery range at Crow Valley. Flying the F-4D, we hung gun pods under the fuselage, and I was again Top Gun in strafing with runs of ninety-six per cent. Then the F-4Es arrived from Thailand, and we had the latest models in the air force. Again, I got to fly the Phantom with the internal gun.

Shortly after that I was moved to the 13th Air Force staff at Clark, to be the planner in charge of a new training exercise, which we called 'Cope Thunder', the Pacific Red Flag. The air staff had just inaugurated the Red Flag series of large, combat training exercises at Nellis Air Force Base, Nevada, and we needed a smaller one to prepare our aircrews spread over the Pacific theatre. The need for this large-scale, integrated training was becoming apparent because as a squadron commander, I was surprised at how fast our combat experience in the unit evaporated. Barely two years after the end of the Vietnam War, we had only a couple of flight commanders and a very few aircrew who had combat experience.[2] We were in danger of losing our edge and falling back into peacetime habits. Historical analysis of World War One and Two air battles had shown that most of the losses occurred in the first ten engagements. If we could somehow train to provide those first ten engagements in peacetime, we could drastically improve aircrew survivability. Cope Thunder and Red Flag were to reverse that trend and create a venue where crews and planners could innovate and continue to develop front-line tactics. That first exercise in the Philippines was conducted in the summer of 1976, shortly after my family and I were reassigned to the National War College, Washington, DC.

Dick Kuiper and I were to meet again in Washington as he headed up the famous Soviet Awareness Group that taught Russian tactics and equipment characteristics to thousands of young recruits and old heads during their operational and staff tours of duty. I went from the war college to the Joint Staff and NATO where, as the deputy commander of 5 ATAF, I was one of the Phantom boys who planned an air interdiction campaign to defeat a Soviet invasion of Western Europe. I guess we helped bring down the Soviet Union and end the Cold War.

After another couple of years on the Air Staff in Washington, I retired from the air force to work another twenty years in industry. Over these thirty-one years of military service, I had flown sailplanes, the F-100, the A-1E and the F-4 Phantom for over 3,000 flying hours and almost as many landings. From a boy in Iowa who only wanted to fly, I had the opportunity to fly supersonic aircraft, earn a PhD, teach and become a general officer, which is not a bad way to make a career.

---

2. For an explanation of pilot experience metrics in combat, see Chapter V in the author's *Oswald Boelcke: Germany's First Fighter Ace and Father of Air Combat,* published by Grub Street Publishing.

CHAPTER 18

PHANTOM FAREWELL

RICHARD PIKE BOWS OUT

If the past is another country – and a curious one at that – then it's surely curious, too, the way that an unexpected event or a certain ambience can arouse memories of that foreign place. Take, say, the potent atmosphere that can be stirred up by stormy weather. I recall, for instance, a recent scene when a sudden shower with strong, squally winds accompanied by rain driven in droves affected a group of friends who were cross-country walking. We were forced to seek shelter as various objects were sent clattering along the track. While Homer's thoughts 'for wreaking havoc upon a strong man, even the very strongest, there is nothing so dire as…' may have overstated the situation a bit, nonetheless on that day, like wrestling jelly, our control over events seemed more than a little inadequate. The elements were in charge and in the infinite catalogue of possibilities it appeared that almost anything could happen. Not far from our chosen spot a smoking stack of fetid manure puffed away as if cheerfully indifferent to ambient conditions."Don't worry," laughed one of the men, "we'll just have to remember to bring gas masks next time!"

I pulled a sceptical expression and prepared to dismiss his jocular remark from my mind. Instead, however, something else happened. Perhaps it was observation of the symmetry of movement, the mesmeric effect as the trees swayed in the wind; maybe it was the atmosphere generated by the storm itself, but whatever the reason, my thoughts, as if coerced by some unknown force, were taken back to incidents that had occurred on a summer's day some forty years previously. On further reflection, maybe the memory-trigger was provided by the mention of those gas masks – those dreaded gas masks – for it was hard to forget the way in which these clumpy creatures, along with other NBC gear (nuclear, biological, chemical – a neat summation of the diverse horrors that might be thrown at us in the event of war), had to be worn during the numerous exercises held at that time on military units, including the RAF airfield at Leuchars where I was a Phantom pilot on 43 Squadron, 'The Fighting Cocks'. To counter this NBC threat, personnel were issued with no-nonsense charcoal-lined green suits, over-boots, gloves, a World War One-type tin hat that would have made the television character Captain Blackadder proud, and, finally, one of those grim gas masks.

Sometimes this paraphernalia had to be carried – some of it even worn – in cockpits when we were ordered airborne in our Phantoms to conduct exercise missions. There was a degree of general dissension, I recall, but not much, for this was the year of 1974, we were military heroes and we were used to 'getting on with things'. Such an approach, in fact, was not prevalent amongst the overall population, for changes, big changes, were underway that year. In the United States, President Nixon was embroiled in the Watergate scandal, in the United Kingdom the political scene was marked by two general elections, strikes, wage restraint, the Three-Day Week and the collapse of several large companies. Even Princess Anne had a spot of bother when some foolish fellow attempted to kidnap her near Buckingham Palace.

It was one Thursday in the mid-summer of that year, a day when I was on duty at Leuchars, that events surrounding a particular flight fixed themselves within my memory cells. Along with my navigator and two other members of aircrew I sat that day in a crewroom in the so-called interceptor alert force (IAF) shed. Our small room was adjacent to the duty engineers' crewroom and next to specially designed hangars that housed two fully-armed Phantoms. In the event of a 'scramble' order from the fighter controller we could be airborne within minutes. Until that moment, however, we had to wait around while listening to the steady background tick of a 'telebrief' device with its direct connection to the controller. Inevitably, a certain lethargy would develop as we read newspapers, talked occasionally about squadron and other issues including, I seem to remember, a discussion on the Eurovision Song Contest held in Brighton in April of that year and won by the Swedish group ABBA with their now-famous song *Waterloo*.

If time appeared to drag while on IAF duty, a good plan was to try to stay as active as possible and attempt to coax the mind into positive territory – to think positive thoughts. Although contemplation of idealised communist figures whose faces were radiant with dreams of heightened productivity might take the notion a little too far, nonetheless it was important to remain alert and focused in case the controller ordered a sudden scramble. In any case, within our hectic lives there was surely value in pausing to reflect from time to time with benefit to be gained from the simple observation of, for instance, falling snow, or an aurora borealis light-show, or perhaps the great, desolate mysteries of outer space.

If, regardless of such tactics, a sense of weariness eventually overcame the crewroom atmosphere, this might be assuaged once in a while by the occasional visitor. One time, when a young squadron navigator roared up in a car, we became instantly alert as he rushed into the room with, we assumed, some compelling news. With almost breathless excitement he said: "The boss has just heard on the grapevine that we can expect a Taceval at any moment." He paused to let this information sink in before he went on: "He sent me round to warn you discreetly. You'd better be ready!" A Taceval, or tactical evaluation, involved a visit (in theory, a surprise visit) by a specialist team tasked to assess the efficiency of a military unit. "We're already ready," I said. The young navigator shrugged. "In that case," he grinned, "now you can become even more ready." At that he waved a brisk farewell, turned on his heels and scurried back to his car.

After this pithy interjection, and as relative tranquillity returned, I began to ponder previous Tacevals, including one a year earlier when, as now, I happened to be on IAF duty. The arrival of a Taceval team was usually announced by the shriek of a siren along with Tannoy messages – the cause of much angst as everyone rushed here and there trying to look keen. Aircrew on IAF duty would be expected to dash to their Phantoms, climb into the cockpits and await further instructions. Naturally, we'd be prepared for anything, but on that occasion we were caught on the hop, as they say, for the first thing we knew, even before the siren had sounded, was the arrival of a sour-looking squadron leader who barged into our crewroom without saying a single word. He then sat down in one corner of the room as if in a sulk. We stared at him; he stared at us, but still he just sat there like a ventriloquist's dummy. Bastard. We should have 'twigged', of course, and did so at once when, quite quickly, the awkward silence was broken by the shriek of the Taceval siren. We leapt up from our seats, sprinted to the Phantoms and did all the right things although we were admonished later for failing to check properly the identification of that squadron leader. They said that we should have verified his identification card down to the last dotted 'i' and crossed 't' and if there was the slightest doubt had him marched off to the station guardroom to sit in silence there. Certainly, we were naive and foolish and taken-in by surface theatricals, but the thought of that only made the whole episode even more annoying.

I could remember, too, another Taceval, one that had taken place some years previously and which had ended in tragedy. It happened when I was based in Germany as a pilot flying the English Electric Lightning with 19 (F) Squadron. I'd been asked to join a Taceval team which had been organised to evaluate a Dutch air force airfield where a couple of Lockheed F-104 Starfighter squadrons were based. Having travelled by train to Holland, I met up in a local hostelry with the rest of the Taceval team. Proceedings were highly clandestine and it was early evening by the time we had been briefed to the 'nth' degree and made ready to 'hit' the air base at dusk. Together with another qualified Lightning pilot I climbed into a waiting car and we were whisked away to be taken directly to the air base's IAF set-up. Grasping clipboards, and just as the alert siren was sounding, the two of us, with earnest expressions and feeling rather important not to mention officially officious, burst into the pilots' crewroom. These feelings would not last long.

Exactly as planned, the two F-104 pilots raced to their waiting Starfighters. Within moments they were both ordered airborne by the fighter controller. On my clipboard I scribbled down information about timing, crew reaction, engineering support – all of it well-intentioned, admirable stuff even though, regretfully, most of it was about to prove irrelevant. After some forty-five minutes, one of the F-104s returned to base and landed safely but the other one failed to respond to increasingly urgent radio calls from air traffic control. Speculation rose as we waited and waited until at length news was received that F-104 wreckage had been found in a field. Soon after that, the leader of the Taceval team announced that the pilot had been killed and that consequently the Taceval was cancelled with immediate effect. Later, it was deduced from radio transmissions that the young pilot had suffered disorientation in cloud. From conversations with fellow members of the Taceval team it was clear that we all felt a sense of guilt even though, of course, not one of us could be held to blame for the sickening turn of events.

It was with a heavy heart and a sense of bitter irony that I'd returned to my squadron to brief fellow pilots on what had occurred for, as with most accidents, there were lessons to be learned. I learned, too, how such events concentrated the mind on what mattered in life, that worldly vanities could suddenly appear meaningless and spiritually empty.

"Leuchars...Leuchars...this is Buchan...alert one Phantom..." the crewroom telebrief now promptly sprang into life; at once, all hell was let loose as we reacted to the fighter controller's order. With newspapers, magazines, writing materials hastily thrust aside, the four aircrew together with duty engineers rushed to the Phantoms. Prudent preparation helped to expedite proceedings: carefully-positioned flying helmets were placed onto heads; cape leather flying gloves draped across the canopy coaming were slipped onto hands. In practically no time at all, the four cockpits were manned and in the front cockpit of Phantom XV585 I announced tersely on the aircraft radio: "Q1 checking in."

"Q2 checking in," said the pilot of the other Phantom. The 'Q' call sign, from the abbreviation QRA, remained in general use by crews on alert duties. The 'Q1' would be the first aircraft scrambled; the 'Q2' machine was manned as back-up in case of problems with the first Phantom.

"Buchan acknowledging," replied the controller, "both aircraft remain at cockpit readiness. We have radar contact with a possible zombie."

"Copied," both pilots replied in turn.

"Standby for further details."

This exchange, despite the brevity, had given us significant information. For one thing, we knew that the alert was for real and not a Taceval or other exercise. The term 'zombie' referred to Soviet Bloc aircraft. Sometimes, but not always, the fighter controllers received advance information from NATO allies of Soviet aircraft movements; IAF crews might even be given an anticipated scramble time, though it appeared that today we'd been denied that luxury.

While sitting in the cockpit I glanced at the engineers who scurried around to make sure that everything was in order. The external power unit was plugged in; fire extinguishers were in position; wheel-chock ropes were laid out for quick removal; a myriad other details, many learnt from past hiccups, helped to facilitate proceedings. Meantime, I double-checked around the cockpit to make sure that everything was ready for a scramble start procedure... fuel switches, flight instruments, throttles, warning panels, missile switches...

Suddenly we heard: "Leuchars this is Buchan," there was an urgent edge to the controller's voice, "one Phantom...I say again one Phantom...*standby...*" There were some background crackles, then: "...head 025 degrees, climb to fifteen thousand feet initially, *scramble, scramble, scramble...*acknowledge."

At once I acknowledged the controller's orders while simultaneously reaching for the engine-start master switches. The small hangar began to fill with the racket produced by Rolls-Royce Spey engines as I went through the scramble start procedure. Soon, with both engines fired up and functioning satisfactorily, I signalled 'chocks away' to the ground crewmen who reacted with typical efficiency. The duty 'chief' gave me a thumbs-up sign and I released the Phantom's parking brake. Now, as I hastened the machine forward towards the runway, air traffic control cleared me for an immediate take-off.

Without stopping, and with the nose wheel lined up on the runway centreline, I pushed the twin throttles forward to the full 'cold power' position. After a short pause, I rocked the throttles outboard into the minimum reheat position, paused again, then selected them fully forward to engage maximum reheat. The consequent commotion as the reheats lit, even though experienced many times, still stimulated a sense of thrill as we accelerated down the runway.

While we proceeded, and as with any well-conducted flight, regular sequences of checks were routine, nonetheless there was a great sense of freedom when we climbed. Looking up, our presence seemed like a tiny entry into vastness but even so, to soar above earthly constraints could, like a breath of fresh air, feel more than a little satisfying. Perhaps part of this was an incongruous aspect – the knowledge that our flight was a demanding military one with consequences (indeed, severe consequences if things went wrong).

When we approached the demanded height, and as I spoke to the ground radar controller, I noticed shafts of summer sunshine light up puffballs of cumulus cloud below and I could imagine whitecaps on the surface of the North Sea. Although the weather on that July day was generally fair, we'd been warned that increasing cloud to the north could give problems. The controller instructed us to continue northwards: "Standby for an update on the zombie," she said. I acknowledged then, looking down, noted the fixed North Sea oil installations dotted across the sea's surface. These provided useful navigational aids to cross-check against the Phantom's inertial navigation system (INAS).

"Turn left ten degrees," said the Buchan controller, "your target is on your port side flying left to right at a range of 160 miles."

"Copied," I said.

"Shouldn't be too long before I pick him up on Doppler," muttered my navigator Barry.

Photographs of the Soviet Bear taken by the author's navigator, 18 February 1975.

"Maintain your heading," said the controller, "target is just over 140 miles."

The controller continued to count down the range until my navigator interjected: "He's beginning to paint now."

"Okay," I said, "happy with this heading?"

"Hold it there for the moment." My focus now was on flying accurate parameters to facilitate the navigator's intercept geometry. When he said: "He's just through fifty-five miles," I tried to assess whether high-level cloud in the area ahead was sufficiently widespread to cause problems.

"Range forty miles," said Barry, "turn left twenty degrees." At this, my heartbeat began to quicken; before long I should be able to spot the zombie visually.

"Range twenty-five miles," said Barry, "this heading looks okay."

"Roger," I said, "still no visual contact." As feared, some wisps of high level cirrus cloud were beginning to affect local visibility. At twenty miles, I was given a minor height adjustment but the zombie was still hidden by cloud.

"I'll be turning you starboard shortly," said Barry, "the target's approaching ten miles away."

"Understood," I said. As well as searching visually, and with the need to concentrate on precise flying to meet the navigator's demands, I became so engrossed that I almost jumped with shock at his next call: "Range five miles. Standby for a turn onto target heading."

Within moments, as he called: "Turn right now!" I reacted immediately and it was during this turn that, finally, the silhouette of a large aircraft started to emerge.

"I'm beginning to make him out visually," I said, "but there's patchy cirrus around – I may lose sight of him again."

"Okay. I'll keep up the patter."

Fortunately, as the range counted down, I was able to maintain visual contact and soon, as we closed up on the target's right side, I could identify the aircraft type.

"What's your assessment, Barry?" I asked my navigator.

"It's a Bear 'D'," he said.

The NATO-designated Bear 'D', a maritime reconnaissance/targeting and electronic intelligence version of the Russian Tupolev Tu-95, entered service with the Soviet Union in the 1950s with the expectation of service until at least 2040 – an anticipated life-span that far exceeded anything normally planned in the West. (I'm intrigued, incidentally, to see at the time of writing that my colleagues in their Typhoon aircraft are intercepting the selfsame Bears.) The length of this Bear brute, at over 150 feet, exceeded that of our Phantom by some ninety feet. In the past I had intercepted quite a few, even so I could not avoid a sense of awe as I gazed at the distinctive swept-back wings and the unusual contra-rotating propellers attached to each of the four Kuznetsov NK-12 engines (the propeller tips moved faster than the speed of sound making this one of the noisiest aircraft in the world). For many, the image of a Bear 'D' was the very essence of Cold War frostiness.

While my navigator took photos, noted serial numbers, external features and any particular markings, I manoeuvred the Phantom to give views from various angles. Fine judgement was needed: we wanted to fly close enough to pick out details and to make our presence known, on the other hand there was no communication with the Bear's crew and it was not unknown for some of the Soviet pilots to turn aggressively towards an intercepting fighter. The danger of collision always threatened. At night, a known hazard was for the Bear's tail-gunner to shine a bright light at the interceptor's crew thus causing a perilous interference with night vision.

In addition to the tail-gunner, the Bear had five, sometimes six, other crew members – two pilots, a flight engineer, a communications system operator, and a navigator or two. That day, as I flew the Phantom level with the Bear's tail area, I scrutinised the cramped-looking 'bubble' where the tail-gunner was ensconced. I could see him stare at us, apparently solemn behind his Perspex bubble, his eyes maybe flashing angrily as if to urge us to leave them be. For a moment or two I wondered if there was a reason for him to be selected for separation from other crew members. He appeared to be a big fellow, and perhaps rumbling up from his large body I surmised that he was inclined to produce noises like an avalanche which seemed to surprise no-none. Ill-tempered in his confined environment, no doubt he gave the impression that the subsequent tsunami was best left unchallenged.

It was not speculation about the tail-gunner, however, that triggered a move but our fuel state. An in-flight refuelling tanker was not available and a discussion with my navigator confirmed that, if we were to land back at Leuchars, we needed to leave without delay as our lone Bear continued to head back towards Siberia. I moved forward to fly level with the very Soviet-looking cockpit, and was gratified to see, after my quick 'wing waggle', one of the pilots raise his hand in a gesture of farewell. I assumed that it was intended as a gesture of friendly-ish farewell although, on second thoughts, it might have meant something else altogether.

The flight back to Leuchars worked out as planned and, after landing, I taxied the Phantom directly back to the IAF set-up. It was while I was dealing with the post-flight paperwork that an unexpected visitor entered the crewroom. "Wonderful surprise!" I beamed, though I may have appeared a bit startled by my wife's unusual visit. In her arms she held our six-month-old baby daughter, Lizzie.

"Tomorrow's a busy day," said my wife. "Someone, remember, reaches the grand old age of thirty-one."

"My birthday! Of course!"

"You've been a little preoccupied, I suppose."

"Just a bit."

"And there are rumours about a Taceval," she said.

"How on earth do you know about that?"

She grinned: "The wives' net, of course! We're usually the first to know what's going on around here." There was a pause after this, and I noticed a worried frown develop on her face as she gazed at me. Eventually she continued: "But I'd better not hang about this place for too long..." she hesitated, "...only I just wanted to...well...you know..." her voice had become strained and I was surprised to see her eyes begin to fill up.

"Everything will be okay," I tried to console her but we were both conscious of the special difficulties faced by the serviceman's wife. This seemed especially true for the wives of aircrew even though we knew well enough that flights were well regulated and professional. Great dramas were uncommon. There were dangers, of course, and occasionally things went wrong and perhaps the thoughts of wives and families tended to over-focus on this aspect.

I glanced at our daughter. "Toodle-oo, Lizzie," I mumbled, almost to myself, "see you later on...look after your mum." She gurgled and smiled by way of reply. I smiled back, confident of a safe return, sure in my mind that a brief au revoir was more appropriate than the gracelessness of an unduly theatrical and therefore somehow phantom farewell.

SELECT BIOGRAPHIES

ALAN WINKLES, born in Torquay, Devon, was a member of the Air Training Corps. Aged seventeen, he gained a pilot's licence and joined the RAF to become a fighter pilot. His first appointment in 1966 was as Lightning air defence pilot on 5 Squadron at RAF Binbrook. After this tour he transferred to the Phantom and became a qualified weapons instructor serving on 54 Squadron and then on 17 Squadron. In 1973 he became a flight commander on 43 Squadron (Phantoms) at RAF Leuchars, he then commanded the Royal Navy's Phantom training squadron and spent six months with 892 Naval Air Squadron on HMS *Ark Royal.*

After a tour on the weapons staff at HQ 38 Group RAF Upavon, he attended staff college at RAF Bracknell and was posted to the MoD London. Following promotion, he took up duties as wing commander training at HQ 11 Group at RAF Bentley Priory. From there he was posted to assume command of 43 Squadron (Phantoms).

From 1987 onwards he was posted to the Sultan of Oman's Air Force, returned to the RAF Staff College, the Defence Evaluation and Research Agency (now QinetiQ) at Malvern in January 1996 before eventually retiring from the RAF in 2001, having flown more than 5,000 hours. In retirement he became an A2 flying instructor with the Air Training Corps flying Vigilant (Grob 109) motor gliders.

ARCHIE LIGGAT

1977   Universities of Glasgow & Strathclyde Air Squadron. SA Bulldog

1980   Graduated BSc (Hons) Aero Eng. RAF Cranwell; Initial Officer Training

1981   RAF Cranwell; Basic Flying Training. Jet Provost Mk5

1982   RAF Valley; Advanced Flying Training. Hawk T1
          RAF Leeming; QFI Course. JP Mk3

1983   RAF Linton-On-Ouse; B2 QFI, JP Mk3 & 5

1984   A2 QFI

1985   RAF Brawdy; Tactical Weapons Course. Hawk T1A

1986   RAF Coningsby; F4 OCU. Phantom FRG2
          RAF Leuchars; 111(F) Squadron, Phantom FG1

1987   IRE and QFI on F4

1989 RAF Leuchars; F4 OCU, F4 Standards. Phantom FGR2 & F4J

1991 RAF Wattisham; 74(F) Squadron. Phantom FGR2. A1 QFI

1992 F4 display pilot. Queen's Commendation for Valuable Service in the Air
RAF Valley; OC 234 Squadron. Hawk T1 & T1A

1994 OC CFS Hawk Squadron

1995 RAF Valley; OC 19 Squadron

1996 Retired to civil airlines

PENNY WILD joined the RAF as a direct entrant, attending the Officer Cadet Training Unit at RAF Henlow beginning in September 1966. After training as a fighter controller at the School of Fighter Control at RAF Bawdsey, Penny was posted there for her first tour of duty, followed by tours at 280 Signals Unit (RAF Akrotiri), RAF Buchan and RAF Neatishead. On leaving the RAF in 1975, she joined Hawker Siddeley Dynamics, conducting trials on the Skyflash air-to-air missile at the Pacific Missile Test Center in California. She married an American in 1978 but was widowed in 1990. She remarried in 1996, became Penny Smith, and is involved with her husband in a Reformed Presbyterian ministry to the poor in a crime-ridden area of Atlanta, Georgia. She has one son and is the proud grandmother of six grandchildren.

JACK HAMILL joined the RAF in 1960. After training he flew Vulcans for six years and became the training captain on 27 Squadron at RAF Scampton. After this he became a qualified flying instructor (QFI) on the Gnat and instructed for three years at the advanced flying training school at RAF Valley. This was followed by conversion to the Phantom in the air defence role and tours at Leuchars (43 Squadron), Wildrenrath Germany (19 Squadron) and Coningsby (29 Squadron).

The 29 Squadron tour was cut short by a posting to the Phantom Operational Conversion Unit (OCU) again as a flying instructor. However this only lasted for about nine months until he did a tour on loan to the Sultan of Oman's Air Force (SOAF). This was on the Hunter in the ground-attack role and also as QFI to the Omani students on their advanced flying training.

On return Jack went back to the Phantom OCU and also became a display pilot on the Battle of Britain Memorial Flight flying the Spitfire and Hurricane for four years. In the middle of this he converted to the Tornado F2/3 and remained as an instructor on the Tornado OCU. He joined a small unit that was set up within the OCU to train Saudi air crew on the Tornado and after the first crews had completed their training, went to Saudi Arabia on secondment to British Aerospace to help in the set-up of the Saudi squadrons. Initially seconded for eighteen months but this was extended and eventually Jack retired from Saudi Arabia in 1999 having spent ten years there.

PETER DESMOND joined the RAF as a boy entrant, aged fifteen in 1948. Then in 1953 he was commissioned as a navigator.

1953-1958	Flew Meteors, Venoms and Javelins air defence
1959-1963	Navigator instructor
1963-1966	81 PR Squadron Canberras RAF Tengah, Nav leader.
	QCVSA Borneo list
1966-1970	Boscombe Down PR Canberra photo trials. First Phantom ride 1969
	Phantom recce pod trials flying. QCVSA
1970	Promoted to squadron leader
1970-1973	Brüggen Phantom Wing. Chief mission planning, radar prediction
	Stayed current Phantom
1974-1977	Flight commander 43 Squadron Leuchars. MBE
1977-1980	UK Staff founder member . AAFCE Tactical Leadership Programme
	Germany. Stayed current Phantom
1979	Promoted to wing commander. Last Phantom ride
1980-1983	Maritime Air Defence leader. RN maritime tactical school
1983-1986	Branch chief ops. HQ AIRBALTAP. Karup, Denmark
1986-1988	Selection board chairman Biggin Hill
1988	Retired from the RAF

JOHN WALMSLEY joined the RAF in 1963 and was one of the very few teenage Lightning pilots. After a tour on Lightnings with 5 Squadron, he transferred to ground attack with the new Phantom on 54 Squadron at Coningsby. Qualifying as a fighter weapons instructor (FWI), he returned to 54 Squadron until becoming an instructor with 228 OCU. During a four-year tour he qualified as an electronic warfare officer and qualified weapons instructor (QWI [AD]) serving on the QWI staff. A tour as QWI with 56 Squadron was followed by becoming a USAF instructor pilot on the staff of the USAF Central Instructor School at Luke AFB, Arizona, flying the F-4C in air-to-air and air-to-ground roles.

After a brief tour with the Central Tactics and Trials Organisation (CTTO) and staff college, he became a flight commander with 43 Squadron in 1983, followed by 23 Squadron in the Falklands. He then had another tour with the CTTO as AD (air-to-air missiles) and AD (fighters), flying trials of missile firings and Phantom modifications. In 1989 he was promoted to wing commander and commanded the Phantom OCU/64 Squadron until its demise in 1991. Of his 4,500 flying hours, over 3,000 were on the F-4 Phantom.

After a tour in the Plans Branch of HQSTC at High Wycombe, he became the defence and air attaché at the British Embassy in Stockholm, Sweden. He retired from the RAF in 1994.

ROLAND TOMLIN

1974-1977   Canberras (98 Squadron Cottesmore, 100 Squadron Marham)

1977-1980   JP / Hawk QFI (Leeming, Valley)

1981-1986   Phantom QFI (92 Squadron Wildenrath, 228 OCU Coningsby)

1986-1988   Tornado QFI (229 OCU Coningsby)

1988-1990   Squadron QFI (5 Squadron Coningsby)

1990-1992   Squadron Leader Ops (MoD UK Air Team Riyadh)

DICK NORTHCOTE

1963-1966   Cadet at RAF College Cranwell

1967-1969   208 Squadron Hunters in Muharraq, Bahrain

1969-1974   54 Squadron Phantom FGR2s at RAF Coningsby

1974-1976   Pilot instructor and flight commander on 4501st TFRS, MacDill AFB

1976-1979   111 Squadron AD Phantoms RAF Leuchars (Squadron Leader OCA
    Flight)

1979-1983   Staff jobs

1984-1986   OC 74 Sqn RAF Wattisham (Awarded OBE for reforming the
    squadron   from scratch)

1987   Wing Commander AD Ops Falkland Islands

1988-1990   Staff Officer, RAF Innsworth

1990-1991   CTTO Group Captain AD at Boscombe Down

1991   Retired from the RAF

PHIL OWEN joined the RAF in 1966 and after flying training he served his first tour as a qualified flying instructor (QFI) at the RAF College, Cranwell. He was then posted to fly the Lightning, serving tours on 19 Squadron and 92 Squadron at RAF Gütersloh. The demise of the RAF Germany Lightning Force in 1977 brought a move to the Phantom, and tours flying on 111 Squadron and the Operational Conversion Unit (OCU), 64(R) Squadron, as a flight commander and QFI.

Four short tours on the ground followed: HQ 11 Group as the Tornado F3 project officer, staff college, HQ RAF Germany on the air defence staff, and HQ Allied Forces Central Europe as chief of defensive operations.

In 1989 Phil returned to flying with command of the Tornado F3 OCU, 65(R) Squadron, before a tour serving on the MoD Central Staff in London. His last two tours, in the rank of group captain, were as deputy commander British Forces Falkland Islands and director of tri-Service Elementary Flying Training.

Phil retired from the RAF in 2000, but then spent the next ten years as a reservist; first as a QFI and latterly as an AEF flight commander.

RG HEAD is a graduate of the US Air Force Academy and was one of the first fighter pilots in Vietnam. He flew 325 combat missions in the A-1 Skyraider, earned the Silver Star, Distinguished Flying Cross and thirteen Air Medals. Earning a PhD in Political Science, he taught cadets at the academy, had a second tour in South East Asia and commanded the 90th Tactical Fighter Squadron in the Philippines. He graduated first in his pilot training class, 'Top Gun' in advanced fighter training, distinguished graduate of the National War College and top graduate of the Maxwell School at Syracuse University.

He was a military fellow at the Council on Foreign Relations in New York City where he published a book, *Crisis Resolution.* He served in the Office of the Secretary of Defense as the military assistant to the Under Secretary for Policy and in the Joint Staff as the special assistant to the director for JCS matters. When promoted to brigadier general he served in Italy as deputy commander of 5 ATAF and the Air Staff.

RG is the author of *Oswald Boelcke: Germany's First Fighter Ace and Father of Air Combat* (Grub Street Publishing, 2016). He lives with his wife, Carole, in Coronado, California.

INDEX

PEOPLE

PLACES

RAF Neatishead, 37, 39, 42, 178
RAF St Mawgan, 39
RAF Valley, 16, 19, 116, 117, 118, 119,
    177-178, 180
RAF Waddington, 156-157
RAF Wattisham, 19, 32, 100, 106, 107,
    108, 178, 180
RAF Wildenrath, 91-95, 96
Skopje, Macedonia, 9-11, 15
Thailand, 45, 51, 55, 162, 165, 166-168
The Philippines, 167-168, 181
Ubon air base, 7, 9, 45, 46, 49, 54, 55, 59
Udorn AFB, 162, 165, 166, 167
Vietnam, 7, 43, 45-49, 50, 53, 61, 101,
    161-162, 164, 166, 181

AIRCRAFT

Blackburn Bucaneer, 24, 25, 27, 29, 35,
    36, 78, 132
Boeing 707, 74-75
Cessna 182 Skylane, 94
Douglas A-1 Skyraider, 51, 161, 181
English Electric Canberra, 33, 39, 123,
    147, 179
English Electric Lightning, 11, 12, 24,
    33, 34, 35, 39, 80-81, 85, 92, 106, 114,
    153, 155, 171, 177-179
F-104, 78, 128-132, 138
F-105 Thunderchief, 49, 50
Fairey Gannet, 24-25
Folland Gnat, 61, 178
Grumman F-14 Tomcat, 120
Hawker Siddley Harrier, 58, 59-64, 72
KC-135, 161, 167
Lockheed C-130 Hercules, 17, 20, 46, 69
Lockheed TriStar, 65
Martin 2-0-2, 34

McDonnell Douglas Phantom:
    F-4, 7-8, 9, 10, 11, 12, 15, 43, 44-51,
        53-55, 101-103, 104, 105, 106,
        110, 111, 120-123, 125, 126, 128,
        129, 130, 132, 138, 159, 162-165,
        167, 168, 180
    FG1, 132, 139, 147, 177
    FGR2, 16, 109, 152, 178, 180
MiG-21, 3, 8, 104, 105
Northrop F-5 Freedom Fighter, 104,
    105
Panavia Tornado, 10, 110, 127, 128, 129,
    131-133, 136, 137, 152, 178, 180
Sikorsky S-61N helicopter, 9, 66
Tupolev Tu-16, 33
Tupolev Tu-95, 175
Westland Wessex helicopter, 25, 29, 144,
    146

SQUADRONS

17 Squadron, 109, 110, 114, 177
23 Squadron, 66, 67, 74, 106, 179
29 Squadron, 67, 178
34 Squadron, 124
43 Squadron, 58, 61, 67, 77, 119, 139,
    169, 177, 178, 179
54 Squadron, 85, 101, 177, 179, 180
74 Squadron, 19, 100, 106, 178, 180
90th Fighter Squadron, 167, 181
92 Squadron, 91-99, 180
111 Squadron, 127, 128, 129, 139, 151,
    177, 180
234 Squadron, 16, 19, 178
280 Signals Unit, Cyprus, 33, 178
306th Tactical Fighter Squadron, 161
308th Tactical Fighter Squadron, 161
421st Tactical Fighter Squadron, 166

MISCELLANEOUS